'A deeply fascinating, highly informative and entertaining account of an overlooked subject. This brilliant book offers unique insights into the stories of would-be terrorists and foiled plots that could have changed the course of Britain's recent history.'

— Julia Ebner, author of *Going Dark: The Secret Social Lives of Extremists*

'A gripping, vivid and important book. By expertly analysing foiled and failed terrorist plots, Dearden presents highly original insight into the complex phenomenon of modern terrorism.'

— Richard English, author of *Does Terrorism Work? A History*

'Terrorists try to present themselves as ruthless and calculating; Plotters shows that most of them are sad, lonely and inept. Yet these stories also reveal the enormous challenges facing the security services trying to keep us safe. Highly recommended for anyone wanting to learn more about terrorism, beyond the headlines.'

— Brendan Cox, anti-terror campaigner

'A fascinating, forensic and highly engaging account of the diverse lives, motivations and backgrounds of Britain's terrorist plotters—and the impossible challenge facing the police and intelligence agencies in trying to stop each and every one of them. This is a must-read.'

— Dame Sara Khan DBE, former UK Counter-Extremism Commissioner

'The terrorist threat to Britain is mutating, and we need to adapt. This gripping and informative book explains why.'

— The Lord Anderson of Ipswich KBE KC, former UK Independent Reviewer of Terrorism Legislation

'Dearden paints a disturbing portrait of today's terrorists, but even more chilling is her account of the near-misses, where only good intelligence and smart policing has saved us from further tragedies.'

— Sir David Omand, former UK Security and Intelligence Coordinator, and author of *Securing the State*

'Excellent reporting and analysis that puts the threat of terrorism in perspective by revealing its often hidden dimension: the many plots that fail on their own, or are foiled by the authorities.'

— Martha Crenshaw, Senior Fellow, Center for International Security and Coooperation, Stanford University

'An alarming portrait of the terror threat the UK faces in all its confusing complexity.'

— Raffaello Pantucci, author of *'We Love Death As You Love Life':
Britain's Suburban Terrorists*

'A compelling deep dive into UK terrorism and counterterrorism.'

— Petter Nesser, Senior Research Fellow, Norwegian Defence Research Establishment, and author of *Islamist Terrorism in Europe*

PLOTTERS

LIZZIE DEARDEN

Plotters

The UK Terrorists Who Failed

HURST & COMPANY, LONDON

First published in the United Kingdom in 2023 by
C. Hurst & Co. (Publishers) Ltd.,
New Wing, Somerset House, Strand, London, WC2R 1LA

Distributed in the United States, Canada and Latin America by
Oxford University Press, 198 Madison Avenue, New York, NY 10016,
United States of America.

A Cataloguing-in-Publication data record for this book
is available from the British Library.

ISBN: 9781787389298

This book is printed using paper from registered sustainable
and managed sources.

This book is printed using paper from registered sustainable
and managed sources.

www.hurstpublishers.com

Printed in Great Britain by Bell and Bain Ltd, Glasgow

CONTENTS

ACKNOWLEDGEMENTS

The idea for this book struck me, quite unexpectedly, while I was in a shower block on a post-lockdown camping holiday in 2020. It was not until months later, when another coronavirus lockdown found me living in hiding after being targeted by a far-right extremist, that I had enough time on my hands to develop it. My first thanks goes to my agent, Andrew Gordon, for taking a chance on me and helping me turn a mess of ideas into something remotely book-shaped. I also owe a debt to Julia Ebner and other great authors who kindly shared their experience of the book-writing process when I was entering the publishing world as a novice.

I have covered terrorism for several years as a journalist at *The Independent*, which sent me to report on many of the cases that feed into this book and gave me free rein to delve into security issues of all kinds. My role as home affairs and security correspondent, and later home affairs editor, brought me into contact with the sources and interviewees whose expertise run through these pages. It would not have been possible to create this work without the support of my editor, David Marley, who allowed me to take the necessary time out of my day job to research and write it. I have also learned much from my colleagues, including security journalist Duncan Gardham, and our post-trial chats. My writing has been overseen by the beautiful Tricia, a peace bear knitted by Figen Murray, the mother of Manchester Arena bombing victim Martyn Hett—who has conducted a powerful campaign for increased security at venues. Although this book focuses on the perpetrators of terrorism, its victims are always in my thoughts.

It is a reflection of the work of countless people, from police and MI5 agents to prosecutors, who discovered these plots and threw them into the glare of open justice. I thank all those who have assisted my research, whether on the record or off, and helped me track down key pieces of evidence. I am immensely grateful to the police officers, officials, academics and others who gave up their time for interviews that imbued this book with expertise far greater than mine. It would not exist without my publishers, Hurst, and my greatest thanks goes to my editor Lara Weisweiller-Wu, whose thoughtful and exacting input immeasurably improved this book. Any mistakes left after the phenomenal work of all those who have reviewed this work are my own.

Writing this book has been a long and challenging journey, which I would not have been able to complete without the love and support of my family and friends. My partner has been encouraging me to write a book for years, and I owe the self-belief to finally complete it to him. His support, from reading my first proposal to keeping me fed and watered during frenzied bouts of writing, made this work possible. I started it while living under someone else's roof, after being given shelter when we had to flee our home in one of the worst periods of our lives. You know who you are—this one's for you.

INTRODUCTION

It took less than two minutes to change the course of modern British history, although few who were there realised the full consequences of the horror they saw unfolding. Wednesday, 22 March 2017 should have been an unremarkable day. Britain's news was focused on its departure from the European Union and Michel Barnier, then the European Commission's chief Brexit negotiator, made a speech warning of the potential for 'serious repercussions' if the two parties remained at loggerheads. In Westminster, the weekly prime minister's question time was dominated by arguments over school funding. By 2.40 pm, MPs were debating the minutiae of a new law on pension schemes.

At that moment, a grey Hyundai Tucson mounted the pavement on Westminster Bridge and started speeding west across the River Thames towards the Houses of Parliament.[1] The SUV repeatedly veered into pedestrians, striking more than 30 victims. Four people were fatally mowed down, including a mother walking to pick up her children from school, an American holidaymaker who pushed his wife out of the car's path and a Romanian tourist who was taking photos of London landmarks moments before she was killed.

As the driver, Khalid Masood, reached the other side of the bridge, he smashed into the ornate metal railings surrounding the Houses of Parliament. The crash briefly appeared to be the end of his rampage, but Masood emerged from the car uninjured and armed with two knives as tourists and passers-by started to flee. One stunned pedestrian who asked the terrorist what he was doing was told: 'Fuck off, you don't want to mess with me.' Masood ran around Parliament's perimeter, heading for a grand official entrance to New Palace Yard which was guarded only by unarmed police. One officer, PC Keith Palmer, stepped forward to challenge Masood and was ferociously attacked, being stabbed multiple times even after falling to the ground. The onslaught only ended when a government minister's armed bodyguard ran into the scene after hearing the car crash and screams. He shot the terrorist dead at 2.41pm, after Masood ignored shouted warnings and charged towards officers.

In just 82 seconds, Masood had murdered five victims and breached the gates of the Houses of Parliament. Armed with a car and two kitchen knives from a Tesco supermarket, he had penetrated one of the most secure and symbolic sites in the UK. The British public were shaken and terrified, as intended, while the jihadist terrorist group Isis triumphantly claimed responsibility for yet another attack by a 'soldier of the Islamic State'. As news of the bloodshed reverberated around the world, countless would-be terrorists saw an opportunity, and started to make their own plans.

British security services had long feared a bloody 'spectacular' by battle-hardened militants who had fought for Isis in Syria and Iraq, like those who had wreaked such terrible carnage in Paris and Brussels over the previous months. But as the then head of UK counter-terror police later admitted, officials had been looking in the wrong direction. 'Despite thinking that our biggest threat was returning foreign fighters, it wasn't—the threat was already here,' Neil Basu told a national security conference in 2018.[2] While working to tamp down the ability of returning fighters to execute plots mounted in Syria, MI5 and police resources were directed away from the seething pool of disaffected extremists who would soon reveal themselves to be Britain's greatest terror threat. The miscalculation had deadly consequences, and set off a chain reaction that continues to this day. The Westminster attack was the first of 15 terrorist atrocities to strike Britain over the following five years, with 42 victims killed and hundreds injured, while nine attackers died during their rampages. Each one sent shockwaves through the country, as targets spread from major cities like London and Manchester to unremarkable towns like Reading, Stanwell and Leigh-on-Sea. But the horrific events are only the tip of the iceberg for terrorist activity in the UK, where many more jihadists, neo-Nazis and anti-Muslim extremists have been plotting carnage and bloodshed.

In the period since Masood struck in March 2017, 37 terror attacks have been foiled by the security services.[3] The largest number were by jihadists, followed by the extreme right wing and a small minority labelled as 'single-issue terrorism'. These are the three main categories currently used by Britain's counter-terrorism machinery, encompassing a huge spectrum of beliefs. The jihadist side has been mainly composed of Isis supporters in this period but many also had links to the UK-based al-Muhajiroun network, led by notorious radical Islamist preacher Anjem Choudary, and sought inspiration from ideologues linked to al-Qaeda—the international jihadist terrorist group founded by Osama bin Laden. The extreme right wing encompasses neo-Nazis, white nationalists and a much more widespread strain of anti-Muslim extremism, while the third category includes any other motivation that falls under the definition of terrorism in the UK—the use or threat of violence for a 'political, religious, racial or ideological cause'.

These failed terrorists do not get the chance to die in a blaze of glory, as they see it, or be martyred for their cause. Instead, they are arrested and prosecuted—their homes searched, their phones and laptops seized, their friends and families interviewed. Many end up seeing their motivations and actions dissected in court, with no humiliating detail too small to be aired before a jury. Such prosecutions reveal much more of the true picture of terrorism in Britain than the 'successful' attacks by terrorists whose secrets often die with them.

Part of the power of terrorism is the shock of it. Plotters design their attacks not just for maximum casualties, but for maximum impact. Horrific rolling news coverage, political rows over how to deal with terrorism, the inevitable questions about how and why someone could do what they did, can easily be anticipated each time. In our interconnected world, we can all be affected by an attack on some level, even if it's just reconsidering where to go on holiday, or not feeling safe enough to go for dinner in the city centre that night. For the victims killed, the survivors and their loved ones, the effects last a lifetime. Every death, every injury, every tear shed, every pang of fear, every shred of discord is a victory for terrorists. They don't mind being labelled 'fanatics' or 'animals' or 'monsters', they welcome it. Because it masks the truth—that they are only human. They don't want us to know how they came to this point, about their families, their relationships, their mental health, their addictions. They don't want us to see behind the curtain of their lives, to look squarely at their vulnerability, and sometimes their sheer stupidity. They most definitely do not want to be laughed at.

Terrorists who fail have no such luck. We can rip off the mask and see precisely how and why their plots were stopped. We can expose the embarrassing details they never wanted us to know, from the Uber driver who was directed to a pub rather than his target because of a SatNav error, to the would-be bomber who bought the wrong ingredients for his explosives, and the amateur rapper who unwittingly blurted his plans to an undercover police officer. Some of these would-be terrorists were intercepted at an early stage, long before they were ready to realise their murderous intentions. Others were thwarted only by their own mistakes or mere chance, and some attacks were averted at the last possible moment as armed terrorists closed in on their targets. More alleged plots are going through the court system and arrests for suspected attack planning are being made every few months in Britain.

The MI5 director general, Ken McCallum, has admitted that the service was having to make 'difficult judgements' as potential threats 'come at us faster and more unpredictably'.[4] He added: 'Which fragments of information seem most likely to be pointing towards real risk? Which fragments—usually the majority—are misleading or exaggerated, or indeed accurately reflect terrorist discussions—but discussions which will forever remain aspirational, and never translate into concrete plotting? So many of the hardest decisions we take in MI5 come down to prioritisation. Every decision to investigate X is, in effect, a decision not to investigate Y or Z.' While trying to maintain coverage on a complex spectrum of threats, the security services are also racing against the clock, and know they will not always cross the finish line first.

* * *

Masood's profile is one that would become grimly familiar through successive attacks and plots that have since struck the UK. Born Adrian Elms, the 52-year-old had a lengthy history of domestic abuse, crime and extreme violence, which saw him spend several spells in prison. He converted to Islam sometime before his final release in 2003, after which he moved to Saudi Arabia and changed his name.[5] Masood first appeared on the security services' radar in 2004, as a contact of someone linked to a jihadist cell planning to bomb the Ministry of Sound nightclub in London.[6] He was not deemed to be directly connected to the plot but repeatedly popped up on the periphery of terror investigations, including one into a group seeking to travel to an al-Qaeda training camp in Pakistan. Masood was made a 'subject of interest' by MI5 in 2010 but quickly downgraded, and the probe was closed after the agency found no evidence of a security threat. As the years counted down to his attack, Masood surfaced again and again in intelligence reports as a contact of extremists in Anjem Choudary's banned al-Muhajiroun Islamist network, but an investigation was never reopened. At the inquests into his victims' deaths, an MI5 agent defended the service's decisions as 'sound'.[7]

The failure to prevent Masood from attacking one of Britain's most heavily guarded sites triggered a domino effect. Terrorists primed by years of violent Isis propaganda calling for attacks on non-Muslims around the world were galvanised into action. Those already plotting moved to act, and many others started planning their own attacks after seeing the apparent ease with which Masood smashed through the British establishment's armour.

I meet Dean Haydon, the UK's senior national coordinator for counter-terrorism policing, at New Scotland Yard. The Metropolitan Police headquarters sits overlooking the River Thames, metres from the Houses of Parliament and Downing Street. We speak in its press room, as tourists wander past and photograph the iconic revolving sign outside. The room appears light and airy, with floor-to-ceiling windows onto the street outside, but the blast-proof glazing is several inches thick. Haydon is a deputy assistant commissioner of the Metropolitan Police, but has held the senior national coordinator role since 2018. Previously the head of the Met's Counter Terrorism Command, he is no stranger to the field. He became a police officer in 1988, when the IRA was continuing its campaign of bombings on targets in England. He was on patrol on Wembley High Road when a bomb detonated outside an army recruitment centre in 1990. Two years later, he was standing on a flyover at the Staples Corner road junction as another IRA van bomb detonated metres away. By the time the planes hit the Twin

Towers on 11 September 2001, Haydon was working in anti-corruption, but was pulled into the effort to identify British victims, contact their loved ones and repatriate their bodies. When the 7 July 2005 bombings struck London, he was drafted into the investigation as part of Scotland Yard's anti-terrorist branch and has rarely strayed from the field since.

Haydon became the only police officer with the power to declare an incident a terror attack in the UK, and was charged with coordinating terrorism investigations and prevention activities. He says that the 7/7 bombings sparked the construction of Britain's current counter-terrorism policing network, but then the 2017 attacks 'changed the landscape completely':

> It threw everything up in the air really because there we were seeing a phenomenon of self-initiated terrorists, lone actors, individuals consuming material online, probably inspired but not directed by terrorist groups, who went on to launch an attack ... a lone actor with no real network to infiltrate, who's consumed propaganda material and looked at instructions, then got hold of weaponry.[8]

Security machinery developed after 9/11 and the 7/7 London bombings was geared up for complex, internationally networked plots that required extensive preparations—not lone, untrained fanatics attempting massacres with minimal planning and using hire cars and supermarket knives. The new modus operandi caused timeframes to 'collapse', Haydon says, with the security services left with far fewer opportunities to spot, infiltrate and disrupt plots.

The threat of attacks on British soil had already been on the rise for three years. In 2014, Isis emerged after splitting from al-Qaeda following an internal power struggle. The group was originally al-Qaeda in Iraq (AQI) but expanded into neighbouring Syria after the start of the country's brutal civil war. Even for al-Qaeda, AQI's excesses of violence had become too extreme at points. In July 2005, Osama bin Laden's second-in-command, Ayman al-Zawahiri, sent a 6,500-word letter to AQI's leader that took issue with some of his strategies. Zawahiri told Abu Musab al-Zarqawi that his main goals must be 'removing the Americans' from Iraq, and then establishing an Islamic emirate or caliphate. He warned of the necessity of 'popular support from the Muslim masses' in Iraq and surrounding countries and said that AQI should strive to increase it. Zawahiri said that ordinary people did not find 'scenes of slaughtering hostages palatable', after AQI issued graphic videos of beheadings. In a portentous message, he told Zarqawi:

> And your response, while true, might be: 'Why shouldn't we sow terror in the hearts of the crusaders and their helpers? And isn't the destruction of the villages and the cities on the heads of their inhabitants [by US bombs] more cruel than slaughtering? And aren't the cluster bombs and the seven ton bombs and the depleted uranium bombs crueller than slaughtering?' All of these questions and more might be asked, and you are justified. However this does not change the reality at all, which is that the general opinion of our supporter does not comprehend that ... we are in a media battle in a race for the hearts and minds of our *Ummah* [global Muslim community].[9]

AQI militants had also been bombing and murdering Shia Muslims, who follow a different branch of Islam than al-Qaeda and other Sunni Salafi jihadist terrorist groups. Zawahiri told Zarqawi that 'Muslim admirers amongst the common folk' did not understand attacks on Shia mosques, and that such attacks 'won't be acceptable to the Muslim populace, however much you have tried to explain it'. He called for AQI not to 'lose sight of the target'. But the tactics that Zawahiri took issue with would become commonplace years later, when AQI expanded into Syria and rebranded itself as the Islamic State of Iraq and Syria (Isis). Al-Qaeda's influence of global terror was starting to wane, and Isis was on the rise. Zarqawi had been assassinated in a targeted airstrike by the US in 2006, and his successor was picked off in 2010. A veteran AQI official, Abu Bakr al-Baghdadi, took the reins and spearheaded the violent conquest that saw him declaring himself emir of a new Islamic State four years later.

Isis' initial priority was attracting people to populate its caliphate in Syria and Iraq and to help it expand and prosper. But as security services around the world clamped down on would-be foreign fighters trying to make the journey, Isis called for them to launch attacks in their home countries instead. The start of a bombing campaign by a US-led international coalition in August 2014 lent the terrorist group fresh justification in its mounting incitement. It pumped out propaganda claiming to show civilian casualties from indiscriminate air strikes, which it characterised as an attack on all Muslims. As a result, Isis told its supporters that all Muslims had an obligation to strike back against the coalition's member nations and kill civilian 'disbelievers' who were complicit in the bombing.

'The best thing you can do is to strive to your best and kill any disbeliever, whether he be French, American, or from any of their allies', came the instruction from Isis' official spokesman in September 2014.[10] 'If you are not able to find an IED [improvised explosive device] or a bullet, then single out the disbelieving American, Frenchman, or any of their allies. Smash his head with a rock, or slaughter him with a knife, or run him over with your car, or throw him down from a high place, or choke him, or poison him.' Isis dramatically lowered the bar for such 'operations', telling supporters that they could act on the group's behalf without prior contact, without permission and without training. It backed up the call with online guides in multiple languages, including several on how to carry out lone attacks using vehicles and knives. Through a propaganda network of unprecedented reach and sophistication, Isis amplified news of each attack and glorified the perpetrators, and the success of its strategy became brutally clear.

From 2015 onwards, jihadist terror attacks were launched across Europe at an unparalleled rate, and the onslaught gave birth to a new threat from the far right. As public anger was exploited by extremist figures to present all Muslims as a threat to Western lives and 'civilisation', a phenomenon developed known as 'reciprocal radicalisation'. While more and more Isis-claimed attacks struck, anti-Islam radicals started to believe that violent retaliation was not just justified, but necessary. Meanwhile, neo-Nazi groups took notes from Isis' attack methods and propaganda techniques, and started to call for their own 'white jihad'. A feedback loop developed, where terrorists used activity by opposing extremists to incite their followers and justify their actions, creating an endless cycle of violence. In the UK, the result was the highest rate of terrorist plotting ever known.

This book begins in 2017, a watershed moment for terrorism in Britain. It was the start of a wave of deadly attacks and plots of a new kind whose ramifications continue to be felt. It was also the year I started focusing on terrorism in Britain, having previously covered Isis-inspired attacks in Europe and around the world for *The Independent*. The UK was no stranger to terrorism, following decades of unrest linked to the Troubles in Northern Ireland, followed by a growing threat from al-Qaeda that culminated in the July 2005 London bombings. But to cover the totality of that history would be the work of more than one book, and to limit the present book to plots inspired by just one ideology would not do justice to the full picture of the threat, nor to the way opposing groups drive each other towards violence.

But my decision to begin in 2017 is not just due to a lack of time or space: we are in a new age of terror, one in which movements as diverse as neo-Nazis, jihadists and cultural nationalists are plotting eerily similar attacks on increasingly unpredictable targets. Part One of this book concerns plots thwarted at an early stage, looking at what the would-be terrorists intended and why. By delving into plotters' mental and material world and looking at their journeys towards radicalisation, we can see how the profile of attackers and their methods changed. The second part covers more advanced plots, where weapons and bomb-making materials had been acquired. Several of these failed attackers were the subject of elaborate security service stings, which demonstrate the evolving challenges for agencies working to prevent terrorist bloodshed in Britain. Part Three of the book details attacks that were stopped at the very last moment, with plotters armed and ready to carry out their plans. It looks ahead to the likely profile of terrorist plotters in the near future, and questions whether it will even be possible to categorise the increasingly murky motivations driving them. It also raises a variety of moral, political, legal and social questions about the meaning of terrorism.

By late 2022, 43,000 people have appeared on MI5's radar for posing a potential threat to the UK. Of those, 3,000 are current subjects of interest (SOIs) and 800 priority investigations are running. Probes into the remaining 40,000 have been closed for now, but official documents acknowledge that situation 'could change at any time'.[11]

Masood and the Manchester Arena bomber, Salman Abedi, had been in that pool of closed SOIs, while the London Bridge attack ringleader Khuram Butt was under active investigation—but his plot was still missed.[12] There was no monitoring or intelligence of any kind ahead of the deadly Finsbury Park terror attack that struck in the same month, where the perpetrator was a far-right extremist who set out to kill Muslims partly as revenge for the Manchester Arena bombing. Several other terrorists would strike without being known to the intelligence services, including a man who went on a knife rampage inspired by the 2019 New Zealand mosque shootings. It was not until 2020 that MI5 took primacy for extreme right-wing terrorism from the police, putting the security response on an equal footing to jihadists.

By that point, the far right had become the fastest-growing threat in the UK, following the emergence of neo-Nazi terrorist organisation National Action and a surge in Islamophobia and support for white nationalist groups. But the British security services' response was still split along the archaic lines of 'international terrorism'—mainly jihadism—and 'domestic extremism'—the far right and everything else. MI5 led on the former, while ever-stretched local police forces were left to deal with the latter. In November 2017, an expert charged with reviewing internal MI5 and police assessments of what went wrong with the attacks of the preceding months issued a withering assessment of the situation.[13] He wrote to the home secretary:

> I was not impressed by the analysis of the threat from domestic extremism that was presented to me … the international/domestic distinction is outdated, and the contrast in apparent seriousness between terrorism and extremism is just the sort of factor that—were it more widely known—would be grist to the mill of those who falsely allege state-sponsored Islamophobia and seek to attract fair-minded citizens to their cause.

At the time of writing, counter-terror police still class jihadists as the largest risk, but the extreme right wing is responsible for up to a fifth of their work, while a new category is growing. Known as 'mixed, unstable or unclear ideology', it encompasses people—often teenagers and those with mental health issues—who appear intent on violence but have no clearly discernible motivation. Some are obsessed with school shootings and mass murder, some are driven by conspiracy theories, and some consume such a wide range of propaganda from different terrorist groups that they are not classed as subscribing to a single ideology.

The way to describe and define these groups is a matter of ongoing debate. This author uses the term jihadist to describe the Salafi-jihadist ideology furthered by al-Qaeda and Isis, and Islamist to encompass a broader set of political and religious ideas. The far right covers ideologies including cultural nationalism, white nationalism and neo-Nazism. Direct quotes have been faithfully reproduced and the terms may be used differently by varying speakers and documents. The British security services, for example, officially use the designations 'Islamist extremist terrorism' and 'extreme right-wing terrorism' to describe the two largest threats. Where terrorist propaganda and documents are referred to, the records used are the author's own and have been obtained for legal journalistic purposes. For security purposes, it has not been possible to name or directly quote some interviewees.

There has been an overall shift in the profile of attack plotters, away from being a part of real-world networks with training and direction from terrorist groups, to being lone actors who 'self-radicalise' online and keep their plans to themselves. Teenagers and people with autism and mental health issues are taking up an increasing proportion of suspects prosecuted for terror offences. Police believe the phenomenon has been enabled by the ease of consuming terrorist propaganda and networking with like-minded people on social media, and then worsened by the isolation enforced by the Covid pandemic, as support from mental health services, schools and councils fell away. 'People can access literally anything online,' senior counter-terror officer Haydon says:

> In the past, people were pretty much stovepiped in relation to different groups. You're either wearing an al-Qaeda badge and you stuck to al-Qaeda, or wearing an Isis badge and you stuck to Isis, or you were supporting the IRA or some other group, whereas now you see youngsters experimenting with all of it because there's so much extremist material online from different organisations. We're seeing the age profile going down and becoming younger because of the accessibility of the internet.[14]

Officials acknowledge that they do not have the resources to track all potential terrorists flagged to them, and several perpetrators of recent attacks were not known to counter-terror police or MI5 at all. Sir Mark Rowley, who was the head of UK counter-terrorism policing from 2014 to 2018, likens spotting the extremists who will move to violence to finding 'a needle in a haystack'. 'There's tens of thousands of them in this wider pool of people who have the mindset but haven't yet had the spark to act and it's hard to judge when and how that spark will come,' he adds.[15] When it does come, it may only take weeks, days or even hours to plan and carry out an attack.

PART ONE

NIPPED IN THE BUD

FALSE FRIENDS AND FAILURES

The Westminster attack was not the first Isis-inspired attack planned in the UK, just the first that got through. As Khalid Masood launched his atrocity, others were hatching their own plots to wreak havoc and death, and they have not stopped. But the majority of plots are nipped in the bud at an early stage, before would-be terrorists have completed the necessary preparations for slaughter. Some plots counted by the security services are stopped too early even to result in a charge, either because intelligence evidence cannot be used in court or there is simply not enough proof to pass muster with the Crown Prosecution Service. Many of these early-stage plotters have previously been known to the authorities for extremist connections or criminal offences, and are already being watched. Some unwittingly spill their intentions to undercover police officers and MI5 agents who are posing as like-minded terrorists. Others make mistakes that alert the authorities to their plans, or spark concerns with friends, colleagues and officials who have no choice but to report them. For the security services, the question is often when—not if—to move in.

Before 2017, it was common to set up complex infiltration and surveillance operations to intercept plots over many months. An al-Qaeda-linked attempt to bomb potential targets including the huge Bluewater Shopping Centre and the Ministry of Sound nightclub was foiled in 2004 when MI5 bugged the terror cell's homes and vehicles and police replaced their stock of ammonium nitrate with a harmless substance. In 2006, a plot to take down transatlantic flights using explosives hidden in sports drinks bottles was stopped after a similarly extensive surveillance operation, as was the 2010 al-Qaeda-inspired plan to bomb the London Stock Exchange. Until the emergence of Isis, these were typical plots—seeing groups of people planning complex attacks over several months, or even years. But then everything changed. Suddenly, terrorists weren't waiting for instructions from an emir abroad to act, they weren't travelling to training camps in Pakistan or Afghanistan, they weren't bringing together cells of like-minded people to plot, they weren't taking months and months trying to build bombs, they weren't aiming for 'spectaculars' in the model of 9/11 or 7/7. They started to pick up guns, knives and vehicles and launched attacks alone, and the security services were caught off-guard.

I meet Sir Mark Rowley in a bustling café inside St James' Park underground station, a short walk from his former base at New Scotland Yard in the heart of Westminster. It is almost four years since he retired as the head of UK counter-terrorism police, but he won't be out of uniform for much longer. Months after we meet, Rowley will become Britain's most senior police officer as the new commissioner of the Metropolitan Police. But as we sit down with our coffee, I've come to talk to him about his former role, known within the force as ACSO—standing for Assistant Commissioner of Specialist Operations. Rowley took the post in June 2014, shortly before Abu Bakr al-Baghdadi declared Isis' 'caliphate' from the Great Mosque of al-Nuri in Mosul. It was, as he jokes, 'not nice timing'. Previously, the biggest terror threats to Britain emanated from al-Qaeda and the IRA. 'They were very secretive organisations which were hard to join and attack methodologies were big, complicated—they were aiming for what they would see as a spectacular,' Rowley explains. 'That complexity makes it easier for policing and the security services to pick up on these cases, and you've got more time to build the evidence so by the time you arrest them you know you've got them completely bang to rights.'[1]

Isis did away with all that. While some of the deadliest attacks launched by the group's adherents, such as the November 2015 Paris attacks, were carried out by combat-trained jihadis who networked in person, the vast majority were not. That was because Isis had specifically ordered its followers not to seek permission, not to bother with complex methods, and not to wait. Supporters around the world only had months to join the new 'caliphate' in 2014 before governments clamped down on travel to Iraq and Syria, and before US-led airstrikes began. And so Isis' strategy shifted, and a call went out that still echoes today. The group's spokesman, Abu Muhammad al-Adnani, told Muslims that they were religiously obligated to 'support your brothers' against a 'new campaign by the crusaders'. 'O *muwahhid* [Muslims], we call you up to defend the Islamic State,' he said. 'Dozens of nations have gathered against it. They began their war against us at all levels. So rise O *muwahhid*. Rise and defend your state from your place wherever you may be.' Adnani claimed the coming battle would be critical in the history of Islam, urging: 'Do not let this battle pass you by':

> You must strike the soldiers, patrons, and troops of the *tawaghit* [transgressors against Allah]. Strike their police, security, and intelligence members, as well as their treacherous agents. Destroy their beds. Embitter their lives for them and busy them with themselves. If you can kill a disbelieving American or European—especially the spiteful and filthy French—or an Australian, or a Canadian, or any other disbeliever from the disbelievers waging war, including the citizens of the countries that entered into a coalition against the Islamic State, then rely upon Allah, and kill him in any manner or way however it may be. Do not ask for anyone's advice and do not seek anyone's verdict. Kill the disbeliever.[2]

The audio message was put out on Isis' propaganda channels on 22 September 2014, and was then amplified, transcribed and translated into multiple languages by supporters around the world. Dean Haydon, who was the UK's senior national coordinator for counter-terrorism policing from 2018 to 2022 and previously led the Metropolitan Police Counter Terrorism Command, says the security services were immediately 'extremely concerned'. 'Adnani's rhetoric in 2014 absolutely had an effect,' he adds. 'This message was "just go and attack anybody in your country". That changed the threat completely and certainly had an impact on the current threat as we see it.'[3]

Despite the paradigm shift triggered by Isis, the idea of lone wolf jihadist terror attacks was far from new. It was first promoted to Muslims in the West by Anwar al-Awlaki, a Yemeni-American jihadist ideologue who became an international attack planner for al-Qaeda in the Arabian Peninsula. Such was his influence that he was assassinated in an American drone strike ordered by Barack Obama in 2011. The US president hailed his death as a 'major blow to al-Qaeda's most active operational affiliate', saying Awlaki had directed international terror attacks including attempts to take down planes in 2009 and 2010. 'He repeatedly called on individuals in the United States and around the globe to kill innocent men, women and children to advance a murderous agenda,' Obama added. 'The death of al-Awlaki marks another significant milestone in the broader effort to defeat al Qaeda and its affiliates.'[4]

But his influence lived on. Awlaki's work, which used stories from Islamic scripture to justify terror attacks, has been a common inspiration for jihadist terror plotters in the UK for over a decade. Alexander Meleagrou-Hitchens, the author of *Incitement: Anwar al-Awlaki's Western Jihad*, says that Awlaki and Samir Khan, a fellow al-Qaeda in the Arabian Peninsula ideologue who was killed in the same 2011 drone strike, 'essentially invented the jihadist version of the lone actor terrorist'. He adds:

> Awlaki developed a religious justification for committing attacks at home in Western countries without needing permission from a scholar or a direct connection to al-Qaeda, or to an official terrorist group. Awlaki was really the first in the West to provide this as an option ... prior to all that the idea was that to be a proper jihadist you had to go to Pakistan or Iraq, go to get trained and come back like the 7/7 types. The idea that you could just do this on your own hadn't really occurred to many people. It was Awlaki and Samir Khan in particular who created this new propaganda and this new ideology around lone actors—and of course Isis took that and put it into hyperdrive.[5]

Tellingly, some of Isis' first English-language propaganda videos were overlaid with voiceovers by the then-dead Awlaki that supported its message. Meleagrou-Hitchens says he acted as 'a bridge from the al-Qaeda jihadism to Isis jihadism'. Isis was originally a faction of al-Qaeda and developed out of a power struggle during the Syrian civil war. Militants from the expansionist al-Qaeda in Iraq, led by Abu Bakr al-Baghdadi, crossed the border and tried to merge with local faction Jabhat al-Nusra, which was aligned with al-Qaeda's central leader Ayman al-Zawahiri. But Jabhat al-Nusra refused to take orders from Baghdadi, sparking a violent dispute that ended with al-Qaeda formally cutting ties with Isis in February 2014. The group then seized control of large parts of Syria and Iraq and issued its instructions for followers to either travel to its new caliphate or launch attacks at home.

Despite the direct competition with al-Qaeda, Awlaki has remained revered by Isis supporters abroad. Meleagrou-Hitchens says that the ideological schism on the Syrian battlefield was 'not something most Westerners are bothered about really, they're just backing the strongest horse ... overall you're talking about groups that are very close together ideologically'. He says that although Awlaki was operating in a period where al-Qaeda was struggling following the Iraq and Afghanistan wars, he 'kept the pot boiling' on the jihadist movement by using news events like cartoons of the Prophet Mohamed to drive perceptions of a global war on Islam. 'He was keeping it relevant, keeping it alive, constantly updating it and reacting to events and giving the jihadist spin on those events to Westerners,' Meleagrou-Hitchens says.

Born in New Mexico, Awlaki was initially a mainstream Islamic imam at prominent American mosques and considered to be a legitimate authority on the religion.[6] His status meant that as his teachings became more openly jihadist, he already had a large and devoted audience who accepted them as religiously justified. He joined al-Qaeda in the Arabian Peninsula in 2009 and became explicit in his calls for 'open source jihad'—lone attacks by jihadists in the West without direction or permission from al-Qaeda—through its English-language magazine. Awlaki's editorials appeared alongside manuals for carrying out attacks, including a widely used article on how to 'make a bomb in the kitchen of your mom'.[7]

Meleagrou-Hitchens first came across Awlaki in the late 2000s, while he was giving remote lectures to audiences in London. 'This name kept on coming up—Awlaki—and at that time he was being promoted a lot among non-jihadi Islamist groups,' he recalls. 'He was very charismatic, very smart tactically and strategically. He was well-read, he could recite the Quran and Hadith, he respected education, he respected reading and scholarship and intellectual discussion. He just knew what made people tick.' Meleagrou-Hitchens says that although Awlaki had already released work that justified terror attacks, in the UK he was 'being presented by people who should have known better as a legitimate scholar'. Awlaki was also held up as a victim following his imprisonment in Yemen for terrorist activity, which he publicly denied at the time. Some British groups had advocated for his release and after he was freed in 2007, he became a celebrity on the Islamist scene. Evidence of his links to two of the 9/11 bombers had been published and made public by the official commission into the attacks in 2004,[8] but Awlaki's compelling speaking style allowed plausible deniability over the threat he posed to continue for years. Meleagrou-Hitchens says that much of Awlaki's earlier work, including titles such as *Constants on the Path of Jihad*, which remain popular with British terror plotters, were translations of others' work. He expanded on texts by Arab Salafi scholars and placed them in a Western context, while applying the same process to Sirah—the early histories of Islam. 'None of this stuff was available in English until Awlaki started translating it,' Meleagrou-Hitchens says. 'He gives them modern relevance. This is very important, firstly in terms of explaining his early popularity and his mainstream appeal, but also in terms of his ability as a recruiter because when he becomes an open jihadist he's doing the same thing by taking stories from the early periods of Islam, which are also some of the most violent.'

Awlaki told Muslims that they were in the same position the Prophet Mohamed had been in—under attack from all sides—and that they should follow his example by responding with violent jihad. He did not initially call for terror attacks explicitly, instead 'giving people the impression they were making those conclusions by themselves'. 'He essentially pushes you right to the edge but gives you the feeling that you are educating yourself and making an objective decision,' Meleagrou-Hitchens says. It was a powerful technique that enabled Awlaki to evade censorship, while having the desired effect on growing numbers of followers who started travelling to fight for jihadist groups abroad and planning terror attacks. Awlaki spent several spells in the UK in the early 2000s and after he moved to Yemen, supporters broadcast his lectures and held question-and-answer sessions by phone and video link. He was an early adopter of the internet, using blogs, YouTube and the chat service Paltalk to reach his audiences in the US and UK when it became impossible to address them in person. Importantly, he characterised what he called 'www jihad'—'following the news of jihad and spreading it', disseminating extremist works and 'fighting the lies of the Western media' online—as ways to support jihad.[9]

Over a decade after his death, his teachings continue to circulate on the internet and inspire terrorists around the world. Meleagrou-Hitchens says that Awlaki 'essentially lowered the bar for what it meant to be a jihadist, he made it something that many more people could do':

> When Isis emerged, there was a pool of people who were primed for recruitment because of their interaction with Awlaki's work in particular. They weren't coming in cold, they were speaking to people who were familiar with jihadist ideology because of Awlaki's work … he knew that terrorism is not really about the numbers. It's about the message it sends, it's an act of propaganda. He knew that while these attacks were going to be low tech and low casualty they were still going to have a propaganda impact and that mattered.[10]

Isis clearly endorsed the message. An issue of its English-language propaganda magazine released in October 2016 contained graphically detailed instructions on how to commit knife attacks, including advice on how to select weapons, targets and where to strike vulnerable parts of the body. The article added:

> It should be stressed that the objective of a knife attack is to attain a reasonable kill count, while equally—if not more importantly—to inflict terror on the Crusader citizens of the land in which the operation is carried out … the overall objective of any just terror operation is to bring horror and misery to the enemies of Allah, and to remind them that their efforts to wage war against Islam and the Muslims will only lead to more and more mujahideen appearing in their very midst, ready to strike them mercilessly on their own soil.

Isis backed up its call for lone attacks with videos, religious songs, magazines, newsletters and countless posts on its social media accounts—ensuring that the key pieces of incitement were disseminated not just in Arabic, but in English, French and other languages.

The group then started claiming responsibility for attacks around the world, regardless of whether it had any contact with perpetrators or, in some cases, any proof of their allegiance at all. A generic form of wording emerged, hailing 'soldiers of the caliphate' for launching attacks and saying they were in response to its call for violent retribution on countries in the US-led coalition. Terrorists were further glorified in propaganda magazines, which contained sections on 'just [meaning justified] terror tactics' with detailed instructions on how to launch attacks using knives and vehicles. Introducing an instruction manual for knife attacks, Isis told readers: 'A hardened resolve, some basic planning, and reliance on Allah for success are enough for a single mujahid to bring untold misery to the enemies of Allah.'[11] The result was that it became 'much easier for somebody to become a terrorist,' Rowley says:

> Isis made terrorism open source in some ways, they threw all that propaganda material out there which was being picked up by all sorts of people, particularly the vulnerable at home and in bedrooms ... if all you need to do is read a bit of propaganda, talk to a few people, have a few ideas, buy a knife, use a car, and off you go and do a much more low-tech simplistic attack, then it's quicker from conception to execution of the idea.[12]

The spate of four deadly attacks in England during 2017 were proof of the difficulties this began to cause for police and MI5. Until that point, Britain had been spared the horrors inflicted by Isis supporters in France, Belgium and Germany, but security officials had been watching the European mainland nervously and working urgently to stop any returning Isis fighters slipping back into the UK unnoticed. Counter-terror police were pulling in intelligence reports from the Middle East and EU partners and running 'faster and faster' to prevent attacks. Rowley, who was knighted following his retirement for his 'exceptional contribution to national security at a time of unprecedented threat', says eventual failure felt inevitable. 'I knew there would be attacks on my watch,' he admits. 'There just had to be, it would be extraordinary if there weren't. You're hoping there won't be but you sort of know there will be.'

Just 17 weeks saw four deadly terror attacks leave 36 victims dead and more than 200 injured. The first three were claimed by

Isis, but the fourth—in Finsbury Park—was the result of a dangerous far-right backlash. But in the same four months, a further six
attacks were thwarted and that number would carry on rising.
While jihadists are still behind the greatest number of plots—
around half of all attacks foiled since 2017 at the time of writing—a
large proportion now stem from the extreme right wing, including
neo-Nazis and anti-Muslim fanatics. Many adopted Isis' modus operandi, attempting indiscriminate bombings or vehicle and knife
rampages, while others aimed for targeted assassinations. The plotters' ideologies could not be more opposed, but they share many
common characteristics which police broadly label 'vulnerabilities'.
They can include mental health issues, learning difficulties, unem-
ployment, social isolation and a lack of purpose in their lives.
Sometimes, the vulnerability comes from their age. One convicted
plotter in the first part of this book was arrested by counter-terror
police when he was just 16 years old. 'The profile of the terrorist
has completely changed,' Haydon says. 'We're seeing the age profile going down and becoming younger because of the accessibility
of the internet. These lone actors can self-radicalise online and
decide, "Tomorrow I'm going into a supermarket, buy a knife and
commit an attack".'[13]

'I-S-I-S, YOU LIKE THAT?'

THE 2017 DOMINO EFFECT

As Masood ploughed his vehicle into victims on Westminster Bridge, a young man was awaiting trial in HMP Belmarsh, one of Britain's most secure and most notorious jails. Haroon Syed, then aged just 19, had been hoping to become the first Isis supporter to murder 'disbelievers' in the UK. The teenager was following in the footsteps of his big brother, Nadir Syed, who had been jailed for life over a 2014 plot to behead members of the public on Remembrance Sunday.[14] But Haroon had even bigger aspirations. From his home in the west London suburb of Hounslow, he attempted to procure a bomb or machine gun from online contacts and researched potential targets including Oxford Street, an Elton John concert on 11 September in Hyde Park, 'packed places in London' and military bases.[15]

Syed made his preparations on the secure Threema messaging app, where he told a contact: 'Machine guns, we need someone who can make a vest ... after some damage with machine gun then do *istishhad* [martyrdom], that's what I'm planning to do'. The teenager attempted to obtain 'gear' to commit mass murder in the name of Isis. 'You have to find out the price for the machine gun, any gun,' he wrote to an online contact he affectionately called '*akhi*, meaning brother in Arabic. 'If the weapons don't work then we can make a bomb ... middle of a crowd, blow it up.' Syed met his contact, a man who called himself 'Abu Yusuf' at a Costa in Slough to finalise their plans, and handed him £150 for a nail bomb to be constructed. 'Those sharp things, lots of them inside, good, good man, can't wait,' he enthused. 'After it's all done yeah it blows up everything, after whatever, if I got go to prison, I go the prison; if I die, I die. You understand? I got to get to *jannah* [paradise].'

Unfortunately for Syed, his co-conspirator was an MI5 officer. 'Abu Yusuf' was merely a character played by the security service, with multiple agents playing the role in online messages as they drew out Syed's plans over five months. Police moved in on 8 September 2016, three days before the Elton John concert he had considered as a target. The unkempt teenager, who was trying to grow out a straggly beard, was not shy about expressing his allegiance. When asked for the password to his mobile phone, he replied: 'Yeah, "I-S-I-S.". You like that?' Syed pleaded guilty to the preparation of terrorist acts at the Old Bailey after a last-ditch attempt failed to get his case thrown out over alleged entrapment. Jailing him for life, Judge Michael Topolski KC said he was 'intent upon carrying out an act of mass murder in this country'. He told Syed: 'You were moving ever closer to being ready to carry out your attack. You were not lured, you were not enticed, you were not entrapped ... you remained deeply committed to the ideology of a brutal and barbaric organisation that has sought to hijack and corrupt an ancient and venerable religion for its own purposes and you indeed wanted to be part of it.'[16]

Syed is among several attack plotters who had previously been flagged to a core British government counter-terrorism scheme called Prevent. Intended to do what its title suggests, the programme aims to intervene in extremists' lives to stop their path towards terrorism before offences are committed. Its mission is a controversial one, and has triggered years of criticism by groups of all political leanings. It has been accused of being ineffective, but also of being overly intrusive, of demonising legitimate beliefs, discriminating against Muslims and having a chilling effect on free speech. At the time of writing, a government-commissioned review has been underway for almost four years but its conclusions have not been published. Syed was reported to Prevent by his sixth-form college, where teachers noticed his behaviour started to change after his older brother's arrest for attack planning in 2014. He became withdrawn and began paying less attention to schooling, professed to have become more religious, started wearing traditional Islamic clothing, and was generally 'less social and more angry'.[17] At one point, Syed spoke to another student about a desire to help those 'being killed in Syria'. Staff at West Thames College voiced concerns that he was being 'groomed to have radical views', could be 'easily brainwashed', and that the views he expressed were not his own. His defence lawyers later contended that he had been indoctrinated by other, older jihadists in the banned al-Muhajiroun network, while consuming Isis propaganda online.

In legal papers prepared for his defence, Syed was described as 'highly vulnerable due to family history, lack of education, addiction to violent online games and the arrest and imprisonment of his brother'. Judge Topolski concluded that Syed's radicalisation had started before 2014, but that his brother's arrest had 'triggered a strong sense of anger'. A psychiatric report presented to the court said that 'lacking knowledge or any proper religious guidance, and certainly lacking any parental guidance, he turned to the internet and quickly developed an interest in Islamist propaganda and narrative … he accepted the ideology of Isis as correct'. The judge found that although the teenager was 'susceptible to being impressed and persuaded' by others, he was 'deadly serious' about wanting to commit an attack in support of Isis. Syed's defence barrister told his trial: 'The proper response of the state should have been to engage Prevent to help this young man, to steer him away from the path it was feared he was going down, rather than guiding him down it.' The argument did not persuade Judge Topolski to reduce his sentence, and an attempted appeal accusing MI5 of entrapment was thrown out the following year. 'Far from the role-players conducting themselves abusively and bringing the justice system into disrepute, they are to be commended for an undercover operation conducted with scrupulous care,' the judges ruled.

'We are a death squad sent by Allah'

For some plotters, a terror attack is their primary act in support of their cause. For several of those in this book, it is actually plan B. Plan A was to become real-life soldiers of the caliphate, fighting for Isis in Iraq, Syria or other territories that sprang up in the Middle East and Asia. The terrorist group's propaganda around building an idyllic Islamic state persuaded thousands of people to migrate from around the world from 2014 onwards, including at least 900 from the UK. By 2018, the British government estimated that at least a fifth had been killed and 40 per cent had returned home—mostly women and children or men who performed a U-turn very quickly in the early stages of the 'caliphate'.[18] The 900 are only a fraction of those who considered or attempted the journey, because as time went on British authorities became ever more adept at thwarting their ambitions—and keeping tabs on those left behind.

Key routes to Syria, often via Turkey, became closely watched and people were grilled on their reasons for travel. If an ambition to join Isis was suspected, foiled foreign fighters could have their passports seized, be put under surveillance or even be prosecuted for preparing to commit acts of terrorism abroad. The aim, Sir Mark Rowley explains, was to stop Isis bolstering its numbers and to prevent British jihadis becoming involved in the atrocities it was inflicting on religious minorities, prisoners, enemy combatants and anyone who resisted it in Iraq and Syria. 'Some people were saying, "Well if people want to go and fight over there, let them go,"' he recalls:

> It's nonsense. You're saying that if you want to go and slaughter people overseas that's ok? That can't be right, and secondly if people who are in Britain want to go and do horrible things overseas and get more trained and more angry, and then potentially come back here that doesn't sound like a good idea either. So stopping it and interdicting and trying to prosecute people for that was in my mind obviously the right thing to do.[19]

But the strategy had consequences. The would-be Isis fighters stopped at airports and confined to the UK became frustrated, with no outlet for their desire to wage violent jihad. So they redirected it. As Neil Basu, who succeeded Rowley as the head of UK counter-terrorism policing, admitted at a security conference in 2018, the biggest terror threat did not in fact come from returning Isis fighters: 'The threat was already here—and there are still plenty of aspirant or frustrated travellers who now have nowhere to go.'[20] Several years later, Haydon agrees. The then senior national coordinator for counter-terrorism policing says that while the Syrian war and other conflicts overseas are still inspiring people in the UK, 'the main threat we currently see is from people within this country that are being self-radicalised'.[21] Haydon says he is aware of several cases where people plotted terror attacks after being prevented from travelling to join Isis, but that British police still worked to prevent such journeys—as well as those to conflict zones elsewhere like Afghanistan and Ukraine. 'We've got to be realistic that in their minds what that actually does is frustrate them further and could even accelerate their attack plans,' he admits. 'Rather than going out and joining a group overseas, instead they decide to commit an attack here.'

One such frustrated traveller was a man called Umar Haque. When he was 23 years old, he quit his job at an Islamic school in east London, moved out of his parents' home and booked a plane ticket from Heathrow Airport to Istanbul. Counter-terror police stopped him before he could board the flight on 11 April 2016, interviewing him and seizing his two mobile phones. Haque, whose spots and wispy beard made him look younger than his age, claimed he was merely travelling to Istanbul for a few days' holiday before going on to Saudi Arabia. The story didn't stand up. His phones showed that he had been researching Isis activity in Syria, including beheadings, and recent terrorist attacks in Belgium and in France. Police seized Haque's passport on the spot and weeks later, the government stripped his entitlement to hold British travel documents.

Having been prevented from joining Isis in Syria, Haque became 'angry and frustrated'.[22] Alive to his sympathies and the potential consequences of their intervention, police reached out to Haque through Prevent, but he refused to engage with the voluntary counter-terror programme. Within weeks, he was drawing up plans to orchestrate attacks in London, listing potential methods, targets and ideas for recruiting others to his cause. He was following Isis' official instructions to the letter—if you cannot reach the caliphate, launch an attack wherever you are. Haque referred numerous times to the group's official spokesman and collected Isis propaganda. He accessed a May 2016 speech that said:

If the *tawaghit* [transgressors] have shut the door of *hijrah* [migration] in your faces, then open the door of jihad in theirs. Make your deed a source of their regret. Truly, the smallest act you do in their lands is more beloved to us than the biggest act done here; it is more effective for us and more harmful to them. If one of you wishes and strives to reach the lands of the Islamic State, then each of us wishes to be in your place to make examples of the crusaders, day and night, scaring them and terrorising them.[23]

Handwritten entries in Haque's notebooks at his home showed the scale of his ambition—multiple attacks in London using dozens of terrorists he was to recruit himself. Haque had scribbled down violent to-do lists including: '(1) Learn how to make it[24]—buy a phone, (2) Purchase *silah* [weapons], (3) Purchase a van, (4) Develop recruitment pack.' He had detailed the 'result of the actions', 'recruitment methodology' and 'what we require', referring to leaders, financial backers, weaponry and a minimum of ten 'soldiers'. Potential targets included the police, the Queen's Guard, courts, transport networks, Shia Muslims, the Westfield shopping centre, banks, Heathrow Airport, Parliament, far-right protests, the American, Russian and Chinese embassies, and even the MI5 building. For such grand plans, Haque needed support, and he let two friends he had met at his local mosque in on the plot. Plans were underway when the Westminster attack struck in March 2017, and Haque was inspired by Khalid Masood and accelerated his activities. He 'hero-worshipped' Masood and frequently talked to his friends about what they could learn from his methods. In a sudden burst of activity, Haque started efforts to buy a gun and ammunition from a local drug dealer. Four days after the Westminster attack, Haque told one of his two co-conspirators, Muhammad Abid:

> What I want to personally is launch different attacks in all the different areas, one in Westminster, one in Stratford, one in Forest Gate, one in so many different areas, yeah. Immediately there's one focus to all the police. Get off the streets. Civilians get off the streets, not just Westminster attack, entire London … we're here to cause terrorism my brother. We are a death squad sent by Allah and his messengers to avenge my Arab brothers' blood.[25]

MI5 agents were listening to the conversation, having bugged Abid's home earlier that day. Listening devices were also inserted in Abid and Haque's cars, as they carried on unaware they were being closely watched. While making his preparations, Haque had returned to teaching, despite his lack of qualifications, and was put in charge of managing religious classes at the Ripple Road Mosque in Barking, east London. He decided that the young boys he taught there would become his soldiers. Their parents had paid for after-school religious instruction on Thursdays and Fridays. Instead, Haque indoctrinated his class of 16 children with his jihadist ideology and started training them to become part of a 'death squad'. He told the boys, aged between 12 and 14, that he had contact with Isis and was intent on dying as a martyr—and that others could join him. Haque played the children the terrorist group's propaganda videos and told them the UK was bombing innocent people, asking them how they would feel if their families were dying. Haque went to cruel lengths to keep the true nature of his teaching secret from both the mosque and the children's parents. He ordered the boys to swear on Allah's name that they would not tell anyone about his classes, and claimed that if they broke the vow they would go to hell and their homes would burn down.

Soon, Haque had the boys doing push-ups, races and grappling, shouting 'Allahu akbar' [Allah is great] as they performed the exercises. On at least two occasions, he made the children act out terror attacks involving knives and car bombs. The class were split into two groups—'martyrs' and police, Christians or Americans—and they would then role-play fighting and killing. The martyr group were taught to launch an initial attack and then a second wave as emergency services responded. Haque told them that in the future they would be able to make the exercise real. The training continued for six months before Haque was arrested, and a psychological report on his pupils later found that they expressed 'confusion and some frustration surrounding Isis, Islam and non-Muslims, specifically on war and the killing of other humans'. The children were left feeling 'conflicted', suffering flashbacks from gory videos and nightmares about going to hell, the report said, warning that without ongoing therapy they may 'develop into religious violent extremism as a result of their exposure to Haque's teaching at a later stage in their lives'.[26]

He was not completely reliant on the 'mini-militia', as a judge labelled them, to carry out his plans and had also downloaded videos on making bombs and discussed with co-conspirator Abuthather

Mamun which 4x4 vehicles would be best to mow people down with. When police searched his Ford Focus after his arrest in May 2017, they found a large, sharp kitchen knife wrapped in newspaper and hidden in the passenger footwell. Haque had already started drafting a pages-long statement addressed to the British people, and intended for release after his attack. Jailing him for life, Mr Justice Haddon-Cave said the 'sheer scale of his ambition was extreme and alarming', and that although he told contacts his plans would take three to five years, a 'more immediate attack was entirely possible'. Mamun, who had been radicalised by Haque when he was only 17, was jailed for 12 years for assisting the plot and raising money. Abid was convicted for failing to alert authorities to the plot and was imprisoned for four years and three months.

The wrong nail-polish remover

By now, the security services were running several undercover operations where agents were playing various roles to track potential terrorists. But in some cases, hapless plotters would be the architects of their own failure. While Syed and Haque were planning their attacks, an unusual online relationship was being developed on the otherwise ordinary SingleMuslim.com dating website. On his profile, 35-year-old Munir Mohammed described himself as a physicist who was looking for a wife and partner and to have children. With a neatly-trimmed beard and severe eyebrows, he posted the headline for his profile as: 'Think deep about your end and day after'.[27] Rowaida el-Hassan, a 32-year-old divorced single mother who wore glasses and had a penchant for brightly coloured headscarves, said she was a pharmacist and wrote: 'I am looking for a simple, very simple, honest and straight forward man who fears Allah before anything else. I am looking for a man I can vibe with on a spiritual and intellectual level. Someone who can teach me new things and inspire me.' The pair lived more than 120 miles away from each other, with Munir in Derby and Rowaida in north-west London, but the distance was no barrier to their shared interests. At the time, Mohammed had been in the UK for two years after arriving from Sudan and was awaiting a decision on his asylum application. El-Hassan was also of Sudanese origin and gave Mohammed money while trying to support his claim.

By spring 2016, they were in regular contact, and particularly liked to share Isis propaganda videos with each other via WhatsApp. They included beheadings, shootings, suicide bombings, stabbings and executions carried out by children. Munir would send the videos and Rowaida would give her verdict. 'Send some more,' she messaged at 11pm one night, while her two young children slept in her bedroom. Their relationship mainly existed online, with only three brief face-to-face meetings taking place in a London park. While romancing Rowaida, Munir was also attempting to radicalise other women, including his estranged wife and niece. The duplicitous online campaign was a form of personal jihad—the desktop background on his computer showed an anonymous fighter, with his face covered, using a laptop displaying an Isis flag. But Munir wanted to go further. Within weeks of beginning his relationship with Rowaida, he started discussing martyrdom, and making use of his new girlfriend's knowledge. The pharmacy graduate directed him to websites containing instructions on making the deadly poison ricin. Days later, Rowaida told Munir she loved him.

His job, at a factory making supermarket ready meals, was mundane. In reality, he was killing time until he could carry out his real mission—a terror attack directed by Isis. On Facebook, Munir was in touch with a man operating under the nom de guerre Abubakr Kurdi, who he later told police was an Isis commander. Munir pledged 'compliance and obedience' to the group's emir, Abu Bakr al-Baghdadi and received a message in reply saying: 'Pray forgiveness to Allah, my dear brother, I hope Allah will put you on the right path and give you what you want. We will be in contact with Allah's will to organise something new.' The commander was not specific at that stage, but between frequent phone calls, Mohammed and el-Hassan were sharing YouTube links justifying the killing of unbelievers and a manual on the construction of explosives. Munir was eager, contacting Kurdi weeks later to complain about the lack of news and asking for information on 'how we make dough for Syrian bread and other types of food'. Prosecutors said the message was unsophisticated code for bomb instructions, and Kurdi replied: 'I want to organise a new job for you ... I ask Allah to accept your deeds and make you an asset for Islam and Muslims.'

Munir got hold of Isis propaganda videos showing how to manufacture the explosive triacetone triperoxide (TATP), which was used to deadly effect in the November 2015 and March 2016 attacks in Paris and Brussels. He collected instructions on creating a remote detonator connected to a mobile phone, and then started shopping. On a dark evening in December 2016, Munir went to an Asda in Derby and purchased a bottle of nail polish remover. At home, he already had two of the chemical ingredients for TATP, hidden in nondescript bottles stashed in his wardrobe and the freezer. Acetone—commonly used in nail polish remover—is the third necessary component. But Munir had made a mistake. Presumably not being a regular user of nail polish remover, he did not know that acetone-free versions are widely available because the solvent is harsh on the cuticles. And so, he did not buy the final ingredient for a powerful bomb, but a harmless bottle of Sally Hansen acetone-free nail polish remover. As far as he was concerned, he was continuing on his path to destruction while sharing messages supporting Isis with Rowaida. When the pair were arrested days later, police found that she had purchased face masks and a bottle containing sulphuric acid, which can also be used in the manufacture of TATP and another explosive called HMTD.

After being arrested in coordinated raids on their homes, Munir Mohammed and Rowaida el-Hassan denied everything and maintained their innocence. Mohammed said he had only sent Isis videos to show 'how unacceptable their conduct was' and to ensure his girlfriend 'realised which path was correct'.[28] El-Hassan, perhaps contradictorily, said she had seen nothing to suggest Mohammed was radical, but also that she felt pressurised by him. Her defence team argued that she had been emotionally vulnerable at the time, while trying to parent two children under five alone following the breakdown of her marriage. When questioned on her views of Isis, el-Hassan's reply hinted that she had swallowed the group's narrative on coalition bombings. 'I believe Muslims are not terrorists,' she said. 'My understanding is that terrorists are those who harm innocent people.'

The couple's case was presided over by the same judge as Haroon Syed, Michael Topolski KC. He said they had worked together to produce either a bomb or poison to be used in acts of terrorism, and that Mohammed may have introduced jihadism into their online relationship, but el-Hassan 'embraced it' and came to believe that a terror attack was her 'religious duty'. The judge told el-Hassan: 'You are an intelligent, resourceful, well-educated, professional woman ... not someone who would have allowed yourself to become involved in participating in a plan to launch an attack in the name of Islamic State had you not been willing to do. What drove you to reach that point only you know.' Judge Topolski said Mohammed had deliberately targeted her because of her pharmaceutical training and qualifications, and that el-Hassan's research helped him obtain the chemical components of TATP. 'It is submitted on your behalf as I said and because you actually bought acetone-free nail varnish remover that should in some way be seen as a mitigating factor,' the judge told Mohammed. 'I do not agree. You just made a simple mistake.' Mohammed was jailed for life and el-Hassan for 12 years.

A double life

Making a bomb, fortunately, is a complicated business, and Mohammed is far from the only plotter to fail at such a mission. Mohammed Abbas Idris Awan was studying dentistry at Sheffield University when his older brother travelled to join Isis with his wife in May 2015. The couple kept their intentions secret from Awan's parents, leaving a letter at their family home saying that they were making a pilgrimage to Mecca and then settling in Saudi Arabia.[29] Instead, they journeyed to the so-called Islamic State and offered their services. Rizwan, now going by the nom du guerre 'Abu-Musa al-Britani', did not keep his location secret from his little brother. The pair remained in contact and Awan started consuming Isis propaganda videos and speeches and writing notes showing him fantasising about fighting for the terrorist group.[30] He kept documents sent by his brother, which celebrated beheadings, the burning of people alive and terror attacks including the *Charlie Hebdo* shooting in Paris in 2015.

In March 2016, the messages from Rizwan stopped. He blew himself up in a car bomb attack on an Iraqi military convoy while fighting for Isis in Anbar province. Isis hailed the attack on its propaganda networks, releasing a photo of Rizwan smiling and holding a rifle, dressed all in black. He was identified only as Abu-Musa al-

Britani, but as news of the attack by a British suicide bomber spread around the world, his relatives recognised him from the photograph. By that point—still a year before the first Isis-inspired attack would strike the UK—Rizwan had become highly radicalised and embraced the ideals of Isis. Over the coming months, he started moving to take action of his own. A judge would later find that he 'looked up to' his brother and was radicalised both by his actions in joining Isis, and the communications sent from Iraq.

It is one of numerous cases involving radicalisation inside families, which have resulted in relatives joining Isis together or plotting and carrying out attacks on its behalf. Brothers were involved in deadly acts of terrorism including the January 2015 Paris attacks, the November 2015 Bataclan massacre and the March 2016 Brussels bombings. When the global migration to Isis territories started, many of those travelling from the UK included married couples and families. In 2017, an academic report described jihadism in Britain as a 'family affair'.[31] Researchers at the Tony Blair Institute for Global Change found that out of 113 British men who had engaged in or supported violent jihad, almost a third had a 'family link to jihadism'. The report said that siblings 'tended to join the same jihadist groups and support each other's jihadist activity', often travelling together or following each other to war zones. Mohammed was never able to follow his brother to Iraq, but he did support his jihad at home.

He continued to study for his dentistry degree at university and outwardly appeared innocent, respectable and shocked at his brother's transgressions. But Mohammed had acquired a notorious terrorist guidebook called *How to Survive in the West*, and started to live by its advice. The manual, published online by an Isis supporter in 2015, said:

> A secret agent always lives a double life, he has a public life and he has a secret life. His public life is to act normal, do his daily chores, and portray himself as a normal citizen in society. His secret agent life is totally different, in this life he will look different, and act different because he has to complete missions secretly without exposing his true self to anyone ... being an undercover agent requires knowledge and skills. In this book, you will be taught these skills. You will be taught; how to live a double-life, how to keep your

secret life private, how to survive in a threatening land, how you can arm and strengthen the Muslims when the time for jihad comes to your country, and neighbourhood. In simple terms, from this guidebook—you will learn how to become a sleeper-cell which activates at the right time when the *ummah* [global Muslim community] needs you.[32]

The guide runs to more than 70 pages and offers advice on how to 'hide the extremist identity', maintain privacy online and conceal evidence of terrorist activity from the police. It also contains instructions on how to make primitive weapons and build bombs, including devices packed with ball bearings as shrapnel. Mohammed purchased 500 ball bearings as part of preparations for what a judge said was an 'unspecified act of terrorism'. He also purchased a catapult, and claimed during his trial that the equipment was for hunting rabbits. Mohammed had also downloaded videos on making fuse igniters, booby traps and knives that could be easily concealed or disguised. He had searched online for information about the injuries ball bearings fired from a slingshot could cause, but Judge Watson KC concluded that the catapult was 'part of a cover story' to explain the ball bearing purchase to police, who were 'closely involved' with the family because of his brother's actions.

The security services had been monitoring Awan's activities and decided to move in after he purchased the ball bearings—often used as shrapnel in homemade bombs—fearing he was getting close to an attack. Police raided Awan's student accommodation in Sheffield and family home in Huddersfield in June 2017. 'I'm quite sure that what you intended in the medium term was something much more violent,' the judge told him. 'It is fortunate that your activities were picked up by the police at an early stage before you, possibly with others, could put your plans into practice. What you would have done if you had remained undetected will thankfully never be known.' The judge jailed Mohammed, who was then 24, for ten years. He told him:

You had all the advantages of a young man growing up in this country in a family of respectable, caring and dedicated parents. Even now they are unable to comprehend that their devoted youngest son should have allied himself so completely with the forces of extremism. The devastation for them is barely imaginable. Your older brother not only went to Syria in 2015, but then killed himself in a suicide bombing in 2016. Now their youngest son stands convicted of possessing material useful to terrorists and of preparing for an act of terror himself.

A remote-controlled car bomb?

Many terror plotters are prepared to die committing an attack, often planning how to ensure they are 'martyred'. Others want to make good their escape and live to fight another day, but such a feat can be difficult when faced with rapid responses by armed police. One man hoped to use emerging technology to inflict mass casualties while getting away unharmed, by creating a driverless car bomb. Farhad Salah was working to improve on the huge vehicle-borne suicide bombs used by Isis on the battlefield with such deadly effect, and avoid the need to sacrifice himself upon detonation. In December 2017, he told a Facebook contact he was working on 'controlling a vehicle with laptop and without a driver'. Salah wrote: 'My only intent is to find a way to carry out martyrdom operation with cars without driver everything is perfect only the programme is left.'[33]

Salah, then 22, was another 'frustrated traveller' who had been unable to travel to Isis territories. The Iraqi national had arrived in the UK in 2014 and claimed asylum on the basis he had suffered repression in Iraqi Kurdistan. No decision had been made three years later and the pending application meant that he was unable to legally work. He was left living in limbo at a community centre in Sheffield and at some point he decided he wanted to leave the UK. In August 2017, he wrote to a friend on Instagram: 'I just need help … I want to go somewhere like Sham [Syria].' He asked if the person knew of any smugglers who could transport him, adding: 'I will pay some money to anyone who can show me ways to enter Syria.' For months, he wrote to different people of his desire to join the 'jihad' in Isis territories but lamented: 'I have tried so hard to go over there but there is no way at the moment.' Salah said that one of his friends had been arrested and jailed for three years for attempting the journey, adding: 'We don't want to go to see our families when we … we have been trying for this for a long time, whenever we can return back from here because none of us has leave to remain in here [the UK], we all return back illegally with Allah's permission.'

Salah never gave up on his aspiration to fight for Isis, but because he had no way of travelling, he instead focused his attempts on developing explosives for an attack to demonstrate his allegiance. While viewing gory Isis propaganda videos showing car bombings and executions, Salah researched and experimented with explosives. By the time of his arrest, he was in possession of black powder, pyrotechnic fuses and highly flammable nitrocellulose. He had explored several ideas of what to do with them, discussing with one friend the possibility of using a drone to drop a bomb—another method used by Isis on the battlefield. But writing to a fellow Isis supporter on Facebook, he said he was still focused on the 'car/vehicle design'. Salah added:

> Only one tiny point is outstanding to find and that is the data. The data for between the vehicle/car and the control this is for big vehicle/cars not small ones. Then there will not be any problem, with a laptop you will move it there will not be any problem. None of our brothers need to get inside it, it is safe for them all of it is laptop with camera will be controlled to the place you want to take you can, the data is remaining. Some people have found it I will buy it off them for money *inshallah* [Allah willing].

He did not get that far. Counter-terror police had been watching Salah for several months, after identifying him as the contact of a man using Facebook to disseminate Isis explosives manuals—including the one used by the Manchester Arena bomber. Armed police raided Salah's home six days before Christmas in 2017 after Salah sent a series of messages suggesting his preparations were close to completion. 'I have the last version [of the explosive] and am going to test it on Tuesday,' he wrote on 16 December 2016. 'Do pray for us, our situation is critical … we are all terrorists. May God judge us.' Detective Chief Superintendent Martin Snowden, the head of the counter-terrorism unit covering north-east England, said officers felt they had to move in before a target was identified rather than waiting for preparations to become more advanced.

'With the extremist mindset that we had identified, and the increasing manufacture and testing of the explosives, it was considered that we needed to disrupt and arrest,' he added. 'All the component parts were there for a serious terrorist attack in the UK, with a significant threat to members of the public.'[34]

Salah denied preparing an act of terrorism and claimed the Facebook account used to send the incriminating messages was 'hacked', but he was convicted of preparing an act of terrorism. Jailing him for 15 years, a judge said that while his preparations were 'very much in their infancy', his intended attack would have 'caused the loss of life or the infliction of terrible suffering'.[35] Judge Paul Watson KC said Salah had betrayed both the faith of Islam and the country that had offered him sanctuary from the oppression he claimed to have suffered.

The Eagle

Adherents of Isis have made up by far the largest group of jihadist terror plotters in the UK since 2017, but another group has cropped up time and again in the background of both thwarted and successful attackers—al-Muhajiroun (ALM). The thread of its influence links terrorists including the Westminster attacker Khalid Masood, London Bridge ringleader Khuram Butt and plotters in this book including hapless Haroon Syed, who blurted his plans to an MI5 officer in Costa. Meaning 'the Emigrants' in Arabic, the network was formed as an offshoot of the international Islamist group Hizb ut-Tahrir in 1996.[36] Fearing a government ban, founder Omar Bakri Muhammad publicly disbanded the group in 2004, but it re-emerged again and again under new names.

The first new incarnation was proscribed as a terrorist organisation in 2006 and the British government was then drawn into a continuous game of whack-a-mole as ALM repeatedly regenerated in new guises. At the time of writing, 11 aliases of ALM are banned,[37] but no one has ever been successfully prosecuted for being a member of the group. Its stated aim, creating a religious theocracy in Britain grounded in its interpretation of Islamic scripture and history, is unrealistic in the extreme and its protests, preaching stalls, speaker events and study circles have proven insufficient for some impatient supporters. When Isis declared its caliphate in 2014, a large number of ALM followers saw it as the realisation of the Islamic state they had been working towards and travelled there. On 2 July that year, Anjem Choudary and other ALM figures formally pledged allegiance to Isis and its leader Abu Bakr al-Baghdadi—an act that saw Choudary finally jailed.

His imprisonment followed years of intensifying police action, which left ALM weakened and unable to carry out the provocative street activism that grabbed national attention and sucked in followers in the 2000s. But it is still cited as a main concern by counter-terror police, who are keenly aware that the group could re-activate as members are freed from prison and have legal restrictions lifted. A report for the UK's Commission for Countering Extremism warned:

> A number of persistent activists are now free to reconnect with their colleagues and re-engage in their activism. Despite participating in compulsory 'deradicalisation' programming, these leading and veteran activists have not changed their beliefs. For them, the ideological struggle continues. Mindful of their hostile environment, they proceed with caution, testing the waters in various online and offline settings. The loss of Isis' territorial caliphate does not deter them. In their view, the Islamic State came back before and will come back again. They also insist that the ultimate reward for their activism comes not from creating the Islamic state in this life, but in reaching 'paradise' in the next.[38]

ALM supporters have carried out terror attacks as far afield as Israel, India and Sri Lanka, but many preferred to wage their jihad closer to home. Former members include the 2019 Fishmongers' Hall attacker Usman Khan, 2017 London Bridge attack ringleader Khuram Butt and the men who murdered a British soldier in Woolwich in 2013. Many more aspired to carry out attacks in Britain but had their plots thwarted. Among them is Lewis Ludlow.

Ludlow, who is autistic, was diagnosed with attention deficit hyperactivity disorder (ADHD) as a child and dropped out of school at 14 because of bullying. He converted to Islam at the age of 16 and, months later, his Kent college reported him to Prevent over concerns about his religious beliefs and his habit of carrying a knife. The teenager would not engage with the programme and explored his new faith not through his local mosque, but through the internet and particularly ALM.[39] By 2010, when Ludlow was still just 18, he was a regular at protests. Dr Michael Kenney, a University of Pittsburgh professor who spent years following ALM activists for his book *The Islamic State in Britain*, recalls seeing him at numerous street preaching stalls that year.[40] White, overweight and with a distinctively patchy mousy brown beard, Ludlow stood out. He was present at a notorious stunt on Remembrance Day in 2010, when ALM activists—then going by the name Muslims Against Crusades— burned replica poppies outside the Royal Albert Hall in London. The group stationed themselves at the end of a charity march by members of the armed forces and veterans, brandishing signs reading 'British soldiers, burn in hell!' and faced off with members of the far-right English Defence League. Kenney says Ludlow came across as an 'enthusiastic supporter' of ALM, but also appeared 'mentally slow and obtuse'. He adds: 'The al-Muhajiroun activists and supporters were very patient with him and treated him warmly. Lewis clearly revelled in their attention and the fellowship of his "brothers".' In time, that fellowship would not be enough to satisfy Ludlow's ambitions.

By January 2015, he was expressing a desire to join Isis in Syria. While messaging a British foreign fighter who would be killed in a drone strike months later, he said he was 'planning *hijrah* [migration]'—but also that he was considering using his job in a Royal Mail warehouse to send 'something lethal'. In August 2015, Ludlow was arrested on suspicion of supporting ALM but no further action was taken. His online activity made clear that his mindset was becoming more dangerous, and Prevent officials tried again to engage in 2017. Using the encrypted messaging service Telegram, he told a contact he had 'resisted the same programme twice in the past' but was now 'sticking to the programme'.[41] His friend replied: 'Even if u dont believe it, fake it.' In the same year, Ludlow claimed that MI5 had attempted to recruit him as an undercover intelligence source but that he rebuffed their advances. By the end of October 2017, he was under surveillance.

The operation revealed that Ludlow was trying to hide evidence of his ongoing jihadist ideology, while planning to travel to a part of the Philippines where Isis controlled territory. He was stopped at

Heathrow Airport on 3 February 2018 and questioned under terrorism laws, resulting in him having his passport seized and being returned home. Searches of his mobile phone, which he had thrown into a neighbour's garden, showed the truth of his plans and revealed that he had been communicating with a militant going by the name of Abu Yaqeen al-Ansari. After Ludlow received a letter confirming that he had been banned from holding a passport, he switched his attention to planning an act of terrorism in the UK—as fellow plotter Umar Haque had done two years before.

Ludlow used internet cafés to research potential targets including 'busy shopping centres' and Oxford Street, then printed out images of Isis' flag, and used encrypted messaging services to communicate with Abu Yaqeen. On 16 March 2018, Ludlow carried out hostile reconnaissance in Oxford Street and took photographs at the Madame Tussauds waxworks attraction. Later that same day, he used one of his Isis flag printouts to write a pledge of allegiance to the terrorist group, in large child-like script. It was signed 'The Ghost' and read:

> I give my *bayah* [oath] to *Ameer ul Mumineen* [leader of the Muslims] Abu Bakr al-Baghdadi and live to serve as one of the soldiers of the *khilafah* [caliphate]. Oh kuffar [disbelievers] of Britain we are ghosts in your midst. *Wallahi* [I swear to Allah] we will take revenge for we love death as you love life. So wait we too are waiting.

Ludlow started detailing his plans in a series of handwritten notes. A list headed 'potential attack sites' included Oxford Street, Madame Tussauds, St Paul's Cathedral and a site of worship for Shia Muslims. Another note described attacking Oxford Street on a Saturday under the heading 'Crowded London Areas'. It envisaged a van mounting the pavement at the busiest time for shoppers, between 11am and noon, claiming that 'nearly 100 could be killed'. Ludlow had researched for hotels where he could stay before the attack and for the prices of rental vans, which had already been used to deadly effect in the previous year in the London Bridge and Finsbury Park attacks. Ludlow did not hold a driving licence and lamented to Abu Yaqeen that he had never learned because 'it's expensive plus [I'm] a bit scared of crashing'. Nevertheless, he started preparing videos to be released after his expected martyrdom in the attack. Ludlow recorded himself pledging allegiance to Isis, calling himself The Eagle and saying he would 'die in the cause of Allah'. In a second video, he pronounced:

> I have grown up amongst you filthy *kuffar* [disbelievers] I learnt your culture, your ways of life and your disgusting debauchery. I reject all of this, I am amongst you. As someone who has given dawah [invitations to Islam] for many years and as one who has studied the *deen* [religion] of Islam. It is therefore appropriate, that I make my [unrecognisable word] from you, manifest there is nothing between us except animosity and hatred. You the *Taghut* and those who worship you therefore, I pledge allegiance to the Islamic State. We love death as much as you love life so therefore, my allegiance is to Islamic State, I have nothing for this country of Britain. I spit on your citizenship, your passport, you can go to hell with that. So be ready.

MI5 and counter-terror police were tracking Ludlow, who was continuing to attend Prevent meetings throughout the period as part of his attempted deception. On 13 April 2018 his contact Abu Yaqeen expressed concerns that he was under surveillance. He and Ludlow started moving to change their social media accounts and destroy potential evidence. Concerned that a spooked Ludlow could swiftly launch an attack, police moved in five days later.

After he was taken into custody, a mental health assessment found that Ludlow suffered from anxiety and depression. At his eventual trial, he claimed Abu Yaqeen had pressured and 'bullied' him into the terror plot, and that he had decided not to carry it out and ripped up the plans. A judge found that Ludlow had made the videos of his 'own free will' and was truly dedicated to carrying out a vehicle attack in London. Jailing him for life, Judge Nicholas Hilliard KC acknowledged that such an attack could not happen until a suitable driver was found—who may not have been Ludlow himself—but told him: 'You were engaged in preparations to launch a spectacular, multiple victim attack on innocent civilians on the streets of London for ideological reasons with the intention of causing death and terror ... your participation in these offences is explained by your adherence to violent jihad. In my judgment that was the predominant and precipitating factor and time and again, the result of free choices made by you.' The judge said that it was easy to speculate over what would have happened if Ludlow's life had been different, and that he was bullied, struggled to establish healthy relationships and became 'infatuated' with a woman living abroad. He said Ludlow was not 'manipulated' by Abu Yaqeen, although the terror plot was a joint endeavour, telling him: 'You were no one's unwilling instrument or tool.'[42]

If at first you don't succeed...

During the period covered in this book, between March 2017 and December 2022, the security services count 37 foiled terror attacks.[43] You will notice that the number detailed is lower. That is because not all plots in the tally kept by MI5 and counter-terror police have resulted in a prosecution for preparing acts of terrorism. In some cases, the intelligence involved cannot be used in court, for example if it comes from an undercover source who would be identified through its use. In others, hard evidence is gathered by the police but it does not pass the threshold required for a charge by the Crown Prosecution Service (CPS), which judges if there is a 'reasonable prospect of conviction' before any case can go to court. In such cases, police may fall back on other ways to ensure someone goes to prison, such as less serious terror offences or different crimes linked to a plot, such as the illegal possession of firearms or explosives. The true scale of the person's plans never reaches the public domain, and the result is that such plotters cannot be included in this book for legal reasons—with one exception.

By day, Sudesh Amman appeared to be a normal 18-year-old student, studying for A-levels in maths and science at the College of North West London. But by night, he was 'Abu Malik', an Isis supporter active in jihadist groups on Telegram under the handle @strangertothisworld.[44] He had been gorging on the usual diet of gory propaganda videos and Islamist screed, but moved into a far more sinister phase in April 2018. In a pro-Isis Telegram chat group, he posted a photo of a knife and what appeared to be a handgun on top of a black flag associated with jihadist groups. The image was overlaid with the text: 'Armed n rdy #april3.' The next post mentioned that he had tried and failed to buy an Isis flag on eBay, with a sad face emoticon. Amman suggested that an anti-Muslim activist who regularly attended Speaker's Corner in London's Hyde Park should be targeted, posting videos of him to the chat. The posts would be his downfall.

A Dutch blogger who had infiltrated the Telegram group was alarmed and wrote an article including screengrabs of the posts by the 'British nutcase Abu Malik'.[45] Counter-terror police in the UK were alerted to the blog and started an urgent investigation to identify the poster. Within 24 hours, they had traced Amman and armed officers arrested him, on suspicion of preparing acts of terrorism, as he walked down a street in north London on 18 May 2018.

The investigation discovered that Amman had a 'plethora of terrorist material' on his phone and laptop.[46] He had discussed wanting to fight for Isis in Syria, pledged allegiance to the terrorist group and wrote in a notebook that his 'goals for life' included dying as a martyr and going to paradise. Amman had extensively discussed his wish to carry out a terror attack with his girlfriend, debating ordering a machete to be delivered to her house to evade detection and encouraging her to behead her 'disbeliever' parents. The teenager posted photos of a machete online, as well as of himself with an Isis flag superimposed on the background, and had searched online for weapons, camouflage gear and potential targets including Speaker's Corner, Jewish shops and the Westfield Stratford shopping centre. In a family WhatsApp group including his mother and siblings as young as 11, he had shared Isis propaganda and speeches by the al-Qaeda-linked preacher Anwar al-Awlaki.

Amman was not known to the security services but was no stranger to the police, having previous convictions for possession of an offensive weapon and cannabis. Investigators found that the apparent pistol he photographed was in fact an air gun that Amman had painted black to look more realistic. Despite the teenager's vocal determination to carry out a terror attack, the Crown Prosecution Service did not authorise a charge of preparing acts of terrorism. Instead, Amman was charged with the less serious offences of disseminating terrorist material and collecting of information likely to be useful to a terrorist. In November 2018, he pleaded guilty to 13 counts and was jailed for three years and four months, smiling and waving at the public gallery in the Old Bailey as he was sent down.

It quickly became clear that imprisonment had not changed Amman's intentions, as he began associating with high-profile terrorist prisoners including the Manchester Arena bomber's brother, Hashem Abedi, the Parsons Green bomber Ahmed Hassan and numerous attack plotters. He tried to convert other inmates to Islam and told people he wanted to commit a terror attack.[47] Weeks before his release, a handwritten pledge to the leader of Isis was found in his cell, and official assessments found that Amman was a high risk to the public and may encourage others to commit terror attacks. An intelligence update drawn up by the Metropolitan Police Counter Terrorism Command read:

> The collective view of the senior investigating officer, investigation team and all partner agencies is that he represents one of the most dangerous individuals that we have investigated. Before he was imprisoned he was operating as a lone extremist without a network of like-minded extremists. Since being in prison this situation has changed and he has now built up relationships with other terror offenders and thereby presents a heightened risk.[48]

Police tried to find ways of keeping Amman in prison for longer but they could not and he was released automatically on 23 January 2020. He immediately became the subject of a priority investigation by MI5 and counter-terror police, and was put in a probation service hostel in the south London district of Streatham. He was subjected to a curfew, electronic tagging, licence conditions, assigned ideological mentors and covered by undercover surveillance. The operation intensified even further a week after Amman's release, when he was seen buying items from Poundland that could be used to make a fake suicide vest of the type used in previous UK terror attacks. But police and MI5 decided against arresting Amman and making a second attempt to prosecute him for attack-planning, instead setting a series of 'tipping points' for further intervention.

The 20-year-old was being followed by four undercover armed police officers two days later, when he ran into the Low Price Store on Streatham High Street. Within seconds, Amman grabbed a kitchen knife and launched a stabbing rampage while shouting 'Allahu akbar'. He managed to injure two members of the public, who survived, before he was shot dead by police. An inquest found that Amman was lawfully killed, but that HM Prison and Probation Service had 'missed an opportunity which may have prevented the attack' over the purchases for the fake suicide belt he wore during the rampage.[49]

The Streatham stabbing became a horrific case study on the management of released terrorists, and sparked fierce debates over whether the fault lay with the laws in place or the ways they were enforced. But the UK's watchdog on terrorism legislation says that Amman is far from the only plotter 'disrupted' using other offences. I meet Jonathan Hall KC in the opulent boardroom of his legal chambers in a historic corner of the City of London. He is a barrister with almost three decades of experience, and since 2019 has been the UK's Independent Reviewer of Terrorism Legislation. He scrutinises how existing laws are exercised and looks at any new proposals or emerging issues concerning the laws around extremism and terrorism.

The most common terrorist-related prosecutions in England and Wales at the time of writing concern the collection and dissemination of material, such as Isis propaganda, bomb manuals or manifestos by far-right terrorists. Hall says such offences have been commonly used as 'proxy offences' in the past, as they were with Amman:

> Sometimes the police and MI5 may have good intelligence that a plot is going on and it could be very sensitive, which is forcing them to act, but when they carry out an arrest the only evidence of terrorism offending is for example possession of a terrorist manual. So there have for some time been prosecutions of apparently quite low-level terrorist offences which have actually masked a plot.[50]

But Hall says that increasingly, people are being prosecuted for terrorist material-related offences even if they are 'not actually involved in plotting or preparing themselves to use real-world violence'. Because counter-terror police and MI5 are 'ruthless' at prioritising cases because of limits on their resources, he says that the discussion of attacks or acquiring weapons can sometimes spark investigations. The offence committed by most of the plotters in this book is section 5 of the Terrorism Act 2006—the preparation of terrorist acts. Hall says it is 'unique' to terrorism and that individuals preparing to commit any other type of crime, even murder, alone cannot be prosecuted in the same way. 'If a person is found with some scribbled plans and those plans are sufficiently developed, even if they never discussed it with anyone else, they could be prosecuted for committing a terrorist offence,' he says. In cases that involve young or vulnerable plotters, who have not armed themselves or made concrete preparations for attacks, that threshold has become controversial. But counter-terror police point to Amman's case as an illustration of the dangers of delaying intervention until there is concrete proof of violent intent.

2

REVENGE, RAMIFICATIONS AND THE RISE
OF THE NEO-NAZIS

On 22 May 2017, a bomb went off among children and families leaving an Ariana Grande concert at Manchester Arena. Salman Abedi, a 22-year-old Isis supporter, blew himself up and murdered 22 victims, injuring hundreds more. It was the deadliest terror attack in the UK since the 2005 London bombings, and struck exactly two months after Khalid Masood's rampage in Westminster. Less than two weeks later, three more Isis supporters murdered eight victims in a van-ramming and knife rampage in London Bridge and Borough Market. The terrorists no doubt wanted to inspire other attacks, and they did—but not all of them were in the name of Isis. Britain was in mourning and tensions were rising as far-right extremists, who had long sought to paint Muslims as an inherent threat, seized on the run of terrorist atrocities. The first act of revenge came quickly.

On 19 June 2017, Darren Osborne ploughed a van into a crowd of Muslim worshippers leaving mosques in Finsbury Park, north London. Osborne, an unemployed alcoholic with four children, had been gorging on far-right material online regarding Isis-inspired terror attacks and the sexual exploitation of girls by gangs of mainly Pakistani-origin men.[1] In the van he used for the attack, which left a Muslim grandfather dead and several victims injured, he carried a handwritten note. It called Muslims 'feral inbred rapists' who were 'preying on our children', and raged against liberal politicians and celebrities. The note began: 'Why are there terrorists on our streets today? We've had three recent terror attacks, our children splattered against the walls of concerts.' It ended with a sarcastic sign-off referencing community memorials that had been taking place across the UK: 'Remember peaceful vigils only and please don't look back in anger, God save the Queen.'

Osborne was not the only one seeking violent revenge over the recent attacks, and the Manchester bombing in particular. In Croydon, south London, 40-year-old Steven Bishop was becoming fixated on the attack's youngest victim, eight-year-old Saffie-Rose Roussos. Over more than a year, he repeatedly accessed websites relating to her and the Manchester Arena bombing, while searching for information on other Isis-inspired attacks including those in Paris and London.[2] Commenting on a Facebook video about Saffie in October 2018, he wrote: 'That's a emotional video god bless little Saffie to 8 yrs old because of this scum who people call terrorisism but ther not terrarist there arsehols tbhonest barstards don't worry something bad is going to happen soon mark my words.' Bishop was planning to bomb a mosque, and had already started preparations. He was attempting to create an incendiary device and had purchased fireworks, a remote initiator and various components. Bishop was also gathering recipes for thermite and plastic explosives online, while using virtual private network (VPN) applications that were intended to conceal his online activity. His target was the Baitul Futuh Mosque in Morden, south London, which was local to Bishop and also the largest in the UK.

Unlike most other plotters, Bishop made little attempt to keep the plans to himself. On 26 October 2018, he showed a drug recovery worker a picture of a detonator on his mobile phone. He told her he intended to blow up a mosque and had bought Semtex on the dark web. Unsurprisingly, the woman called 999 and police swiftly arrived at Bishop's flat. He confirmed that he had purchased the detonator but said it had not yet arrived, stating that 'he wanted to get revenge for the eight-year-old girl killed in Manchester'. A cursory search of his home found nothing suspicious but Bishop told officers: 'I'm really upset about the attack in Manchester ... I think it would be justice if someone did to them what they do to us'. Asked what he meant, Bishop backtracked and said he did not mean any harm. The police present, believing he was suffering from mental health issues, warned him against making similar comments about mosques in future and left. At the time, Bishop had been receiving therapy for crack cocaine use, which worsened pre-existing psychiatric problems including paranoid schizophrenia and personality disorder. Thin, balding and sallow, Bishop was also diagnosed with ADHD, learning difficulties and possible autism. Unemployed and living on benefits, he was not previously considered a security threat, but was known to police due to his 18 previous convictions for 34 offences. They included numerous violent crimes and a recent racially-aggravated assault on an Asian police officer. Bishop called him a 'fucking Paki cunt' and threatened to cut off his head.[3]

Police returned to his home three days after their initial visit and a full search uncovered a tampered-with fireworks pack. They also combed through his mother's home, and in the garden shed they found a suitcase full of potential bomb components, including fuses and batteries, alongside handwritten notes on explosives. The detonator that Bishop had ordered online was seized on arrival and he was arrested. After being taken to a police station, Bishop told officers that he experienced hallucinations and delusions. 'I heard the voice of a victim of the Manchester Arena bombing who told me to do this,' he added. He described the victim as a 'young girl', in an allusion to Saffie, and in a phone call to his mother that was overheard in custody officers heard him say it was for her that he 'was doing this retaliation'.

The Crown Prosecution Service initially charged Bishop with preparing an act of terrorism but changed it to an explosives charge, which does not require proof of an ideological motive, in light of his mental health issues. He was jailed for four years for the possession of explosives and documents useful to a terrorist. A judge found that the explosives offence had a 'terrorist connection', telling Bishop: 'The object of your revenge was selected because it is an Islamic institution. As such, your actions were for the purpose of advancing an ideological cause, namely an anti-Islamic mindset, even if confined to retaliation against one group of Muslims for the perceived actions of another.' Defence lawyers said Bishop's offending was not terrorist in nature, and that his mental health issues meant his plans would never have come to fruition and the mosque was never 'truly in danger'. But Judge Peter Lodder KC told Bishop: 'Terrorist acts are not limited to those who do not have similar vulnerabilities to you … I accept that you are easily fixated, and have been badly affected by issues within your family, but I do not find that your condition at the time of offending was substantially reduced by mental disorder or learning disability.'

The mosque Bishop planned to bomb is a site of worship for the Ahmadiyya community, a minority Islamic sect that has itself been targeted by Isis. At the time of the plot, the building was emblazoned with the words 'love for all, hatred for none'—a slogan displayed on signs by Ahmadi Muslims at a vigil for the Manchester Arena attack.[4]

Bishop's plans, like Osborne's deadly van-ramming the previous year, are among the most violent examples of a phenomenon labelled 'reciprocal radicalisation', where the rhetoric and actions of one extremist group fuel the rhetoric and actions for another. Isis' attacks in the UK and Europe triggered a vicious escalation of the dynamic between Islamists and the far right, which continues to drive deadly attacks to this day. Julia Ebner, who chronicled the cycle in her book *The Rage*, says the security services do not appear to have foreseen the possibility of tit-for-tat terror attacks. 'There was a significant time lag in understanding the threat posed by this phenomenon,' she adds:

> After the Manchester and Westminster attacks in the UK, far-right extremists and influencers like [English Defence League founder] Tommy Robinson knew exactly how to exploit the situation to radicalise people. On the other side of the spectrum the same was true—far-right extremist attacks were used as a factor in the recruitment into Islamist extremist channels because they would have an easier time in convincing people that actually, Western governments are not paying attention to what is happening and how Muslim communities are being targeted. That sparked a lot more grievances than was necessary.[5]

Ebner has continued tracking reciprocal radicalisation in her role as a senior research fellow at the Institute for Strategic Dialogue. She says that national boundaries have not limited the phenomenon, amid an 'internationalisation of grievances' as extremist groups cast their net as wide as necessary to find fuel for the fire. Ebner recalls seeing German white supremacist networks promoting news of the

Westminster attack, while British Islamists focused on Western military interventions in Iraq and Syria, or assaults on Muslim victims in Australia. She says the 2018 New Zealand attack, where a white supremacist shot 51 Muslim worshippers dead at mosques in Christchurch, both accelerated reciprocal radicalisation globally and was an example in itself. Brenton Tarrant's manifesto showed that while his primary motivation was the 'great replacement' conspiracy theory, which contends that white people are being wiped out in Western countries, he was inspired by global events that had become touchstones for far-right violence. Tarrant wrote that his attack was 'revenge for the European lives lost to terror attacks', as well as for the sexual abuse of white girls by predominantly Asian 'grooming gangs' in Britain. He was fixated on the Isis-inspired 2017 Stockholm lorry attack, which killed 11-year-old Ebba Akerlund. Tarrant wrote:

> Ebba's death at the hands of the invaders, the indignity of her violent demise and my inability to stop it broke through my own jaded cynicism like a sledgehammer. I could no longer ignore the attacks. They were attacks on my people, attacks on my culture, attacks on my faith and attacks on my soul. They would not be ignored.[6]

Ebner says that for both Islamist extremists and white nationalists, the strength of their perceived identity means that 'every attack on the group is a personal attack' that needs to be met with a response. 'Every Isis-inspired attack or al-Qaeda inspired attack helps far right extremists on a global scale and the same is true for Islamist extremists,' she warns. 'They use them to mobilise people, and exploit the fears and grievances and deep anger these events spark.'

Accelerating the race war

For some far-right extremists, jihadist terror attacks are an aberration that need to be avenged. For others, they are to be welcomed as a means of awakening the white populace and spurring further racial violence that will cause the eventual breakdown of social order. That is the aim of the neo-Nazi brand of 'accelerationism', which has become the driving ideology behind modern far-right terrorist groups including the US Atomwaffen Division and Britain's Feuerkrieg Division.

Dr Matthew Feldman, an expert on far-right extremism who frequently appears as an expert witness at terror trials in the UK, says the idea dates back decades but was appropriated by neo-Nazis in recent years as they 'seized upon' the work of American fascist James Mason. 'Mason is an accelerationist,' Feldman says. 'He's saying, "We want lone wolves because it is a way of showing our value system. The neo-Nazi political movement is over".'[7] Born in 1952, Mason joined the American Nazi Party and then the National Socialist Liberation Front but became disillusioned by such political efforts and began to advocate for individuals to bring about violent revolution.[8] Over six years, starting in 1980, he published a newsletter called *Siege* that called for the destruction of 'the System'. Mason envisaged a 'period of absolute chaos' where racial groups would 'take up the struggle on newly equalized terms: animal to animal'. He told readers that it was incumbent on them, as individuals, to fight the system and to 'strike hard, strike deep'. Mason argued that tactics including making headlines and rallying white people to the neo-Nazi cause would not work because of brainwashing by Jews and liberals. Instead, he called for people to adopt the concept of the 'One-Man Army and bring the struggle to the enemy'. Mason issued advice on shootings, terror attacks and assassinations that he hoped would trigger a 'full, revolutionary conflagration in the United States', with white people as the ultimate victors. He praised murderers including cult leader Charles Manson and wrote of white supremacist serial killer Joseph Franklin: 'What a man! Pray we can each measure up to him one day.' Mason urged readers to 'cease to be part of the herd of sheep and instead become a lone wolf':

> We must have acts of revolution, the sooner the better, the more the merrier. But these are all of a nature that they can and MUST be carried out by INDIVIDUALS and that removes all requirement for talk, the possibility of "conspiracy", and the danger of a leak! The lone wolf cannot be detected, cannot be prevented, and seldom can be traced. For his choice of targets he needs little more than the daily newspaper for suggestions and tips galore ... for his training the lone wolf needs only the US military or any one of a hundred good manuals readily available through radical booksellers. Equipment is still easily available. His greatest concern must be to

pick his target well so that his act may speak so clearly for itself that no member of White America can mistake its message.[9]

The idea of 'lone wolves' would become heavily associated with Isis decades later, but never left the white supremacist community. Like jihadism, far-right terrorism has also evolved into a decentralised form based around loose online networks that are much harder to detect or track. Pre-dating as they did the social media era of 'easy access' radicalisation that allowed Isis to spread its ideas so successfully, Mason's ravings were initially confined to printed newsletters and looked set to fade into obscurity. But they were collected into a book that was eventually transformed into digital form and given new life on a neo-Nazi internet forum called Iron March. Users started sharing a 2003 digital edition of *Siege*, which Feldman calls a 'dynamic-changer' for the international neo-Nazi movement. 'It would have been a fringe book at that point but it became canonical,' he adds. Members of Iron March republished *Siege* three times from 2015 onwards, Feldman says, and while Mason had called for either 'total attack or total drop-out' from the system, the new version 'put the emphasis on total attack'.

Such was the level of veneration of Mason within Iron March that a teenage member physically tracked the ideologue—by then in his sixties—down to endorse the US neo-Nazi terrorist group Atomwaffen Division and write a foreword for a new *Siege* edition published in 2017. Months later, the Iron March forum was shut down but Feldman says *Siege*'s influence was already starting to 'snowball of its own accord', with the publication becoming required reading for emerging neo-Nazi terrorist groups around the world. 'It's easy to get, it's too easy to stumble across, it's easy to read, it's easy to circulate,' he adds. 'People put Mason's book on their shoulders and said "if you want to be a good neo-Nazi in the 21st century you need to read *Siege*".' And so they did. *Siege* has become a 'common denominator'[10] among neo-Nazis convicted of plotting attacks and for other terror offences. Photos emblazoned with the words 'read *Siege*' have become a ubiquitous neo-Nazi internet meme. At the time of writing, the possession and dissemination of *Siege* had not been prosecuted under terror laws in the UK. In an experiment run for this book, it took the author less than three minutes to find the full text on the open web, in multiple languages.

Jack Reed got hold of a copy in February 2018, when he was 15 years old. He had been immersed in far-right internet culture since the age of 12, when he had become obsessed with the Columbine High School shootings, and already described himself as a neo-Nazi 'with the prejudices Hitler had'. In his diary, Reed recorded how he had read *Siege* and initially thought it was 'retarded rhetoric' but persevered. He drew a picture of a man holding a copy of the book and shooting someone, writing: 'It took quite a while for me to accept what the book was telling me, whether that was ignorance or denial I can't remember. Either way, now that I practice the doctrine I'm a better man for it.' Reed's electronic devices showed that he had read the second edition of *Siege* online and kept a hard copy of the newest edition in his bedroom. Reed had become an accelerationist and started sharing his ideas with other neo-Nazis on the Fascist Forge forum, which was the successor to Iron March. By August 2018, the teenager was describing himself as a follower of James Mason, Charles Manson and Adolf Hitler, and wrote that democracy was 'dead' and 'only political violence can help us … the white race is being silently genocided, the West is dying'. In a journal entry on 28 October 2018, Reed wrote that a race war was 'inevitable' and narrated how his views had evolved:

> I turned away from being tolerant at a young 14 believing we would soon all just 'wake up' and put an end to it. Movementarians and the alt right do romanticise this false notion of an awakening of Europeans. But all this effort of mine that went into debates and activism, it all did nothing. I got the police called on me by my school and interrogated about radicalism. My second stage, I find somewhat hard to articulate. I think it was a transitional period. Aimless, anti-establishment anger. I wanted rid of the liberalism enforced onto me. I tore down LGBT posters, got suspended for it. My phone was found with pictures of Hitler on it. Looking back I accomplished nothing. All I got was a reputation I still struggle to shed today. And now here I am an accelerationist. These social norms are disgusting, but I say let them grow. It'll cause more turmoil and make people less comfortable, sowing the seeds for the systematic downfall.[11]

Reed had indeed been questioned by police, when he was just 14, over a Twitter account containing racist and homophobic posts. It had the handle @mosleywasright, in tribute to the British Union of Fascists leader Oswald Mosley. He claimed the tweets were just 'for a laugh' and that he was not an adherent of fascism. Reed agreed to shut the account down and to take part in the Prevent counter-terror programme. But he stopped engaging and continued to get more extreme, while viewing both neo-Nazi and Isis propaganda. Reed progressed into occult neo-Nazism, immersing himself in material by the satanist Order of Nine Angles organisation and linked Tempel ov Blood. By the time he turned 16, Reed was researching satanic rituals and compiling handwritten to-do lists with targets including 'shed empathy' and 'research Sinister Tradition'. 'It baffles me how some people do not get that empathy is learned behaviour,' he wrote in his journal. 'I believe there is primal enjoyment to be had in sadism.'

Reed did not limit his research to ideology—he was also search-ing online for information on firearms, explosives, ammunition and knives. While living in his family home and studying for his GCSEs, he wrote that he wanted to 'strike the system' and was looking at 'areas that are worth attacking—banks, railways, public transport, bridges'. In January 2019 he said he was planning to conduct an arson spree targeting synagogues in north-east England, using siphoned gas to make Molotov cocktails. At an unknown date that year, Reed started drafting a terrorist manifesto to be released as part of his own lone-wolf attack. He called it 'Storm 88: A manual for practical sensible guerrilla warfare against the kike [offensive term for Jewish] system in Durham City area, sieg hiel'. The hand-written document listed synagogues and public buildings to be tar-geted and had sections on the 'means of attack', 'avoiding the law and staying incognito' and 'should people die'. The potential targets included pubs 'to prevent degeneracy', the passport office as a strike against immigration, schools because they 'serve as centres of indoc-trination for the youth', bus stations, council buildings and banks. A judge found that Reed's document was imitating far-right terror-ists including the Norway shooter Anders Breivik, whose manifesto he had purchased online.

After Reed wrote that an upcoming period of study leave would be 'showtime', police moved in. They arrested him the morning of 13 March 2019 as he was leaving his family home. Officers found him carrying two pieces of paper in his pockets. One contained lines of numerical code, which when deciphered read: 'Killing is probably easier than your paranoid mind thinks. You're just not used to it.' The other document was a crude drawing depicting the beheading of a fellow school pupil who Reed hated. He also wrote of 'exacting judgement' on a gay student, because his 'hypersexual behaviour and flamboyant faggotry aren't compatible with the new world I shall mould'. Prosecutors said that because of the staggering breadth of Reed's hatred they had not identified a 'particular act or acts' of terrorism that the boy was going to commit, but that he had been preparing for some kind of atrocity since October 2017.

During his trial, Reed denied wanting to commit an attack and claimed that his online activity was for schoolwork, to satisfy personal curiosity or an interest in politics. He said he only posted material on the Fascist Forge forum to gain acceptance, be controversial and make himself feel important. His trial was told that he was diagnosed with autism spectrum disorder, but Judge David Stockdale KC called Reed a 'young man of high intellect'. He added:

> Whilst your youth is a powerful mitigating factor, it is also a feature of this case which is, perhaps, its most disturbing. Given the development of your intellect, the breadth of your reading and your obvious thirst for knowledge, it is a matter of infinite regret that you pursued, at such a young age, such a twisted, and many would say sick, ideological path ... the police intervened and tried to set you on a level course.[12]

Reed, then aged 17, was jailed for six years and eight months for preparing acts of terrorism, disseminating a manual on homemade firearms and possessing instructions on making explosives, ricin and Molotov cocktails. It was not the end of his story. Almost a year later, Reed was given a new sentence for sexually touching a girl under the age of 13. His lawyers applied for a ban on making Reed's identity public when his right to automatic anonymity expired on his 18th birthday, claiming that the move would damage the welfare of a 'very vulnerable youth with very obvious social difficulties'. They lost the battle and Reed was named as one of the UK's youngest ever convicted terror plotters.

'I'm sick of people just talking shit online'

Jack Reed is just one of several teenage neo-Nazis convicted of planning terror attacks in the UK. Like him, many have been autistic. Britain's independent reviewer of terrorism legislation has warned that 'more individuals are coming to the attention of counter-terror police who are diagnosed with or appear to have mental health conditions, or neurodivergent conditions such as autism which may affect the manner in which defendants gather or retain material.'[13] In a speech marking the 16th anniversary of the 7/7 London bombings, Jonathan Hall KC said it was necessary to speak about the phenomenon without stigmatising autistic people:

> The incidents of autism and Prevent referrals are staggeringly high. It is as if a social problem has been unearthed and fallen into the lap of counter-terrorism professionals. From the point of view of counter-terrorism legislation, is the use of strong powers to detect and investigate suspected terrorism in children justified? I believe it is because of the potential risk to the general public.[14]

In an interview for this book, Hall says that autism can be 'strong mitigation where someone becomes fixated on a particular kind of material'—for judges to lower sentences for offences like collecting terrorist propaganda—but does not render someone 'incapable' of being a threat. Hall believes the internet has been a great thing for people who are socially awkward and find it difficult to make friends offline, but 'at the same time, people who have in the real world lacked friends and not been part of a group can feel immensely seduced by the friendliness and group mentality they encounter online—particularly if you think about joining a terrorist group'.[15] In Chapter 7, we will return to the challenge this poses for the security services, police and prosecutors—a challenge that looks set to grow throughout the 2020s but has already begun to feature in terrorist plots.

For Paul Dunleavy, autism led him to have an 'obsessional interest in firearms' as a child.[16] At school, he experienced depression, anxiety and social isolation that caused him to retreat into an online world. But the world he chose was the one of neo-Nazism and accelerationism. From the age of 15, he posted vile material online including photos of soldiers doing Nazi salutes, racial and antisemitic slurs. Dunleavy had memes referencing *Siege* and the 'day of the rope', an event where race traitors are dragged from their homes and hung from lampposts, power poles and trees in the 1978 novel *The Turner Diaries*. From the bedroom of his family home in Rugby, Warwickshire, the teenager watched Brenton Tarrant's footage of the March 2019 Christchurch mosque shootings, and downloaded and read his manifesto calling for further attacks. That summer, Dunleavy started joining neo-Nazi groups on the encrypted Telegram messaging app. He offered to make propaganda for one called Iron Dawn and told a fellow member: 'We're going to be taking action. I'm sick of people talking shit online. We're going to crack some skulls.' Through his new contacts, Dunleavy heard of a new neo-Nazi group called Feuerkrieg Division (FKD). There was a test to join, and the teenager's answers showed he was a fitting recruit. He called himself an accelerationist, saying he had read *Siege* and believed in 'rather than sitting back and waiting for the race war to start, going out there and provoking it'. Asked for his views on Jewish people, Dunleavy called them 'a parasite which must be eradicated'. Then 16, he passed the test with flying colours and was accepted into FKD on 20 July 2019.[17]

Unknown to Dunleavy, one of his fellow comrades—a man going by the name British Sun—was an undercover police officer. He was watching as Dunleavy started issuing advice on how to convert blank-firing guns into deadly weapons and claiming that he had access to a drill press necessary for the task. In one-to-one chats with the officer on the encrypted Wire messaging service, Dunleavy unwittingly laid out his plans. 'I'm getting armed and getting in shape,' he wrote. 'I'd urge everyone to do the same.' The teenager posted more and more instructional material on making homemade firearms and ammunition, while praising terrorists including the 2011 Norway shooter Anders Breivik. The leaders of FKD were urging their members to become more active, writing in an online group: 'Get off the grid, get together and organise. Stop sitting behind a computer screen. Get out there and organise. Your race needs you.' Dunleavy said he was 'working on arming us as we speak', but his enthusiasm raised suspicions among fellow neo-Nazis. The leader of FKD, an Estonian teenager who went by the name Commander, accused him of being a police officer and made him undergo a new test. Dunleavy responded to the questions by saying that 'laws that are put in place by the kike [derogatory word for Jewish] system should be broken to further our cause' and that people should be 'willing to die in pursuit of the natural order'. Days later, he wrote in an FKD chat group: 'Appear niggers, we have acts of terror to commit.' But shortly afterwards, Dunleavy abruptly left the group. When Commander messaged him to ask why, he responded: 'I'm wiping my online presence while I get my own operations off the ground IRL [in real life].'

Counter-terror police decided it was time to move in and searched Dunleavy's home on 22 August 2019. In his bedroom, they found two knives, an air rifle and an airsoft handgun and a face covering with a skull on that the blonde-haired and blue-eyed Dunleavy had worn in photos where he performed Hitler salutes. There were handwritten notes and drawings on manufacturing firearms and ammunition, as well as pieces of metal piping and a home-made wooden gun stock. The teenager was arrested almost a fortnight later, when police searched an industrial unit owned by his father, which contained a drill press and other tools. Dunleavy admitted speaking with extremists on the internet and rated himself a nine to ten out of ten on the 'full on Nazi Hitler scale', but said the discussions about making guns had been a fantasy. He denied preparing acts of terrorism at his trial but was convicted by a jury. A judge said autistic spectrum disorder had initially led Dunleavy 'into an obsessional interest in firearms' and that he 'retreated into an online world in which you sought out and read extreme right-wing literature'. Judge Paul Farrer KC concluded:

> I accept that much of what you said within the chat groups was bravado and exaggeration designed to increase your own status within the group. Nonetheless, I have no doubt that you did harbour an intention to commit an act of terror at some point in the future, although I accept that it is unlikely that you would ever have given effect to this intention … the advice and encouragement that you offered to others is of a different calibre. You knew that you were communicating with extreme right-wing individuals who harboured terrorist intentions. In these circumstances, you repeatedly offered them practical advice on the construction of improvised firearms.[18]

Judge Farrer said that Dunleavy's autism had an impact on his maturity, and that while preparing acts of terrorism he was socially isolated and suffering from depression, anxiety and symptoms characteristic of post-traumatic stress disorder. An expert report called him 'a confused, isolated teenage boy with a low sense of worth and self-esteem, desperate for recognition'. Dunleavy was jailed for five-and-a-half years for preparing acts of terrorism and nine counts of possessing terrorist documents, after the judge found his vulnerabilities 'played a significant part' in his radicalisation and offending. Defence lawyers later launched an appeal against the teenager's conviction for preparing acts of terrorism. They argued that Dunleavy's obsessive pursuit of information on guns could be 'viewed as a symptom of his diagnosis of high functioning autism, as opposed to deliberate acts in preparation for an act of terrorism' and that he did not believe his instructions would be acted on by others because autistic people have 'difficulty in understanding the intentions and desires of others'.[19] The appeal failed, with judges ruling that Dunlevy's autism could not amount to a 'reasonable excuse' for the offending in law. A Court of Appeal judgment said:

> The defendant's explanation included the possible future use of the material in a future intended race war. It is sufficient to say that on the defendant's account it is impossible to import any concept of lawful self defence into future terrorist violence of which the defendant maintains he would have been a supporter, not a victim … there can be no question of his autism spectrum disorder making it reasonable for him to possess the information for a particular purpose when it would not be reasonable for anyone else to do so.[20]

3D-printed guns for 'no-fun countries'

On 9 October 2019, a 27-year-old neo-Nazi called Stephan Balliet left the home he shared with his mother in Benndorf, Germany, and started driving towards the city of Halle. It was Yom Kippur, the holiest day in Judaism, and he was heading for the local synagogue. Balliet parked up outside the building and started to livestream footage from a smartphone attached to a helmet. At 11.57am, he uploaded a post on the obscure Meguca imageboard. 'For all of you who live in no fun countries [with restrictive gun laws] this may be of interest,' Balliet wrote. 'All you need is a weekend worth of time and $50 for the materials.'[21] He said he was about to start 'testing' and posted a link to the livestream, manifestos and folders containing detailed instructions on how to make homemade weapons. He then launched what is believed to be the world's first deadly terror attack involving partly 3D-printed weapons.[22]

Balliet tried to force entry into the synagogue, shooting the main door repeatedly and throwing an improvised explosive device at it, to no avail. Frustrated, he shot and killed a 40-year-old woman who happened to walk by and then fired at a man who tried to help her— but his homemade gun jammed. Balliet abandoned the synagogue, which had more than 50 people inside, and drove around Halle until he came across a Turkish kebab restaurant. He opened fire and killed a 20-year-old diner, before going on the run when police arrived. Balliet shot two more people while trying to hijack their car as an escape vehicle, then stole a taxi but crashed and was eventually arrested. According to his manifesto, Balliet's arsenal had included five improvised firearms, which were mostly constructed out of metal and wood but also used some 3D-printed components. Balliet had listed his primary objective as 'proving the viability of improvised weapons', although footage of the attack showed them jamming and failing multiple times as he cursed and called himself a loser.

Balliet's attack may have fallen short of his expectations, but for terrorists around the world it opened up a new means of attack. Among those viewing his manifesto was a former British Army driver from Somerset who became the first person in Britain to be convicted of terror offences involving 3D-printed guns. Dean Morrice, then 34, was arrested in August 2020 after police found parts of homemade firearms and bomb components at his home. The investigation showed he was a virulent neo-Nazi, who had shared violent material supporting the Sonnenkrieg Division and National Socialist Order terrorist groups, but he was not charged with attack planning himself. Detective Chief Superintendent Kath Barnes, the head of Counter Terrorism Policing South East, said at the time: 'This is the first terrorism case which has taken evidence obtained by use of a 3D printer to court.'[23]

Nor would it be the last neo-Nazi terror case in the UK involving attempts to create homemade firearms. Among an oncoming stream

of similar plots was a 'fascist cell' in Yorkshire who had partly constructed a PG22 handgun using 3D-printed and metal parts by the
time they were arrested in May 2021.[24] They were not charged with
planning attacks, but others had grand plans. Matthew Cronjager,
then 17, planned to accrue so many firearms that he was planning
to build a storage bunker. A sketched plan for the construction,
which was hidden among schoolwork at his family home in Essex,
said it would be in a 'secluded area' and concealed with vegetation.
Different sections in it would include 'mortar space, rifle crate,
pistol crate, ammunition, water, food, clothes and first aid'.
Cronjager did not plan to act alone. As head of the internet-based
Exiled 393 neo-Nazi organisation, he recruited followers and created a library of terrorist documents including manifestos, combat
training manuals and instructions on making explosives and
3D-printed firearms. The teenager floated potential targets including 'powerful Jewish figures in banks and stuff', the government,
black and Asian people. Cronjager also said he wanted to 'execute'
an Asian school friend after finding out he had sex with white girls.
He discussed using a conventional shotgun for attacks, or manufacturing 3D-printed firearms for himself and 'the rest of the lads'. In
November 2020, Cronjager told an online contact: 'I don't want to
start anything too soon but I want to conduct at least one offensive
action within two years.'[25]

He did not know that the man he was speaking to was an undercover police officer. He had been deployed to develop a relationship
with members of the British Hand, an online neo-Nazi group whose
leader had voiced a wish to launch a terror attack on Muslim refugees arriving in the port of Dover. Posing as 'Jay Adams', a white
man in this early 20s from the Midlands, he struck up an online
bond with Cronjager. Believing he was talking to a fellow neo-Nazi,
the teenager spilled his plans to buy a 3D printer to make guns and
claimed that a 'shipment' of professionally produced weapons
would be sent to him from Europe the following year. 'Once we've
got them we're illegal,' Cronjager wrote. 'There's no real going
back. We either go full send it or we pussy out and end up like
every other British nationalist group believing we are going to fix
this legally.' 'Jay' claimed to have a friend with a 3D printer and
Cronjager instructed him to make an FGC [fuck gun control] or

Cheetah-9 gun, but the undercover officer repeatedly delayed the task by claiming his contact needed more money. 'See what your mate can do,' Cronjager wrote. 'I'd personally prefer the two shotguns but that depends upon him being able to get two shotguns and it not costing an arm and a leg.'

Police intervened on 29 December 2020, when Cronjager's mother answered the door to their home in Ingatestone, Essex. When the teenager was told that he was being arrested on suspicion of preparing acts of terrorism, and involvement in Exiled 393 UK and the British Hand, he claimed he was actually 'part of antifa' and had only infiltrated the groups to bring them down. He quickly abandoned the lie, but maintained his innocence and told his trial that he had been 'just blowing hot air' online. But police found knuckle dusters and body armour in a wardrobe, alongside hand-drawn plans for the bunker and a large collection of extreme right-wing propaganda, bomb instructions and combat manuals. Asked if he wanted to use the guns to attack black people, Asian people, Jewish people and the government, he replied: 'They would have been used in that way if they had been used, yes.'

Jailing Cronjager for a total of 11 years and four months, a judge said he held fascist beliefs and wanted to violently overthrow the government. Judge Mark Lucraft KC said that the teenager had been diagnosed with autism spectrum disorder, but that it did not have 'any very significant impact on his culpability', telling him:

> You are someone who played a leading role in terrorist activity ... I have letters from your parents, from those who have known you over many years. Many of the letters speak highly of your many qualities and the impact on you of this conviction. Some of the letters state that you pose no threat and that there is no victim. I should simply say that those are matters that are at odds with the evidence.[26]

Cronjager's case may turn out to be a good example of what amateurish attack plotting looks like in the 2020s: a self-radicalised individual taking a DIY approach that can often be a would-be terrorist's downfall—if they lack the skills to develop a plot without drawing attention to themselves—and the constant need for security services to keep on top of emerging technologies as the threat landscape shifts.

PART TWO

ARMS RACE

INTERCEPTING ADVANCED PLOTS

The pool of terror plotters in this part of the book came much closer to achieving their deadly aims. They were not merely aspiring to commit attacks, they were arming up and making their final preparations. Swords, knives, bombs and machetes were the weapons of choice, but thanks to the intervention of the security services, they could not be used for their intended purpose. Some were stopped after members of the public raised the alarm, while others were being closely watched by MI5. In some cases, those watching the would-be terrorists were not aware how close they were getting to being fully ready to attack. A small number of plotters were not on the security services' radar at all. But many of those who were fell into the most severe classification of known potential terrorists—priority one subjects of interest, or P1 SOIs as they're known by insiders.

Every month, MI5 receives hundreds of new leads. They are pieces of intelligence and information that suggest a risk to national security, and fly in from multiple sources, from informants and undercover agents to friendly intelligence agencies or calls to the UK's anti-terrorist hotline, and even emails directly to the security services. The tip-offs are received and assessed 24 hours a day, 365 days a year,[1] and each piece of intelligence is assessed to check if it is credible, the level of risk posed, whether anything can be done, and which agency should take action. Any credible tips are progressed either as a 'trace' or a more pressing 'lead'. A trace sees intelligence that does not immediately hit the bar for full investigation cross-checked to determine potential links to extremist activity, whereas leads describe new intelligence that suggest involvement in 'activities of national security concern'. MI5 looks for any links with existing investigations and sends the information to the agents responsible if one is already in place, or launches a new investigation if necessary.

MI5 and counter-terror police have a joint intelligence handling model, which aims to pool expertise and coordinate what happens next. 'Covert investigative resources', such as undercover agents, online role-players, spying and bugging are directed at the most concerning investigations and those where there is no other available option to ascertain the target's actions, aspirations and capabilities. Many factors are weighed when deciding which of these capabilities to assign. The security services have to make judgements on what would happen if the information is not addressed, how imminent any threat could be, how reliable the information is, what can be done with it and whether any action is proportionate—not just legally and ethically, but according to 'existing priorities and resource constraints'. At the end of that process, leads are given a status of red, amber, green or blue, alongside a band according to the credibility of the information. That makes the most urgent category 'red, band 1'—credible intelligence of an imminent and serious threat to national security, such as a terror plot in its final stages—while dubious intelligence suggesting low-risk activity at the other end of the spectrum would be 'blue, band 3'.[2]

MI5 and police must then decide what action to take. Do they send officers in straightaway, or is it too early? Do they need to develop their lead by identifying any gaps in intelligence and carrying out further research? That work is carried out as far as possible without any covert surveillance or interception of communications, but if undercover operations are approved they often require a cascade of intermediate steps. In a case explored in this section, MI5 set up a fake company staffed entirely by undercover officers in order to bug a car.

Every investigation can contain multiple people, and each is made a subject of interest (SOI). As of October 2022, there are around 43,000 SOIs with files held by the security service. Of those, 3,000 are live SOIs and the remaining 40,000 are classed as closed SOIs. That indicates that they are not currently assessed to represent a national security threat, potentially because they are not in the UK.[3] They are not subject to ongoing investigations but official documents acknowledge that the situation 'could change at any time' if potential terrorists re-activate and become a threat once more.[4]

When SOIs are closed, they are graded as a high, medium or low residual risk and then subjected to periodic reviews. In 2015, MI5 introduced a process called Operation Clematis, which sees people from the pool reviewed and referred for further investigation if there is cause for concern. After the 2017 attacks, when revelations that MI5 had dropped investigations into terrorists including the Manchester Arena bomber and Westminster attacker, the service started work to categorise its entire pool of closed SOIs into risk bands 'and to treat the higher-risk individuals accordingly'.[5]

Live SOIs are currently the focus of around 800 ongoing investigations, which are assigned a priority level according to the threat posed. The lowest classification is mainly comprised of terror offenders who have been released from prison and other SOIs who have previously posed a threat to national security and may re-engage in terrorism.[6] The largest proportion of investigations sit in the next level up, which covers extremist activity that falls short of terrorism, such as the preaching stalls formerly used to spread jihadist ideology by Anjem Choudary's al-Muhajiroun network, but may increase the likelihood of attacks. The number of investigations falls as the priority category gets more severe, with the tier above covering lower-risk extremist activity that is not directly linked to violence in Britain, such as the supply of false documents for foreign fighters. Above that is high-risk extremist activity linked to terrorist violence, such as plans to travel overseas to fight for Isis or fundraising for a terrorist group. The smallest category, thankfully, is 'priority one' (P1). That covers investigations into credible intelligence of active attack planning—plotters in action. Each investigation can involve several suspects and associates, meaning SOIs are themselves split into tiers from one—the main targets of the operation— to three—contacts with no involvement in terrorist activity.

Anyone dangerous enough to reach the category of a P1, tier one, SOI, has the metaphorical kitchen sink thrown at them by the security services. Any and all tactics can be deployed, sometimes in stages and sometimes all at once. That can include informants who are already providing MI5 information from inside terrorist networks, or undercover agents and online role-players being brought into contact with suspects to draw out their intentions and capabilities. There can be in-person surveillance where people are literally followed wherever they go, or remote methods where their electronic devices are hacked to keep tabs on their movements. Phone interception and the bugging of homes and vehicles are also options on the table, as the security services work to fill any gaps in their coverage.

Every priority investigation is a joint effort between counterterror police and MI5. In the intelligence-gathering phase, MI5 are in the driving seat, but at the point where the threshold is passed for a potential arrest, the police take the lead and ensure that the investigation is run to a standard of evidence that can be used in court. An 'executive liaison group' comprised of officers and agents from both sides then decides when and how to move in. They must weigh the risk to the public of waiting to take action against the many risks that taking action creates. Arresting a suspected plotter lets the cat out of the bag. They know they have been watched, and so do the people around them, sparking a potentially dangerous reaction from terrorist networks who could accelerate or change their own plans. Undercover sources must be protected and informants inside terrorist networks may have to be extracted and given new identities to save their lives.

Ideally, the security services would never intervene until they have enough evidence for a prosecution for preparing acts of terrorism, which brings a potential sentence of life imprisonment—the ultimate protection for the public. But sometimes that is not possible. With the rise of low technology attack methods using cars and knives, they sometimes decide to intercept at a point too early in an investigation for attack planning to be proved. In the short term the public is protected, but the cost may be—as in the case of Streatham knife attacker Sudesh Amman—a shorter prison sentence that sees a plotter back on the streets too quickly for comfort.

Dean Haydon, who was the UK's senior national coordinator for counter-terrorism policing between May 2018 and July 2022, says that al-Qaeda's model of using networks of people, with command and control structures behind them, to carry out extensive planning for 'spectaculars' was easier to infiltrate than the currently dominant 'self-initiated' plotters who plan to attack alone. He described how counter-terror police changed their tactics in light of the 2017 attacks and were forced to adapt again during the Covid pandemic. Over a year of national lockdowns and restrictions on gatherings in the UK meant that 'you couldn't deploy surveillance teams in your conventional manner to look at what somebody was up to'. At the same time, people were spending more and more time online, with less and less possibility of mental health services, schools, probation workers and other agencies noticing whether they were becoming a threat. The pandemic also created less opportunities to commit an attack because of the lack of crowded targets, causing security services to fear that risk was being 'stored up'.[7] The fears were borne out on 15 October 2021, when an Isis supporter stabbed Conservative MP Sir David Amess to death at a constituency surgery in Essex. Ali Harbi Ali had been planning a terror attack for over two years, but told police his action was delayed because of 'corona y'know, that was a a write-off year'.[8]

Sir Mark Rowley, who was the head of UK counter-terrorism policing between 2014 and 2018, agrees. He says al-Qaeda and the IRA, who posed the biggest terror threat to Britain before Isis emerged, attempted longer and more complex plots that were 'easier to pick up on'. To his knowledge, none of the seven fatal terror attacks in England since 2017 have been launched by 'priority one' subjects of interest. 'I think it's notable that none of the [fatal] attacks of the last six or seven years have come from those at the highest level of risk, those at the top end of the investigations, because there's plenty of coverage and the system is wrapped around them,' he says:

> The attacks come from further down the system … how do you spot something coming at you? You want multiple different radars, one isn't going to do it. You've got all the informants that police and MI5 run, you've got all the intelligence coming from existing operations where there's someone associated with them, you've got international intelligence from GCHQ and MI6 and partners that tells you 'so and so in Raqqa is directing someone in Birmingham', and then you've got the nosy neighbour who says something weird

is going on. Each of those are very different. Putting GCHQ and nosy neighbours on the same list looks very odd at the first inspection but actually, the more of those differently configured radar systems you have, the better chance you will spot most things and fewer will slip through the cracks. It won't be perfect but that's what you're constantly trying to do.[9]

In this second part of the book, we will move out of the early-stage and sometimes fantastical plots that existed mainly in their makers' minds, and into the fraught world of surveillance operations and life-and-death decisions.

3

BLINDSPOTS AND BUGS

One of the most complex terrorism operations run in the 2010s was the investigation into three men who called themselves the 'Three Musketeers'. The comical name belied the seriousness of their dedication to the cause. They were not newcomers to jihadism, or 'self-radicalised' bedroom fanatics—they were already hardened terror offenders. Naweed Ali and Khobaib Hussain, from Birmingham, had been jailed in 2011 for attempting to travel to an al-Qaeda training camp in Pakistan. They were part of a larger group accused of planning terror attacks in the UK.[10] Fellow 'musketeer' Mohibur Rahman was imprisoned following a separate investigation in 2012, for possessing copies of al-Qaeda's *Inspire* magazine. Again, he was part of a wider cell planning terror attacks in Britain. One of Rahman's original co-defendants was Usman Khan, who would go on to murder two people in a 2019 terror attack at Fishmongers' Hall in London. Following his release from jail, he deliberately targeted employees of a prison education programme he had joined.

Ali and Hussain met Rahman while all three men were serving their sentences in HMP Belmarsh, where they also mingled with other terror offenders. A judge later said that on entering prison, they 'were already exhibiting dangerous signs for the future', and that the networking inside jail 'reinforced' their radicalisation.[11] The friendship was rekindled when the trio were released in 2015. Hussain and Ali moved next door to each other in Birmingham, while Rahman lived around 50 miles away in Stoke-on-Trent. Ali, who was convicted of dealing Class A drugs before becoming a jihadist, was married with two young children and worked two jobs to support his family, while Rahman began working at a peri-peri chicken shop. Hussain moved back in with his family and enrolled on a gas-fitting course. Freedom did not go smoothly, and they swiftly came to the attention of the police once more. All three men breached the conditions of their release, particularly by picking up banned associations with fellow extremists. Hussain was sent back to jail once and Ali twice, while Rahman was recalled twice and violated his terrorist notification requirements by failing to tell police where he lived in early 2016.

By spring that year, all three men were out of prison for the final time, and MI5 launched a priority investigation while trying—and failing—to recruit Rahman as an informant. Officers witnessed numerous meetings between the trio where they seemed to be deploying counter-surveillance measures, such as having lengthy conversations in noisy and bizarre locations, including on a pedalo in a park's boating lake. When meeting, they would turn off their phones or leave them at home. It was a concerning sign. The trio met in their hometowns of Birmingham and Stoke, but also travelled to London. Digital evidence later showed that Rahman blasted a video playlist called 'best music of Isis' from his laptop during the lengthy car journey.

Because of the men's efforts, agents observed them in hours of deep conversation but could not hear what they were saying. Something needed to be done. By this time, in July 2016, Hussain was looking for a job, and the security services decided to give him one. They set up a fake business in Birmingham called Hero Couriers—a surprisingly tongue-in-cheek name given the nature of the operation—and employed Hussain as a delivery driver. He was managed by a man he knew as 'Vincent', but was in reality an undercover police officer, as were all Hussain's co-workers. Tahir Aziz, the d'Artagnan of the group, was only brought into the plot in August 2016. He was a friend of Rahman who lived in his hometown of Stoke-on-Trent. Aziz had no previous terrorism convictions but was part of Anjem Choudary's banned al-Muhajiroun Islamist network, as were the 'musketeers'.

They adopted the name on 11 August 2016, when Ali created a new chat group on the encrypted Telegram messaging app. It was called 'The Three Musketeers', and the group icon was a cartoon of Mickey Mouse, Donald Duck and Goofy from the animated Disney film of the same name. The chat was used to arrange meetings and discuss security measures, with Rahman ordering his fellow plotters not to bring mobile phones with them. He had already taken precautions, ordering basic phones with pay-as-you-go SIM cards off eBay for Ali and Hussain to use for their communications, rather than their 'hot' regular numbers. Months before, Rahman had told Aziz: 'The khanazirs [pigs] are listening ... may Allah protect us and make them deaf and blind.' A court later heard that Rahman and Ali had been the target of 'persistent' recruitment approaches by MI5, while Aziz said counter-terror police wanted to use him as an informant after raiding his home in Stoke. Rahman, who had been offered unknown sums in payment by the security services, resumed his previous contact with MI5 in May and June 2016 in an apparent attempt to find out whether they were on the secret services' radar and to get information.

At the same time, the group upped their security and continued with their plans. They consumed and shared propaganda material from Isis and al-Qaeda-linked ideologue Anwar al-Awlaki, who had developed a religious justification for committing lone terror attacks in Western countries and issued advice on tactics years before Isis did the same.[12] They offered prayers for radical preachers Abu Hamza and Anjem Choudary, and other Islamist extremists being held in prison at the time. They were also focused on previous terror attacks, including the recent lorry-ramming in Nice that had killed 86 victims. The original trio of musketeers got together at Rahman's home to watch a documentary on the 2006 liquid bomb plot to bring down transatlantic flights, which was foiled by the security services. Perhaps they were looking for inspiration, or information on where their fellow jihadists went wrong.

Messages in the Three Musketeers' Telegram channel on 25 August 2016 showed they were gearing up for action. Rahman posted a video on the 'humiliation that would come from not waging violent jihad'. Shortly afterwards, Hussain asked 'what are we doing? Nothing is happening, we just talk', saying he felt depressed. 'We gotta do something,' he added, and Ali replied with quotes about martyrdom, paradise and 'jihad for Allah's cause'. 'May Allah make it easy for us,' he added.[13]

He had also been offered work by Hero Couriers and the next day, 26 August, was his first shift. MI5 officers intended to take the opportunity to bug his car, after he left it parked while doing his delivery rounds in a company van.[14] The operation did not go to plan. While searching the unremarkable black Seat Leon and looking for the best place to insert a covert listening device, the agents noticed a multi-coloured drawstring JD Sports bag under the driver's seat. Hussain had also been seen carrying an identical one in the past. They opened it up, to find it contained a partially-constructed pipe bomb, a meat cleaver with the word 'kaffir' [disbelievers] scratched on the blade, an imitation handgun, 11 shotgun cartridges, a 9mm bullet, latex gloves, tissues and gaffer tape. 'I will admit to being scared and it took some time to pull myself together and fall back on the training I had received,' an MI5 officer later admitted.[15] The 'three musketeers' were a lot closer to carrying out an attack than the security services had realised, and they moved straight in to arrest them. Aziz was pulled over in his car, which contained a CD full of jihadist religious songs. Next to the driver's seat was a samurai sword, which Aziz said he bought from a local sex shop for 'defensive purposes' while delivering food.

The musketeers' eventual trial came at an extraordinary time. The prosecution opened its case on the day of the Westminster attack in March 2017, causing the trial to be paused over fears the jury would be swayed by events. Defence lawyers applied for jurors to be discharged but a judge refused. The trial continued for another four months, during which time a further three deadly terror attacks struck in London and Manchester. When jailing the four defendants, Mr Justice Globe said:

> Those attacks have demonstrated, in stark form, the carnage that can be created by different types of terrorist attack that can be carried out with a vehicle, explosives and bladed weapons. I am satisfied from the evidence and the jury's verdicts that, but for the intervention of the Counter Terrorism Unit of the West Midlands Police and the Security Service, there would have been not dissimilar terrorist acts in this country using, at the very least, the explosives and/or one or more bladed weapons recovered.[16]

The judge said the group's pipe bomb did 'not need much more doing to it to make it a viable murderous weapon', and that the meat cleaver could have been used to kill and injure at any time, while the air pistol would have discouraged anyone from trying to intervene. Mr Justice Globe said the attack 'would have been carried out to promote an anti-West ideology of radical violent jihadists and with a degree of determination that would have included a willingness to die if necessary in the execution of the attack'. All the musketeers had denied preparing terror attacks, with the defence arguing that the JD Sports bag had been planted by an undercover police officer. The claims were rejected by the jury and then thrown out by the Court of Appeal. Hussain's DNA was on the gaffer tape in the bag—an inexplicable occurrence if it had never been touched by him. Ali, then 29, Hussain, 25, and Rahman, 33, were all jailed for life with a minimum term of 20 years. Aziz, then 38, was jailed for life with a minimum of 15 years to reflect his lesser involvement. He was the only plotter in court for their sentencing, with the other three refusing to leave their former stomping ground of HMP Belmarsh.

* * *

They were not the first or last terrorists to network inside the high-security jail, which is among the most notorious in Britain and known for holding terrorists and prolific murderers. Days before the 'Three Musketeers' were arrested, the results of a review of Islamist extremism in prisons were published. The full findings by Ian Acheson, a civil servant and former prison governor, were not made public but a summary said that Islamist extremism was a 'growing problem' in jails and that some inmates were plotting attacks. It went on:

> Some prisoners sentenced under the Terrorism Act 2000 and its successors (known as TACT prisoners) aspire to acts of extreme violence which require not only action within prisons but oversight and direction from experienced operational staff working centrally. A new strategy should focus on greater coordination with the police.[17]

Acheson said the number of terror offenders had increased since the 7/7 bombings in 2005, and that they were both mingling with like-minded extremists and radicalising vulnerable inmates who had been convicted of unrelated crimes. He warned that extremist activity was manifesting in a kind of 'gang culture', linked to violence and drug trafficking, while inmates were openly voicing support for Isis and threatening prison staff. Charismatic prisoners were acting as self-styled 'emirs', exerting a controlling influence on the wider Muslim prison population and forcing conversions to Islam, while running their own prayer sessions and intimidating qualified imams. The review warned that prison staff who tried to challenge the behaviour were being cowed by accusations that they were racist or undermining religious freedom.

The review concluded that the way terror offenders were spread through different British prisons had to change, sparking the creation of three new separation centres to remove the most influential inmates from the mainstream population. But the government did not accept all of Acheson's recommendations, and his report's findings would prove to be terrible portents of terrorist atrocities to come. In November 2019, released terror offender Usman Khan murdered two people at a rehabilitation event in London's Fishmongers' Hall. Then in January 2020, another terror attack was carried out by two of his former associates in the high-security HMP Whitemoor jail. Brusthom Ziamani, a jailed pro-Isis attack plotter, and radicalised violent inmate Baz Hockton tried to murder a prison officer. Weeks later, released terror offender Sudesh Amman was shot dead while launching his stabbing rampage on Streatham High Street. In May 2020, three Isis-supporting terrorist prisoners attacked a prison guard in HMP Belmarsh but the assault was not declared a terrorist incident. Hashem Abedi, the Manchester bomber's brother, Parsons Green bomber Ahmed Hassan and Muhammed Saeed, a terror offender who had discussed committing a knife attack, had mingled in the prison's high security unit. Abedi was working to become its 'emir'. Then in June 2020, a released prisoner who had previously been convicted of violent crimes murdered three victims in a terror attack that struck a park in the town of Reading.

I meet Acheson six years after the review was conducted, in an opulent gold wallpapered room of the Institute of Directors building in Pall Mall. Acheson is now an adviser to the Counter Extremism Project and in the intervening years has been shouting warnings from the rooftops about terrorist activity in prisons. He says he found 'levels of obfuscation, total ignorance, complacency, incompetence and hubris' in the prison service, adding: 'They believed back then, astoundingly, that they were world leaders in combating violent extremism in prisons. It's extraordinary, that level of delusion.' He believes that terrorist prisoners are still not being effectively monitored, and that attempts to manage them using processes originally designed for non-ideological crimes are fatally flawed:

> We need to not forget anybody just because they've got 55 years, because those people are still dangerous and I've said to ministers we have avoided the murder of a prison officer [in HMP Whitemoor] by luck, and our luck will run out as long as we have a large number of people who are determined to complete their mission ... the people I think are particularly dangerous in prison are people who have been scooped up upstream of what they are planning to do. In Islamist terms, although this crosses the ideological threshold, if you believe you've got theological permission to kill and you've been thwarted by the security services what does that mean?[18]

Sir Mark Rowley says it was 'massively frustrating' for counter-terrorism police officers who intercepted plots and other terror offences and saw people arrested and jailed, only to see them become more dangerous. 'The prison service was initially weak,' he adds. 'They didn't quite face up to the scale of what was going on in prisons.' Rowley says the Acheson review was 'rejected' by the prison system when it was published and its recommendations were only taken more seriously following the wave of attacks by freed inmates. He adds:

> The fundamental difference that the prison service is now getting to grips with is that an ideologically driven offender is fundamentally different. In my experience, gang members and organised crime people do some awful things and some of them are prepared to commit murder but it's not really ideological. It's almost like 'I'm on this life path, it works for me and I do these things'. They don't think it's right, it's just pragmatic. That's very different to someone who fundamentally believes that killing people who don't ascribe to your world view is the right thing to do. If that becomes your pur-

pose and your mission then everything else comes second, so you get the disguised compliance. They are a particularly difficult cohort to deal with.[19]

Peter Clarke, who was the head of Scotland Yard's Counter Terrorism Command between 2002 and 2008, agrees that there has been a 'complete failure to understand the difference in the risk that's posed by ideologically driven terrorists as opposed to other serious criminals'. He adds: 'The deception, the risk they pose and their ability to game the system is quite significant.' He says that when he was appointed as the country's chief prison watchdog in 2016, senior officials refused to show him the full Acheson report until the then prisons minister Rory Stewart intervened. 'The prison service were extremely reluctant to take it on board, they were resistant to it,' he recalls. 'They approached the whole thing about separation centres in a very defensive way … it's crazy the resistance there's been to this.'[20]

As of 30 September 2022, there were 239 terrorist prisoners in British jails, and the action taken following Acheson's report has not made the problems go away. Of those, 65 per cent were categorised as Islamist extremists, 28 per cent extreme right wing and 7 per cent as holding other ideologies.[21] In January 2021, the Independent Reviewer of Terrorism Legislation launched his own review of prisons. Tellingly, it was the first time the watchdog had ever initiated a systemic inquiry that was not requested by the government. Jonathan Hall KC said the situation was 'urgent', adding: 'Everything is clearly not fine.'[22] His review, which the Ministry of Justice refused to publish until it had formulated its own response, said that 'limited attention' had been afforded to terrorist risk inside prisons by counter-terror police and MI5. The report said that the jailing of an offender was considered 'job done', until the string of attacks and incidents from late 2019 onwards forced 'belated' change and investment by the government.[23]

'Prisons must not be allowed to become a second opportunity for committed terrorists whose attack plans are thwarted in the community,' Hall warned. 'The impact of Islamist groups has been under-appreciated for too long by the authorities.' The report said that terrorist risk offenders were present in the majority of the 104 prisons in England and Wales, and that activity by Islamist gangs had risen as the prison service budget was slashed and the number of staff plummeted in Conservative austerity programmes from 2010 to 2017. The government has subsequently increased funding, but when Hall's report was released in 2022 there were still 12 per cent fewer staff than in 2010.[24] Terror offences were being committed in prison without criminal investigation and punishment, such as inviting support for Isis, encouraging attacks, possessing and disseminating terrorist publications and launching violent attacks on prison staff that may have had a terrorist motive. Many of the behaviours identified in Acheson's report six years previously were highlighted yet again including self-styled 'emirs' controlling and radicalising the wider Muslim prison population. Hall also found that staff struggled to identify terrorist risk behaviour and 'worry about making false assumptions based on a lack of cultural familiarity with Islam or Muslims'. Hall made a total of 14 recommendations but again, not all were accepted by the government.

In a statement to the House of Commons on the report, the then justice secretary, Dominic Raab, said the government had already strengthened laws to stop terrorist prisoners being released automatically in the way the Streatham attacker was. He said a 'Step Up' programme was underway to improve information sharing between prisons, police and MI5.[25] The Ministry of Justice admitted that only 15 inmates had ever been put in the separation centres set up as a result of Acheson's 2016 report, and that one of the three units was not currently operating. It vowed to make it easier for prison governors to put 'dangerous predators' into separation centres with procedural reforms.[26] The government said it would also draw up an agreement between the prison service, counter-terror police and prosecutors on how to deal with potential terror offences committed inside jails. At the time of writing, ministers were looking at changing the wording of some terrorist legislation, including encouraging terrorism, to mean that the behaviour did not have to be directed at 'members of the public' to be a crime and could be applied to inmates inside jail.

All of this may be too late to have prevented the establishment of jihadist terror networks inside the UK's prisons, but if the promised reforms are properly implemented they could at least stop the danger being replicated by incoming extremists. Speaking after his report's release, Hall says convicted terror attackers and plotters have climbed to 'the top of the tree' within prison hierarchies and that there has been a 'power grab' by Islamist extremists in many prisons. He says that the phenomenon was currently confined to jihadists and that a parallel structure is not yet being seen among rising numbers of far-right terrorists. But Hall found that institutional complacency has not been eradicated. 'Even while doing my report there was a lack of curiosity and willingness to grasp the significance of these groups,' he adds:

> Governors have been able to say, 'Someone else will tell me if that person is a real terrorist risk, and if they are we can move them elsewhere'. The problem was at least some governors tolerated the position of saying: 'I'm happy with what's going on in my prison because if it becomes a real problem it will be someone else's problem'. One of my recommendations was that governors should feel they are all part of a national endeavour about reducing terrorist risk, not just in their own prisons but also within the prison estate, and on release as well.[27]

Hall warns that prison staff are not always adequately trained to spot terror offending, and even if they do police have not seen it as their job to investigate in the past. 'Counter-terror police weren't focused on what was going on in prison because they had done their job, they had conducted an investigation, someone had been convicted, MI5 were happy,' he adds. 'They were in prison now—job done.' Intelligence gathering was prioritised over action and Hall found that prison staff spent too much time trying to work out why inmates were exhibiting extremist behaviour—whether they really believed in the ideology or were just doing it for protection, or paying a drug debt, or showing off—rather than stopping the behaviour. He says that it is 'unrealistic' to keep all terror offenders separate from each other and that there are no legal powers to stop prisoners on the same wing from associating together. 'Most of these people have got to be released, they've got to move through the system,' he adds. 'You've got to be realistic about it and sometimes the answer may be to do as much monitoring as possible, sometimes the answer may be to put people into separation centres, sometimes to disperse them into different prisons. The point is to be alert to the phenomenon.'

Jack Albion

Prisons were far from the only blindspot for Britain's security services in the mid-2010s. With the extraordinarily polished, organised and varied radicalisation operation coming out of Islamic State creating an ever-growing pool of potential jihadist terrorists in Britain, the resources dedicated to other threats dwindled. Unwatched and unfettered, violent far-right movements began to grow and suck in a new cohort of young, internet-based acolytes. Jack Renshaw was only 14 when he became a neo-Nazi. From his online research at his Lancashire home, he became convinced that an international Jewish conspiracy was causing the oppression and eradication of white people in Britain. Renshaw wanted to end that perceived control. First, he joined the British National Party (BNP), which at the time still held council seats across England despite its racist and fascist policies. At the point Renshaw joined, the BNP's most recent general election manifesto had claimed that the UK was facing 'the extinction of the British people, culture, heritage and identity' and that it would take 'all steps necessary to halt and reverse' the supposed decline of 'indigenous British people'.[28] The BNP pledged to stop all immigration, halt asylum processes and repeal racial discrimination laws. Renshaw initially felt at home and did well in the BNP, rising to be made a leading figure in its youth wing. But political success did not follow and Renshaw became the subject of waves of online ridicule.

In May 2014, an 18-year-old Renshaw fronted a BNP Youth video called *Fight Back*, which railed at 'heartless Zionists' and 'banksters' over the 'ongoing attempt to eradicate the British culture and the British identity through the forced assimilation of different cultures and different peoples'.[29] The video went viral and was widely lambasted and parodied by the BNP's many opponents as it made news headlines. Two months later, Renshaw was again the subject of mockery after one of his Facebook posts was shared on Twitter. He appeared to be lamenting that he would have to disown his dog in the belief it was gay. Sharing a photo of his pet, Renshaw wrote: 'I wish my dog would stop licking the penises of other males dogs. I love you, Derek (my dog)—but—don't challenge my principles because my principles will likely win.'[30] The teenager's humiliation continued later in 2014, when he ran for the BNP in a council by-election in Blackpool but received a measly 17 votes.[31] The now-defunct political party claims it expelled Renshaw before the end of a mandatory two-year probation period.[32]

Renshaw did not take the opportunity to step away from far-right politics and focus on his studies. Instead, he found a new home with the new British neo-Nazi group National Action. It was founded in late 2013 by another former BNP member, Alex Davies, who wanted to create a new movement for 'politically homeless' young neo-Nazis and work towards a 'white Britain'.[33] National Action's logo was a nod to Adolf Hitler's 'Sturmabteilung', meaning storm detachment—the Nazi Party paramilitary wing that helped the dictator's rise to power by intimidating, disrupting and fighting political opponents. Unlike older neo-Nazi groups like Britain's Combat 18, National Action initially focused on online activism—drawing in young members through internet forums like Iron March and social media networks, while using striking art-work and memes. It quickly accumulated enough followers to start, albeit small, street demonstrations where members clad in black clothing and face masks performed Hitler salutes and gave racist speeches through megaphones. Renshaw became a familiar face at the stunts in 2015 and was praised by one of National Action's leaders for being able to 'blast Jews better than any Klan leader alive or dead'.[34] He had started studying for an economics and politics degree at Manchester Metropolitan University, but his prolific activism saw him kicked out in September 2015. National Action became even more of a focus and Renshaw threw himself into its demonstrations, speeches, stickering campaigns and increasingly violent online propaganda output.

Branded posters calling for the execution of 'race traitors' and Jews caught the attention of counter-terror police, who had already witnessed the murderous intentions of one of National Action's sup-porters. In January 2015, a 25-year-old neo-Nazi called Zack Davies tried to behead an Asian dentist in a Tesco supermarket in Mold, north Wales. He had previously photographed himself wearing a skull mask and brandishing a machete in front of a National Action flag, and was in contact with leading figure Ben Raymond online.[35] Davies shouted 'white power' during his attack, where he targeted a victim at random solely because of his race, but it was not declared a terrorist incident at the time. Little over a year later, it would become horrifically apparent that the threat from British neo-Nazis had been underestimated by the security services.

On 16 June 2016, exactly a week before Britain's referendum on remaining in the EU, a Labour MP was assassinated outside a library in the West Yorkshire village of Birstall. Jo Cox was shot and stabbed by her 52-year-old constituent Thomas Mair. He was a long-time neo-Nazi, who targeted the mother-of-two after reading about her opposition to Brexit, advocacy for Syrian refugees and previous humanitarian work for Oxfam. Mair's hatred long pre-dated National Action and he had no known links to the group, but it seized gleefully on news of the terror attack. A Twitter account operated by its north-east branch tweeted: 'Only 649 MPs to go.' National Action members publicly hailed Mair as a hero and 'legend' whose 'sacrifice' must not go in vain. Finally, the group had overstepped the line for the British government. In December 2016, National Action became the first far-right group ever banned as a terrorist organisation in the UK. Membership and support was made a criminal offence and the government vowed to combat its 'racist, antisemitic and homophobic' propaganda and promotion of violence.[36] Renshaw and his fellow neo-Nazis were now officially in the sights of counter-terror police, who started combing through years of videos and evidence collected by anti-fascist groups that had long been calling for action.

On 11 January 2017, Renshaw, by then 21, was arrested on suspicion of inciting racial hatred with two speeches made the previous year. The officer leading the investigation was detective constable Victoria Henderson, of Lancashire Constabulary. Speaking under his pseudonym Jack Albion at a rally in Blackpool, he called for counter-protesters to be put 'in the chambers' and called Nazism 'nature's politics'. Renshaw labelled Jewish people a 'disease', adding: 'In World War Two we took the wrong side ... National Socialists tried to remove Jewry from Europe once and for all. Instead we let these parasites live among us.' At a previous meeting of the Yorkshire Forum, a far-right debating group, Renshaw had claimed that Hitler was too merciful towards Jews and called for their total eradication. The crime police suspected him of committing was a relatively minor public order offence, but his arrest set off a chain reaction that culminated in Renshaw plotting his own Jo Cox-style terror attack, where he would kill a female Labour MP and take brutal revenge on the police. He was initially released under investigation but police seized his mobile phone. It revealed evidence of a completely unexpected crime—the sexual grooming of children.

Renshaw had set up two fake Facebook profiles and used them to contact boys aged 13 and 14 since February 2016. He boasted to two victims that he was rich, could give them jobs and offered one of them £300 to spend the night with him. He also requested intimate photographs of the pair before one of the boys reported the messages to his tutor and the police were contacted.[37] While the investigation into stirring up racial hatred continued, Renshaw was arrested over the new allegations in May 2017. He was yet again interviewed by DC Henderson and released, with the same officer remaining his main point of contact after he repeatedly violated his bail conditions. As pressure from the investigations mounted, Renshaw's personal life was going downhill. He had not returned to studying and then got fired from his job at a pub in Blackpool. Renshaw told fellow neo-Nazis he wanted to join the British Army but did not get far in the application process, and was stuck living with his parents. He did not initially tell National Action members the reason for his second arrest, letting them continue to believe it was connected to his antisemitic speeches.[38]

So when he arrived at a meeting at the Wetherspoons pub in Warrington on 1 July 2017, nothing initially seemed out of the ordinary. The Friar Penketh was a frequent watering hole and informal hub for National Action in the north-west, both before and after it was banned as a terrorist group. On that day, Renshaw met up with six other members and quickly started raging against the investigation into his speeches. Claiming that he had done nothing wrong but could be jailed for up to seven years, he complained that the police were destroying his life and trying to make it sound like he was a paedophile, accusing DC Henderson of fabricating evidence against him. But Renshaw declared that he would not go to prison and laid out a different plan. He told his fellow neo-Nazis that he was going to murder his local Labour MP, Rosie Cooper, with a machete. Anticipating a swift response by armed police, he would take hostages in order to lure DC Henderson to his location. Renshaw planned to murder her in revenge for the investigations against him, and then force armed police to shoot him dead by advancing on them wearing a fake suicide vest—as Isis-inspired terrorists had in London's Borough Market just weeks before.

Renshaw's listeners did not discourage him. One told him not to 'fuck it up' and suggested that he commit the attack in the name of National Action, as a bloody signal from the group following the government's ban. Renshaw said he could make a 'white jihad' video to be viewed after his death, using the term coined by National Action co-founder Raymond to describe the group's 'holy struggle to give the white European race its soul back, and to get justice for our people'.[39] Some fellow neo-Nazis advanced alternative targets for the attack, such as the home secretary or a synagogue, but Renshaw was resolute and his preparations were already advanced. He had been researching Ms Cooper's itinerary, knowing that constituency political events were not guarded and would make an easy target, as well as looking up DC Henderson on Facebook. Renshaw had bought a Roman gladius sword-style weapon online—marketed as '19 inches of unprecedented piercing and slashing power at a bargain price'—the previous month and stashed it in an airing cupboard at his uncle's house ready for use.[40] He made a stream of Google searches on how to kill people, and how long it would take for someone to die after having their throat slit.

Despite the ongoing police investigations, Renshaw was not considered a terror threat at the time. He was not on MI5's radar; he was not under surveillance. The security services were completely unaware of the plot until someone very unexpected raised the alarm. Unknown to Renshaw and the rest of National Action, one of the men sat around the table at the Friar Penketh was already working against them. Robbie Mullen had joined the group in 2014 after becoming drawn to far-right politics as a teenager and being put in touch by a recruiter he met at a National Front demonstration.[41] But as National Action began to become more focused on violence, demanding all members started combat training and holding camps where people practised knife fighting, he started having doubts. After the ban, members started to turn on each other as they became increasingly suspicious that various people in their ranks were spies for the police or security services. The paranoia was not completely groundless—by the time Renshaw revealed his plans, Mr Mullen had started secretly passing information to the counter-extremism group Hope Not Hate.

'I was saving myself in a way, I knew something was going to happen eventually,' he tells me. 'No one trusted each other, so it was like the first one to save himself and I was just that person really. Surprisingly no one turned on me first.' We are back at the Friar Penketh, on a cold Tuesday afternoon in January. Outside, the streets of Warrington are dead, but the pub is busy with men drinking, friends meeting and pensioners enjoying a bargain lunch. Everyone, as Mullen points out, is white. We are sitting two tables away from where Renshaw declared his intentions, but the exact spot is occupied by a young couple sharing a burger. Mullen says the pub was once a regular meeting point for National Action, where members would interview new recruits and discuss their plans after training at a gym round the corner. It is the first time Mullen has gone back into the pub since 1 July 2017, and he says that by that point, things were 'getting strange'.

The 23-year-old was already in the pub when Renshaw arrived late, and 'instantly' started talking about his plans. 'He had come to say goodbye, because he planned on dying the next week,' Mullen says. 'He was at ease. I think he was at that stage, where he was like, "This is what I'm going to do".' Mullen believes that Renshaw partly planned the attack in the hope it would either wipe out or overshadow his prosecution for child sex offences, because 'he would have just been this person who went and killed some MP or policewoman or whatever he would have done in the end. That's all he would have been known for. I think he was happy being known for that.' After Renshaw's declaration, the drinks continued at the Friar Penketh. Mullen says he left at 11pm, but Renshaw and others went on to a club. He texted what he had heard to his contact at Hope Not Hate, Matthew Collins, and they spoke on the phone early the next morning. Hope Not Hate then contacted the Labour MP Ruth Smeeth, who used to work for the charity, to inform her they had received intelligence of a murder plot targeting her colleague. She immediately contacted Ms Cooper, the MP for West Lancashire, and she called the police, finally triggering an urgent investigation.

Renshaw was arrested three days later and initially denied the plot, claiming he had made some 'drunken, throwaway comments in jest' but had no intention to harm anyone. Mr Mullen's testimony and CCTV from inside the pub would prove his undoing. In three-and-a-half hours, the group of seven National Action members had consumed just 15 alcoholic drinks between them.[42] Renshaw pleaded guilty to preparing an act of terrorism and making threats to kill and was jailed for life with a minimum term of 20 years. He was also sentenced to three years in prison for stirring up racial hatred with the speeches that were the subject of the initial police investigation, and given another 16-month term for inciting children to engage in sexual activity. A judge said Renshaw had set out to replicate the murder of Jo Cox and targeted Ms Cooper because he held Labour politicians responsible for mass immigration. Mrs Justice McGowan found that although Renshaw, then 23, was young and came from a 'troubled background', he had made detailed arrangements for the attack and remained a dangerous threat to minority groups in the UK. She told him:

> To kill a Member of Parliament because of their political allegiance is an attempt to damage our entire system of democracy. In planning to kill [police officer] Victoria Henderson you would have risked the lives of many others and would, if you had succeeded, have burdened other police officers with the consequences of having to shoot you ... your twisted political ideas were not the only reason that you set out to plan this killing. You wanted revenge on those who had prosecuted you for incitement to racial hatred and the sexual offences you had committed against children. You acted in a polite and respectful manner to detective Henderson, all the while planning how to kill her. But for [the undercover action which led to your arrest], the activity was likely to have been carried out. Your own evidence made it plain that you fully intended to carry out this attack.[43]

Mullen says he thought that after reporting the plot it would be 'job done' for him, but police threatened him with prosecution for membership of National Action, preparing acts of terrorism, conspiracy to murder and funding terrorism. Under pressure, he signed an immunity agreement in exchange for giving evidence against his former friends and comrades for violating the government ban. As they were arrested in waves of police action, but Mullen remained at large, some realised that he had turned informant and he fled his home after receiving warnings that his life was at risk. Despite his actions in thwarting Renshaw's plot, he has reason to believe he remains on the security services' radar. Mullen says he has been stopped numerous times under terror laws at airports, sometimes being held for several hours and having his phone seized. But he does not regret reporting Renshaw and firmly believes he would have gone ahead with the attack. 'I think he would have done it that week, or at least tried,' he says. 'You can never say what would have happened.'

The plot may have been stopped, but it was not a victory for the security services. It was Mullen and Hope Not Hate who had saved an MP's life, through the type of dangerous undercover operation that MI5 was coordinating for jihadist plots. Despite their involvement with Renshaw, police had no inkling of his plans and National Action had been able to continue its training camps and meetings for months after being banned as a terrorist group. As the murder of Jo Cox had the year before, Renshaw's plot exposed a dangerous hole in Britain's counter-terrorism machinery that had to be plugged.

* * *

The emergence of National Action was a turning point in modern British terrorism. Neo-Nazis had long existed in the UK and, as the campaign of London nail bombings in 1999 showed, could be a deadly threat. But in the mid-2010s, the security services were already scrambling to deal with Isis, whose emergence and tactics had also caught them off guard. When National Action was formed in 2013, MI5 had responsibility for 'international terrorism'— mainly jihadism—but 'domestic terrorism'—encompassing the far right and all other ideologies—was left to the police. Initially, the distinction made sense. International networks of jihadists were still planning al-Qaeda-inspired 'spectaculars' involving bombs and planes, while most of the violence emanating from the extreme right wing was assessed to be related to disorder and street fighting at protests. 'We had had in previous decades occasional right-wing terrorist attacks but they had very, very much the appearance of lone actors like the nail bomber, they were much more isolated,' recalls Sir Mark Rowley, who was the head of UK counter-terrorism policing between 2014 and 2018. 'When it starts to become organised, that's different. Rather than having a hate problem that occasionally flips up into an individual terrorist action, which is how I saw it, you have something which is more like organised terrorism. We felt that was what was happening in 2016, that tipping point.'[44]

Rowley says it was police, rather than the security services, who gave the government the evidence leading to the proscription of National Action as a terrorist group later that year. In 2017, he personally requested that MI5 'do the same' for the extreme right wing as they did for jihadists, but the security service did not finish recalibrating its approach until 2020. Rowley says he felt that the banning of National Action was a 'watershed moment' in British terrorism, but the potential threat still was not immediately appreciated. The extreme right wing made up between 13 and 20 per cent of counter-terror police casework in 2022, and a quarter of MI5's terrorism caseload.[45] Much of that is made up of neo-Nazis, and in particular *Siege*-reading accelerationists, rather than other far-right factions such as anti-Muslim groups or white nationalists. In his 2021 annual threat update, MI5 Director General Ken McCallum said the sector involved a high prevalence of teenagers and an 'obsessive interest in weaponry'. He added: 'The online environment is a challenge—with thousands exchanging hate-filled rhetoric or claiming violent intentions to each other in extremist echo chambers—leaving us and the police to try to determine which individuals amongst those thousands might actually mobilise towards violence. This needs new expertise, new sources, new methods.'[46]

Dr Matthew Feldman, an expert on far-right extremism who has given expert evidence at 16 of 19 trials resulting in convictions for National Action membership, says British police are 'further ahead than anyone else in the world' on neo-Nazi threats, but still behind where they need to be. He says 'no one wanted to talk about it' until the assassination of Jo Cox and banning of National Action in 2016. 'All of a sudden people like me started to be listened to,' he adds. 'It's still slow and actually, after Anders Breivik [murdered 77 victims in the 2011 Norway attacks] I did about 80 interviews in the seven days afterwards, thinking, "This is the paradigm shift, this is the moment the world will wake up to the threat." I was profoundly down to find that nothing had changed.'[47] When National Action emerged, it was 'open season' on the internet for neo-Nazi groups, Feldman says. Its website, with the unsubtle address national-action.info, remained accessible on the open web for over three years and was only taken down in the week it was proscribed as a terrorist group.[48]

In an encrypted email to regional organisers days before National Action was banned, leader Christopher Lythgoe instructed them to maintain contact with members and 'reassure them' on how they could continue their activities without being prosecuted. 'Make sure that they understand that the SUBSTANCE of NA is the people, our talents, the bonds between us, our ideas, and our sustained force of will,' he wrote. 'All of that will continue into the future. We're just shedding one skin for another.'[49] And so they did. The group split into regional factions that started to operate under new names in a bid to evade the ban, following an approach that had been largely successful for Anjem Choudary's al-Muhajiroun Islamist network. The number of offshoots only became apparent after counter-terror police found a senior member, Alex Deakin, hiding in an airing cupboard in Birmingham in May 2017. His mobile phone, poorly hidden under floorboards, gave investigators access to National Action's leadership network on the encrypted Telegram messaging app and Tutanota email service.

In September 2017, the British government banned Scottish Dawn and NS131, the rebranded chapters of National Action for Scotland and south-west England. Then in February 2020, it proscribed the System Resistance Network (SRN), which was not an alias of National Action but a successor. Set up by politics student Andrew Dymock in 2017, it was initially intended as a European counterpart for the neo-Nazi Vanguard America movement. Dymock was expelled from his own group the following year over an internal row about his push towards a more sadistic and mystical form of Nazism. A notice from remaining members cited his 'promotion of satanic literature and ties to Satanists within other groups' and 'shifting the focus of SRN from a political to a religious angle/ esoteric death cult'. Dymock went on to form the Sonnenkrieg

Division, which was banned at the same time as SRN. Its slogan, 'Universal Order shall always prevail', was an allusion to the neo-Nazi accelerationist bible—James Mason's *Siege*.[50] Other neo-Nazi groups subsequently outlawed as terrorist organisations in the UK include Feuerkrieg Division (FKD)—the home of young terror plotter Paul Dunleavy—and America's Atomwaffen Division. Despite being based in the US, the group's entry on Britain's list of proscribed terrorist groups says it has inspired several 'loosely affili-ated franchise groups abroad', including FKD.[51]

A 2022 report on extreme right-wing terrorism by parliament's Intelligence and Security Committee warned that the internet had 'removed barriers' by allowing neo-Nazis to network and research anonymously, in the privacy of their own homes. It found that the previous need for real-world contact with like-minded people through events like street demonstrations or music festivals saw many people deterred by cost and logistics, visible policing and the prospect of publicly associating with controversial groups. But the report said that now, 'recruitment can start with an invitation to a closed chat room in an online gaming community, or with a link to a closed forum. This global accessibility means a growing number of people now have access to, and are exploring, extreme right-wing terrorist content online.'[52] Feldman warns that while the suc-cession of terrorist group bans have helped drive action by internet giants to de-platform neo-Nazi groups and begin to check the spread of key manifestos, the 'supply of ideas and groups' continues. 'Since 2019, they are now mostly doing this stuff on Telegram,' he adds. 'If you want to find this stuff, you can still find it all too easily.'[53]

He hopes that the belated efforts will prevent cases he has seen where teenagers initially 'stumbled across' violent neo-Nazi content because of their use of social media networks, online forums such as 4chan and the gaming platform Discord. Feldman says that de-platforming has been 'shrinking the pool' of potential neo-Nazi ter-rorists, but the security services still view the extreme right wing as a growing threat. More than 20 members of National Action and other banned neo-Nazi terrorist groups were jailed in the years fol-lowing the ban, either for being a part of the organisations or com-mitting associated offences, including encouraging attacks, dissemi-nating terrorist documents and making explosives. Following the conviction of National Action founder Alex Davies in May 2022, a senior counter-terror officer said the group itself had been 'dismantled' but police were under no illusions. 'Over the course of a number of investigations we've managed to dismantle National Action,' said Superintendent Anthony Tagg, of the West Midlands Counter Terrorism Unit. 'Clearly people with that neo-Nazi ideology still exist but we will seek to identify them and bring them to justice where we can.'[54]

4

CRIMINAL PASTS, TERRORIST FUTURES

'I'm changing in many ways,' Sahayb Abu told his brother in May
2020. 'I wanna worship Allah and be pure. I'm done with everything, I care about the bigger picture … I don't wanna go back to
no clown bullshit.' Little over six weeks before, the 27-year-old
had been released from jail after serving a sentence for a burglary
conspiracy. It was his third spell in jail, following previous stints
inside for drug offences in France, and for assault and knife possession in the UK. But this time was different. Sahayb had changed,
and security services were concerned about that change. MI5 and
counter-terror police started monitoring him and discovered that
within days of his release, Sahayb was starting to plan an Isis-
inspired terror attack. Using a false name, he purchased a sharpened and deadly 18-inch 'warrior sword' to commit the atrocity,
and a combat vest to protect himself against anyone who tried to
fight back. The security services stopped the items reaching him
from online sellers, but Sahayb already obtained a lock knife, balaclavas, gloves and other items to be used in the attack.[1] He wore
some of his new combat gear in a series of amateur music videos
where he laid out his gory plans. In a clip Sahayb sent to two of his
brothers on 5 July 2020, he rapped:

> One day I was sitting by myself,
> Felt so low picked the Quran off the shelf,
> Started reading chapter 12,
> Next thing you know *shaytan* [Satan] creeped up on the stealth,
> Whispered in my ear about women and mass wealth,
> So I boxed him in his face as he ran back to Beverly Hills,

Bare *akhis* [loads of brothers] out here losing his souls,
Telling me 'big man your missing out on the world' …
Enough jokes and fun,
Why did Sumayyah [Islamic martyr] take a spear to the lung,
Is it so Sadiq Khan can become mayor of London?
Sadiq Khan's a sell-out and a *kaffir* [disbeliever] if I ever saw one,
And one thing that I don't understand
All these brothers all these sisters running round
With Leggings and hijab, Instagram fads, lied to themselves.
I wonder have they got marra bodies burning in Iraq?
They want me to vote Saj –
Fam don't chat to me about no Gandhi Islam or no Sufi Islam.
I'm trying to see many Lee Rigby's heads rolling on the ground,
Man I shoot up a crowd cos I'm a night stalker.
Got my shank, got my guns, straight Isis supporter –
Reject democracy, advocate Sharia supporter,
Five times a day my lord supplicator,
And my RPG through the armoured Humvee of a crusader
invader.
Ya Allah destroy the Saudi traitors and the Shia innovators,
Allah arrest him. My shank penetrate ya,
Got my suicide vest, one click boom and I'll see you later.

Sahayb's pivot from drug-dealing criminal to terror plotter was not a complete surprise—his family contained what police called an 'extraordinary' number of jihadists, and signs of Sahayb's radicalisation had been visible as far back as 2017. On 13 October that year, officers found Sahayb, his brother Muhamed Abu and half-brother Ahmed Aweys putting up posters on a high street in Ilford, east London. 'Britain uses your tax money to kill Muslims in Muslim lands,' they read, displaying a picture of a poppy with a skull in the centre, alongside silhouetted military planes. 'British terror: lest we forget,' continued the anti-Remembrance Day message. 'Don't betray your *ummah* [community] … do not take the Jews and the Christians as allies.'[2] The trio were not arrested over the posters, which were removed by police, but the incident turned out to be part of a long string of terrorist activity. Sahayb's father, who moved to Britain from Somalia in the 1990s, had married twice and he had numerous half-siblings from the other branch of the family. Two of his half-brothers, Wail and Suleyman Aweys, travelled to Syria to join Isis in 2015. Relatives later received news of their deaths, being told that Suleyman had died in battle and Wail was inside a bombed building. In a three-way iMessage chat between Sahayb, his brother Muhamed and a 17-year-old half-brother, the fighters were celebrated. The teenager, who was not prosecuted, wrote: 'We don't belong here. [Suleyman and Wail Aweys] lead the path, let's follow. We shouldn't just watch these videos and feel pain in our heart *akhi* [brother], we still have time.' Sahayb pledged that Allah would make them 'action men and not chatty men,' adding: 'The caravan left without us but *inshallah* [Allah willing] our time will come.'

In January 2019, more of Sahayb's half-siblings were jailed for collecting and disseminating Isis propaganda. Ahmed Aweys, Asma Aweys and her husband originally had their phones seized in an unrelated criminal investigation. It was into a conspiracy to burgle a jewellery shop and Ahmed, Sahayb and Muhamed were all jailed for their parts in the plan.[3] But during the investigation, detectives uncovered a plethora of violent propaganda on the relatives' phones, with Ahmed having told Facebook contacts it was acceptable to kill non-Muslims. Sahayb and Muhamed were only prosecuted for conspiracy to burgle, but Ahmed, Asma and Munye were charged with terror offences. The trio had shared terrorist material, and Asma's phone contained disturbing guides on carrying out attacks using vehicles, knives and firebombs. Their trial heard that several other relatives were sharing Isis propaganda and supportive posts in a family WhatsApp group. Jailing the Aweys siblings and Munye in 2019, Judge Mark Dennis KC said: 'It is apparent that other adults related to the defendants shared similar views and varying degrees of support for the extremist cause.'[4]

Sahayb mentioned his family's terrorist credentials when applying to join an Isis-supporting group on the encrypted Telegram app in June 2020. 'Me and my family have had our whole world turned upside down because my brother and sister and her husband were "disseminating" videos and magazines to each other,' he said. 'The feds came and locked them all up, even my sister for a year and they're still on probation and a bunch of other anti-terror stuff. [They were] posting vids of Dawlah [Isis] and this stuff.'[5] The family are believed to have had links with the al-Muhajiroun (ALM) Islamist network, with Asma Aweys and her husband previously living on the same London street as the family of its founder Omar Bakri Muhammad. While he was planning his terror attack, Sahayb made numerous online searches for Anjem Choudary and other ALM figures. Among his other ideological influences was preacher Abdullah el-Faisal (who has been convicted of stirring up racial hatred), Isis propaganda magazines, and a US cleric called Suleiman Anwar Bengharsa, who he had direct contact with online after being freed from jail. Giving evidence in court, Sahayb said he was originally told about the preacher by a half-sister who had paid £200 to do an 'online course' with him and said he was 'really good'.[6]

Sahayb was active in numerous jihadist Telegram groups, including one called 'Servants of the Unseen', where he went by the name Tariq Bin Ziyad. It was infiltrated by an undercover police officer who kept records of his violent posts celebrating terror attacks around the world. 'Time for talk over 100%,' Sahayb wrote in one of many similar posts. 'The *kuffar* [disbelievers] aren't talking, that's for sure.' The undercover officer, known as 'Rachid', drew Sahayb into one-to-one conversations by dropping breadcrumbs into the group chat suggesting he lived in the UK and knew 'the right people' if anyone wanted a gun. Once he had Sahayb in a private chat, the undercover officer claimed he had the power to smuggle firearms into Britain—'literally anything within reason'. Sahayb swiftly asked if they could meet up for a coffee and on 30 June 2020 they met for the first time. As they sat in a bugged vehicle parked outside a large Tesco supermarket in Surrey Quays, south-east London, Sahayb made his plans clear. After the pair gossiped about the whereabouts of Islamist figures including the radical preachers Anjem Choudary and Abu Haleema, Sahayb started asking 'Rachid' if he could 'get *silah* [guns] in here'. 'I'm just waiting for my brother [Ahmed] to come out of jail man,' he added. 'I'm sure he's gonna tell me [to] fire.' Unaware he was in the company of an undercover police officer, Sahayb gloated about not 'falling for the same trick' as other plotters caught by surveillance operations. 'Don't be an idiot bro,' he had advised. 'These people need to start using their brains man.'

In the days following the meeting, in private messages on Telegram, Sahayb asked 'Rachid' more questions about smuggling guns, using code including 'cloths' and 'toys'. But he never requested a firearm from his contact, instead ordering the sharpened sword online on 1 July 2020 for £57.45. The weapon was described as a 'deadly close combat design, used by warriors from Persia to the Caucasus for hundreds of years'. The security services ensured it was never dispatched. Police moved in to arrest Sahayb on 9 July 2020, finding him living in his father's flat in Ilford. A black Isis flag was found in his bedroom, alongside his new clothing and balaclavas. Despite the incriminating evidence, he denied the plot and made up a series of bizarre excuses to explain his behaviour, saying that his rap videos were parodies of drill music where he was playing a 'character' called the Masked Menace. At his trial, Sahayb told the jury he was a 'man of world peace' who was a fan of British television gardener Alan Titchmarsh, and wanted to start a charity that would grow crops for developing countries. He claimed he wanted the sword to use as a prop in videos and because he enjoyed YouTube videos of people cutting everyday objects, like paper and carpets. Sahayb, who was unemployed and living on benefits at the time, told detectives that he only joined the Servants of the Unseen group because he was 'trying to find a wife'. He added: 'Maybe behind that screen is a flowery princess, you know, who wouldn't mind marrying a beast like me.' The jury was not convinced, and Sahayb was convicted of planning an act of terrorism.[7]

A judge found that had it not been for police intervention, Sahayb would have been 'in possession of all that he needed to carry out a lone attack on a target of his choice and emulate attacks in which he had shown an interest such as had occurred in Westminster, Reading and Streatham'. Judge Mark Dennis KC said Sahayb had become part of a 'seam of extremism in his family' at an unknown stage and was not deterred by the deaths of his half-brothers in Syria, or the prison sentences handed to his other relatives. Jailing him for life with a minimum term of 19 years, he added: 'Within weeks of your own release from prison you had sought out and joined other extremists committed to supporting and promoting that same violent cause, and within no time you were getting ready to carry out your own act of violence on the streets of this country.'[8]

After Sahayb was jailed, Commander Richard Smith, head of the Metropolitan Police Counter Terrorism Command, said the number of convicted and alleged terrorist sympathisers in his family was 'extraordinary'. 'Nobody is born with hatred and intolerance in them, that has to come from somewhere, some malign influence to start that process happening,' he added. 'Certainly being in proximity to people of the same mindset, and it would appear in this family there may have been several of a similar mindset, would enforce some of those intolerant, bigoted and hate-filled beliefs. But exactly what that malign spark or influence was we do not conclusively know.'[9]

* * *

Sahayb Abu is one of at least 20 people with previous criminal convictions or cautions who have planned or carried out a terror attack in the UK in recent years.[10] He is part of a long line of terrorists and plotters who had criminal histories, including the killers who struck in London Bridge, Westminster and Reading, as well as the cell that carried out the November 2015 Paris attacks. Like many of them, Abu also took drugs as part of a hedonistic lifestyle before being jailed in 2017. 'I was in *jahiliyyah* [ignorance],' he told the undercover police officer known as Rachid. 'I should have gone a long time ago, I have two brothers that have gone [to Syria] and they're *shaheed* [martyred] over there.'[11] When giving evidence at his trial, Sahayb said he had changed his lifestyle after being freed from prison and had 'started praying again' while in jail. During their meeting in the shopping centre car park, Sahayb told 'Rachid' he had met and 'loved' pro-Isis propagandist Husnain Rashid, who was jailed for calling for terror attacks on targets including Prince George. Rashid had created a prolific Telegram channel named Lone Mujahid, which he used to issue advice on potential targets and how to use poisons, vehicles, weapons, bombs, chemicals and knives. 'He was telling people go out there and ... go to the nearest Sainsburys and put poison in the ice creams so the royal family will go and buy the ice creams from there,' Sahayb explained to the undercover officer. 'I love you my bro but that wasn't smart ... the *kuffar* [disbelievers] are gonna laugh at you.' Sahayb said he also spent time with Abuthather Mamun, who assisted the Isis-inspired plot to groom a 'mini militia' of children who could launch simultaneous terror attacks across London.

He emerged from jail appearing far more religiously observant than when he went inside for commercial burglary, but he still had an eye on crime. While discussing his attack plans with 'Rachid', Sahayb also invited him to join in a bank card fraud scheme. 'If you target for example a bank and you take a million pound ... that money is halal [permitted],' Sahayb told the undercover officer. 'Is *Dar al-Harb* [territories of war] we're living bro.' Dr Rajan Basra, who has studied the links between terrorism and crime across Europe, says the idea of using illegal activity either to fund attacks or as a form of assault on non-Muslims in itself has 'permeated the jihadist subculture'. 'Some jihadis actually justify engaging in crime as a means of either financing jihad or as a form of jihad in and of itself,' he adds. 'You could commit any range of crimes—fraud, robbery, dealing drugs—whatever it is you consider a viable means of funding your activities.'[12] Not all jihadists agree on the subject, but the argument was vocally advanced by jihadist ideologue Anwar al-Awlaki in an article for a 2011 al-Qaeda propaganda magazine. The lengthy tract, entitled 'The Ruling on Dispossessing the Disbelievers' Wealth in *Dar al-Harb*, argued that stealing from non-Muslims was religiously mandated. 'Jihad cannot depend wholly on donations made by Muslims,' Awlaki wrote:

Since jihad around the world is in dire need of financial support, we urge our brothers in the West to take it upon themselves to give this issue a priority in their plans. Rather than the Muslims financing the jihad from their own pockets, they should finance it from the pockets of their enemies.[13]

Awlaki argued that Muslims could steal from non-Muslim states by avoiding tax, and were also permitted to literally steal from individuals. But he cautioned readers to 'avoid targeting citizens of countries where the public opinion is supportive of some of the Muslim causes', and to target banks, government-owned property and global corporations instead. Sahayb's bank fraud plan and references to theft being religiously permitted in '*Dar al-Harb*' appear to have followed his instructions to the letter. Basra says Awlaki's argument was very appealing to criminals being drawn into jihadism, explaining:

The beauty of this message is that it's essentially telling people who want to be jihadis that if you're currently engaging in crime you can continue to do exactly what you're doing, it's just now you've got some kind of spiritual or ideological veneer or legitimacy to it … you don't really need to change your behaviour, you just need to change your motivation. Instead of it being for yourself, to get more money or whatever it may be, you're now doing it for the sake of jihad.[14]

Years later, the same message was put out by Isis. An issue of its English-language propaganda magazine published in 2017 contained an article entitled: 'The *kafir*'s [disbeliever's] wealth is halal [permitted] for you, so take it.' 'Any attack on the *kuffar*, including that which is financial, is jihad,' Isis decreed:

In this regard, any wealth taken from the *kuffar* through deception or defeat is considered *ghanimah* [the spoils of war] … the Muslim in *Dar al-Kufr* has the opportunity to follow this blessed *sunnah* [tradition], striking terror by stalking the *kuffar* and causing them economic harm. There should be no misunderstanding about the excellence of this deed, as taking this wealth is in accordance with the command of Allah.[15]

Basra says that offenders have also 'utilised their criminal knowledge' for terrorist purposes. The pioneer of the approach was Mohammed Merah, a French-Algerian al-Qaeda supporter who murdered seven victims in 2012 targeting soldiers and a Jewish school in France. Merah had a lengthy criminal history and is believed to have used his connections to obtain the guns used for the attacks.[16] But the incident that really 'planted the flag' for what Dr Basra and his colleagues came to label the crime-terror nexus was the January 2015 Paris attacks. Amedy Coulibaly, who took hostages at a kosher supermarket in the name of Isis, had been mentored by an al-Qaeda recruiter while serving a prison sentence for receiving stolen goods, drug trafficking and robbery.[17] The same recruiter took another prisoner under his wing, Chérif Kouachi, who was accused of trying to become a foreign fighter in Iraq. He and his brother Saïd are believed to have partly financed their massacre at the offices of *Charlie Hebdo* magazine by importing counterfeit Nike shoes from China. Coulibaly was making money by dealing drugs and fraudulently taking out large consumer loans shortly before the shootings.

The same trend can be seen in several deadly terror attacks around the world. The ringleader of the 2017 London Bridge attack, Khuram Butt, was arrested over suspected bank fraud eight months before his rampage.[18] Basra says that militant groups have been funding themselves through crime for decades, but that as the 'nature of terrorism changed' following the emergence of Isis, there has been a 'rise in criminals becoming jihadists on an individual level'. As the International Centre for the Study of Radicalisation's (ICSR) seminal report on the crime-terror nexus noted:

Just like the criminal gangs of which they used to be members, jihadist groups offered power, violence, adventure and adrenaline, a strong identity, and—not least—a sense of rebellion and being anti-establishment. This made the 'jump' from criminality to terrorism smaller than is commonly perceived—especially when considering that, unlike al-Qaeda, Islamic State required practically no religious knowledge or learning, and cared little about the complexities of theological discourse. For criminals with a guilty conscience, the jihadism of the Islamic State could seem like a perfect fit.[19]

The pink post-it note

'I thought that was my way to heaven, I thought that's my way for forgiveness,' Safiyya Shaikh told police officers in a dingy London interview room on 10 October 2019. The 37-year-old mother had been plotting to bomb St Paul's Cathedral and a nearby hotel in an attack inspired by Isis attacks that had killed almost 300 people in Sri Lanka. Those atrocities struck churches and hotels on Easter Sunday 2019, and Shaikh said she wanted to mount her own attack at either Easter or Christmas, the holiest Christian festivals. 'I would like to bomb and shoot til death,' she told an online contact. 'But if that not possible I do other way. Belt or anything. I just want a lot to die. *Inshallah* [Allah willing].' Shaikh carried out reconnaissance at St Paul's in September 2019, taking photos of the inside of the cathedral and sending them to a contact. Under an image of Sir Christopher Wren's famous dome, she wrote: 'Under this dome I would like to put bomb.'

She drafted a pledge of allegiance to Isis on a pink post-it note, and was considering making a video to be released after her expected martyrdom. All Shaikh needed was the bombs, and she passed a jihadist contact a fuchsia Nike holdall and 'girly backpack' to fill with explosives for the task. One bomb would be detonated at a hotel after Shaikh left for St Paul's Cathedral, where she would plant the second device. She would be wearing a separate suicide vest, which she hoped to use to kill herself among crowds fleeing to a nearby Tube station. But all was not as it seemed. Shaikh's contacts were undercover police officers and she was under surveillance as part of a joint operation with MI5. They decided to move in shortly after Shaikh handed over her bags, fearing that she may not wait for them to be returned before she acted.

Shaikh had called the plot the 'best opportunity of her life'.[20] Previously known as Michelle Ramsden, she was a heroin addict who converted to Islam in 2007 after being impressed by the kindness of a neighbouring Muslim family. She had a difficult childhood, being taken into care to remove her from issues linked to drug and alcohol abuse in her family, and her own addiction led to convictions for theft, burglary and heroin possession. Unemployed and living on benefits, she turned to YouTube for help. In 2017, she started making playlists indicating her ongoing struggle with addiction and her deepening extremism. They included videos on exorcisms, on 'overcoming *haram* [forbidden] situations' and making '*dua* [prayer] for addict'.[21] Shaikh appeared to be curious about the concept of magic and drawn to conspiracy theories, including those accusing Jews of responsibility for the 9/11 attacks. Her YouTube journey progressed into extremism, with Shaikh making playlists of videos by prominent jihadists including Anjem Choudary and ideologues in his al-Muhajiroun network, hate preacher Abu Hamza and al-Qaeda co-founder Abdullah Azzam. Her other key influences were an Australian convert-turned Isis propagandist called Musa Cerantonio and jihadist preacher Ahmad Musa Jibril. Shaikh's YouTube profile indicated that she would watch the videos for hours on end and spent significant amounts of time compiling the playlists.

Shaikh's journey towards jihadism appeared to have accelerated in 2016. She had been organising meetings for female Muslim converts in west London, but dropped out of the events and stopped attending mosques to avoid being reported for her extreme views. She later told undercover police that around the same time, she had wanted to journey to Isis' 'caliphate' but was prevented from travelling. Between August that year and September 2017, Shaikh was referred to the Prevent programme three times over her suspected radicalisation, but denied being an extremist. Counter-terror police said they made 'numerous attempts to engage' with her until August 2018 but she turned them away and was not assigned an ideological mentor.[22] Within months, Shaikh had become a propagandist herself. She ran a total of eight channels on the Telegram messaging app, including a notorious group called GreenB1rds, which distributed Isis propaganda and calls for terror attacks.

A threat towards Americans on 11 September 2019 sparked international media coverage. 'Allah will give us victory against them and what America awaits in the coming days is greater and worse than what has passed by the will of Allah,' said the post. 'You are a disease which will be wiped out by the permission of the Allah. Monotheists Brothers in the United Snakes of America.' A poster featured a sepia-toned photo of the World Trade Center's Twin Towers on fire with Isis flags in the background and a call to 'kill the Americans and plunder their money wherever and whenever they find it'. The GreenB1rds channel had previously generated news reports by publishing threats against British targets including London Bridge and Big Ben, as well as videos of Isis executions and bomb manuals. Shaikh loved the publicity. '*Kuffar* always publish my work. They don't even realise they promote for us,' she gloated. She ran the channel with several administrators and went to lengths to keep her identity hidden by using fake names, made-up email addresses and sometimes posing as a man. But her activity would not remain secret for long.

On 18 August 2019, Shaikh was stopped under schedule 7 of the Terrorism Act before she could catch a flight to Amsterdam from Luton Airport. The ticket had been purchased by Yousra Lemouesset, a 31-year-old Dutch woman who had returned to her home country after joining Isis in Syria and marrying a fighter. The women were planning to meet but police did not let that happen. They turned Shaikh around and seized her mobile phone. The ensuing examination revealed her activities on Telegram and triggered the surveillance operation by MI5 and counter-terror police. Two days after being stopped at the airport, Shaikh used the encrypted Threema messaging app to contact a man she believed to be a terrorist operations expert, but who was, in fact, an undercover officer. Known as H, he claimed he would be able to help her create the explosives she needed for her attack.[23] Shaikh told H she was going to 'do a piece of history' and outlined her plans—requesting the holdall and rucksack bombs. She arranged to meet a female undercover officer, who she believed to be his wife, to be fitted for a suicide vest. At their meeting on 24 September 2019, Shaikh boasted of her work on the GreenB1rds channel and handed over her bags.

After her arrest, she admitted the plot in police interviews. Although she later instructed defence lawyers to tell a court she had developed 'cold feet' and would not have gone through with the bombings, Shaikh changed her mind once again after reading media coverage of the barrister's quotes during her trial. Knowing the call would be recorded for security reasons, she phoned one of her character witnesses from prison and she said the claim had been a 'big lie'. Shaikh insisted that she would have carried out the attack and said that she had not attended a second meeting with the female undercover officer by accident, rather than because her intentions had changed. Shaikh claimed she had been smoking drugs and failed to wake up in time. The Isis supporter then instructed her barrister to tell the judge what she had said and that 'her intentions had not waned'.[24]

Shaikh was jailed for life with a minimum term of 14 years for planning the attack and her work disseminating terrorist publications. A judge said that after being prevented from joining Isis abroad or meeting her contact in the Netherlands, she 'decided that she could take better revenge in this country for what the *kuffar* [disbelievers] had done'. Mr Justice Sweeney found that Shaikh's troubled background, mental health issues and addiction did not reduce her responsibility for the plot, and that her daughter's right to a family life was of 'little weight' in the circumstances. He told her:

> The court must be alert, particularly in terrorism cases, to its process being abused by defendants who seek to aggrandise their role or crime, and thus the reporting in the media in relation to it, for

their own perverse purposes and/or the perverse purposes of the cause they seek to espouse. However, in your case, I had already reached the sure conclusion, on all the original evidence, that your claim of doubts to the police and others was a lie, that your intention had been, and remained throughout, strong, and that ... but for apprehension, the activity was likely to have been carried out.[25]

* * *

Shaikh's criminal convictions and continued use of drugs may, on the face of it, appear to be a direct contradiction of her identity as a dedicated jihadist and Isis supporter. The terrorist group prohibited alcohol, cigarettes and drugs in areas under its control, emphasising its opposition with a propaganda video of it setting fire to hashish supplies in Afghanistan.[26] But researchers at the International Centre for the Study of Radicalisation (ICSR), based at King's College London, have found overlaps between current jihadist movements, drug use and wider criminality. A 2019 report found that while most extremists kicked their former habits as part of the radicalisation process, it was not a 'uniform response and many jihadists in Europe continue to use or deal drugs while simultaneously engaging with extremist ideas and networks'. Numerous British terrorists and plotters used drugs in the past, including the Westminster attacker Khalid Masood, London Bridge ringleader Khuram Butt, Manchester Arena bomber Salman Abedi, and Mohammed Emwazi the Isis executioner known as 'Jihadi John'. Several plotters who planned attacks before the period covered by this book continued their drug use at the same time, like Shaikh. Sana Khan, who was convicted of planning an Isis-inspired bombing alongside her husband Mohammed Rehman in 2015, ran an unsuccessful defence claiming that the fact 'she was taking drugs at the time of offending, which is strictly prohibited within the Muslim religion, suggests very strongly that she was not a committed radical Islamist'. The Court of Appeal concluded that adopting some tenets of jihadism but not others, and continuing to dress in a Western style and take drugs, did not 'indicate any diminution of her commitment to furthering the aims of radical Islam'.[27] Security services in other countries were slower to take the same approach. In Germany, authorities halted a surveillance operation on suspected Isis supporter Anis Amri in September 2016 after observing him dealing and taking drugs. Three months later, he murdered 13 people in a lorry attack on a Christmas market in Berlin.[28]

The ICSR's report found that drug use can have an 'indirect role in the radicalisation process', and that since the emergence of Isis, there has been a Europe-wide trend of 'merging criminal and terrorist social networks, environments, and milieus' in a phenomenon labelled the crime-terror nexus. Isis appeared to acknowledge the trend in a December 2017 propaganda video, where a narrator explained how supporters often come from communities where 'deviant behaviour' is common and showed a footage of cocaine being snorted while condemning people who choose 'life's pleasures over worshipping Allah'.[29] Dr Rajan Basra, the author of the ICSR report, says that some former drug users become jihadists as part of 'a quest for redemption' or as Shaikh put it to police, 'forgiveness'. 'That idea to wipe the slate clean and start afresh can be a very powerful one,' he adds. 'What we saw when we looked at cases across Europe is that amongst criminals that are radicalised, they did have this idea that their involvement in jihad was going to purify them, was going to give them a shot at redemption and make up for all the "sins" they've committed before as bad Muslims'.[30]

Isis recruiters and propagandists quickly utilised the dynamic. In 2014, a Facebook post by Isis-supporting British group Rayat al-Tawheed showed a militant dressed in all black, holding an AK-47 rifle and facing towards a bright light. 'Sometimes people with the worst pasts create the best futures,' read the slogan imposed on the image. Basra says similar mottos were posted across Instagram, Facebook and other social media at the time, 'because this was in 2014 and you could do that'. He adds: 'Their message was that it doesn't matter who you are or who you were before you became a mujahid, all that matters is what you do since. It's a very straightforward message, anyone could understand that.' The approach set Isis apart from the more structured and puritanical jihadist terrorist groups that preceded it. Basra says Isis widened its recruitment pool by 'lowering the bar in terms of who they would accept'. 'Groups like al-Qaeda were seen almost as the thinking man's jihadist groups and they would be a bit more rigorous in their vetting processes and so on, but with Islamic State the doors were much more open,' he adds. A cache of leaked Isis forms filled out by foreign fighters entering its territories between 2013 and 2014 showed how open the doors were. Analysis of over 4,600 documents by the US military's Combating Terrorism Center found that 70 per cent of recruits described their knowledge of Sharia law as 'basic'. The most common occupations listed were either unskilled or low-skilled jobs, or 'student'. But a 24-year-old man from Gaziantep, Turkey, was brutally honest. He listed himself as a 'drug and hashish dealer'. A note scrawled on his form by an Isis official stated: 'May Allah forgive him and us!'[31]

5

LOVE AND LIES

'Can we get married already ffs. I want u to kill ppl for me. I have a list,' Madihah Taheer wrote in a text message to her boyfriend, Ummariyat Mirza. He replied: 'The day of *nikkah* [marriage] I'll kill em all. Give me the list. The only thing that stops me is we are not married. I will defo I'm not joking.'[1]

The couple were just 19 at the time, and it would take them longer than expected to prepare for an attack. They were married in April 2016 and set up a home together in Birmingham. Taheer quickly became pregnant with their first child. But despite the appearance of domestic bliss, their intentions had not changed. A love for Isis had been common ground since the earliest days of their relationship. In March 2015, they had discussed travelling to Syria together. Taheer was looking for an escape from living with her cannabis-smoking father, who had tried to marry her off to her cousin.[2] She had met her husband-to-be in sixth form but never passed any of her A-levels. Searching for inspiration in her life, she had been reading a blog called 'Diary of a Muhajirah', which was written by a woman who had joined Isis in Syria and married a fighter, saying she wanted that life for herself. Mirza, one of five siblings, had gone straight from college into an accountancy firm run by his family. He flirted back with a photo of Isis leader Abu Bakr al-Baghdadi but Taheer had already seen it, and the two debated who was more radical. Mirza boasted that he had introduced his girlfriend to Twitter, jihad and 'Dawla'—a term for Isis favoured by its supporters. Taheer joked that she would use the messages in her defence if she got arrested. It was in September 2015, six months after they had first discussed moving to the caliphate, that she sent the message urging Mirza to kill people for her.[3]

The teenagers both had targets in mind. Taheer said she fantasised about Katie Hopkins, an anti-Muslim commentator, being beheaded and called her the 'biggest *kuthi* [bitch] of them all'. Mirza named Paul Golding, then the co-leader of far-right group Britain First, as one of his targets. Following their marriage, the couple moved in together and started preparations in earnest. In May 2016, Taheer purchased a sparring dummy online, and sent a video to her husband of herself punching it. But it was not 'human' enough for him, and Mirza had the dummy returned and replaced with a more expensive model called Century Bob. Six months later, Mirza started knife shopping. He originally wanted to spend £300 on a weapon but Mirza, now pregnant and working as an administrator for a children's nursery, said they could not afford it. 'Can u not use any *dishum* [knife]?' she asked. 'It doesn't have to be bloody state of the art.' Mirza pressed for his weapon of choice, telling his wife: 'This isn't a fantasy … it's real.'

Amid the bickering, he sent her a new Isis propaganda video showing suicide bombers being interviewed before blowing themselves up in attacks on Iraqi forces, and sadistic executions of two alleged spies being beheaded and drowned. The following day, Taheer gave her husband a £100 to £150 budget for a knife, commenting: 'They all do the same frigging thing Ummar, u don't need to spend £300 on one.' They settled on a rubber training knife, which was used by Mirza to stab the £275 dummy. Depicting a white man's torso, it was later found at their home with slash marks on the forehead, throat and abdomen. Mirza's internet search history made his intentions clear. He had looked up the 'best knife to kill with', 'Isis knife', 'best assassin knife', 'silent assassin kill', 'neck knife', 'deadliest daggers' and 'how easy is it to kill someone with a knife?'[4]

In February 2017, the couple decided to upgrade from the training knife to a steel blade. In a text message, Mirza pledged: 'It'll be done, *shaytaan* [the devil] won't be able to delay me any further, once it's there I have no excuse, take any chance I get.' Taheer paid £121.20 for a Cold Steel knife with a 7-inch black blade. Mirza then researched how to conceal a weapon and bought a high-strength length of rope to fashion into a covert harness. He made online searches for potential targets including Army and RAF sites in

Birmingham and Jewish areas of the UK. Mirza appeared to be inspired by the Westminster attack when it struck on 22 March 2017, searching for information on terrorist Khalid Masood. Days later, he responded to a video of a speaker at a local mosque who condemned the attack with a picture of a knife in his family WhatsApp group.

Among the members was his older sister, Zainub Mirza, who shared an affinity for Isis. For months, she had been sending her brother its propaganda videos including graphic footage of child suicide bombers, beheadings and hostages being hung from 'meat hooks' and having their throats slit. After sending one link Zainub, then 23, wrote to Mirza: 'I'm proper ready'. 'May Allah keep you steadfast and your *imaan* [belief] high,' he replied, before conducting online searches for the 'best' knives. Later on the same day, in January 2017, Zainub voiced a wish to travel to Isis territories in Syria. 'I think life would be easy in *dawlah* [the Islamic State],' she wrote. 'I would like to go there lol.' Her brother agreed, writing, 'so much easier'. Zainub repeatedly used Google to search for 'new Isis videos', watching and discussing some of the terrorist group's most graphic output, which her brother described as 'amazing … proper horror movie terror squad'. Zainub was becoming desensitised by the endless decapitations, shootings, bombings, stabbings and stonings, telling Mirza: 'I could slit a throat easy now.' But he was already making his own plans.

Intelligence that Mirza could be planning a stabbing rampage reached MI5 and he was put under surveillance. On 29 March 2017, a week after the Westminster attack, armed police swooped as Mirza drove down Birmingham's busy Alum Rock Road with Zainub. They forced the car to stop and arrested the pair. Officers swiftly moved to search Mirza's home, but they did not initially have any intelligence of his wife's enthusiastic support for the plot. Taheer, then heavily pregnant, was not arrested until investigators examined her husband's mobile phone and discovered their joint conspiracy and bloodthirsty pillow talk. At the time, she was seven months pregnant and was detained after being asked to travel to a police station in Birmingham with her solicitor.

By the time Mirza was arrested, he had already created the harness for the knife, meaning it could be carried over his shoulder under clothing, and it was lying ready for deployment in his home. Jailing him, Judge Christopher Kinch QC said:

> There is a clear and seemingly inexorable progress from interest and enthusiasm in terrorism, through research and study into training, sourcing and acquiring equipment and then researching targets for action. At each stage the discussions between husband and wife demonstrate that Taheer was supportive throughout. The jury were sure that when she ordered and paid for the £120 Cold Steel knife, she intended to assist her husband to commit acts of terrorism. However, there is no evidence of any target being identified or of any actual plan of attack being formed.[5]

Defence lawyers argued that it was not certain that Mirza would commit a terror attack, given his young age and that he had been spouting 'big talk' on jihadism for two years without taking any action. But the judge said that he 'had been moving towards some act of terrorism over a period of many months' and was deeply committed. The difference between online boasting, genuine intent and actual capability is a constant challenge for the security services, and a substantial portion of surveillance operations are geared to pinpointing when the latter stage has been reached. If police had arrested Mirza before he had obtained his Cold Steel Knife, it would have most likely been impossible to charge him with preparing an act of terrorism.

He pleaded guilty to the charge, while his wife denied involvement in the plot and claimed that she had taken on a subservient role as a wife. Taheer was convicted at trial and the judge pointed to her long-standing extremist mindset and vocal encouragement of her husband. Zainub claimed she did not know about her brother and sister-in-law's plot, but inside her home, which was where Mirza had lived with his family before marrying Taheer, police found the training knife, air rifles, a meat cleaver, sword, machete and an array of knives. Defence lawyers said that she had been a 'promising university student' but dropped out of her course with stress and anxiety, retreating to her home and the internet. Zainub, then 24, was jailed for 30 months. Taheer was convicted of preparing acts of terrorism and jailed for ten years, at the age of 22 while Mirza, then

21, received an extended sentence of 21 years. The couple's baby was five months old when they were sent to prison.

* * *

It is one of several foiled terror plots where women gave emotional and material support to their partners' violent ambitions. The role fits with Isis' messaging towards female supporters, which widened their role far beyond that permitted in previous real-world terrorist networks and al-Qaeda's mountain training camps. Women who reached the 'caliphate' were to be wives and mothers, ensuring the continuation of the Islamic State by caring for fighters and populating it for the future. Those who hadn't made it there still had a part to play, but Isis did not explicitly encourage female jihadists to carry out acts of violence themselves. For that reason, international security services did not focus on women as a domestic terror threat in the years immediately following Isis' emergence. Even when female supporters started travelling to Syria from European countries, sometimes alone or with their children, they were not widely considered to be a security threat as individuals.

In an issue of its English-language propaganda magazine, published in February 2015, Isis featured an 'interview' with the wife of Amedy Coulibaly—the terrorist who attacked a kosher supermarket in Paris in an assault synchronised with the *Charlie Hebdo* shooting. The article was entitled 'to our sisters' and praised Coulibaly for sending his wife to Isis territory before the 'blessed' attack. Going by the nom de guerre or 'kunya' Umm Basir al-Muhajirah, Hayat Boumeddiene was quoted as giving a lengthy address to other women. She urged them to disregard imams and Islamic scholars and strive against doubts from their 'inner selves' to adhere to Isis. 'My sisters, be bases of support and safety for your husbands, brothers, fathers and sons,' it continued. 'Be advisors to them. They should find comfort and peace with you. Do not make things difficult for them. Facilitate all matters for them.' The article urged women to follow the example of female figures in the Quran and their 'chastity, modesty and obedience', calling on them to 'be patient while hoping for Allah's reward'.[6] Isis propaganda positioned marriage and motherhood as a form of jihad, saying women's duty was to encourage their husbands and sons to fight the enemies of the caliphate. Instead of protecting them from danger, women should 'bow down in thankful prayer' at their deaths.[7]

As Isis began to lose its territory and face military defeat, the position on women as passive supporters for men's violence shifted slightly, but only insofar as 'defensive' jihad was concerned. An article in an Arabic language newsletter from December 2016 stated: 'While it is known that jihad is not [obligatory] for women in principle, the Muslim woman should know that if an enemy enters her home, jihad is incumbent on her as it is on men and she should repel him by whatever means possible.'[8] Amid more damaging military losses in the autumn of 2017, the position slipped further. Isis justified the change by claiming women had fought in the Islamic Golden Age and cited female companions of the Prophet Mohamed as examples. 'Today, in the context of the war against the Islamic State, it has become an obligation for female Muslims to fulfil their duties on all fronts in supporting the [male] mujahedeen in this battle,' said an official article. 'They should prepare themselves to defend their religion by sacrificing themselves by Allah.'[9] Four months later, for the first time, Isis' video propaganda outlet released footage of women fighting. A group of female jihadists, dressed in black with their faces covered by veils, were shown being driven to battle in a truck flying the Isis flag. A voiceover praised the 'chaste mujahid woman journeying to her Lord with the garments of purity and faith, seeking revenge for her religion and for the honour of her sisters imprisoned by the apostate Kurds'.[10]

Dr Elizabeth Pearson, the author of *Extreme Britain: Gender, Masculinity and Radicalisation*, says the video was one of the 'moments' where Isis praised violence by women, but that overall it remains 'transgressive' in the group's value system. Isis claimed responsibility for a shooting carried out by a husband and wife at a work Christmas party in San Bernadino, California, in 2015 and an attack on a police station by three women in the Kenyan city of Mombasa in September 2016. But Pearson says that praise for such attacks is 'generally inverted—if a woman can do this, then what's wrong with all you men? That's the way women's violence is used, it's a motivation to right that.' Isis' official response to the Mombasa attack, in its Arabic language newsletter, asked: 'What is the matter with those men who continue to remain behind, having laid down their swords, even watching passively as they are surpassed on occasion by the women of the *ummah* [global Muslim community]?' Pearson says the footage of female combatants showed Isis 'flirting with the idea' of embracing a new role for women, but that it previously chose not to publicise reports of female snipers and suicide bombers deployed in the defence of its territories:

> They've got a clear delineation between the roles, it's the backbone of everything. The highest status men are the ones who are martyrs and they're doing that to protect women. If the women are fighting, what is there to protect? Ideologically and religiously there is no justification for the exclusion of women, it's about power and the protection of this male role, which is hugely important for Isis.[11]

Pearson says that women who support their husbands and relatives to wage terror attacks would be fitting the role ascribed by Isis, but any planning to carry out attacks themselves would be overstepping the mark. 'If you're an Isis supporter and you're a woman and you do a violent act you're transgressing,' she adds. That was not a bar to Britain's first, and so far Britain's only, female jihadist terror cell.

The tea party

When Safaa Boular was 15, she made a new group of friends. They were older than her and, she thought, a lot cooler. They were jihadists living in Isis' self-declared caliphate in Syria. She made her first 'friend' on Twitter, where at the time Isis members were able to freely post about their supposedly idyllic lives in the hope of ensnaring new recruits. A woman who called herself Umm Isa al-Amriki set her sights on Safaa, who had already been radicalised by her extremist mother and was fantasising about life as an Isis bride from her London bedroom. Al-Amriki told Safaa of the joys living in the Islamic State with her fighter husband, and sent her videos and religious songs. Safaa eagerly drank in her teaching and retweeted the older woman's posts. They switched their communications to the encrypted messaging app Telegram, for better security, but after several months of chatting al-Amriki suddenly went silent. She had been assassinated in a targeted air strike by the US-led coalition on 22 April 2016.[12]

Al-Amriki, an Australian woman whose real name was Shadi Jabar Khalil Mohammad, was killed alongside her husband, a Sudanese man known as Abu Sa'ad al-Sudani. It turned out Safaa had not been the only teenager al-Amriki had struck up an online 'friendship' with. Pentagon press secretary Peter Cook said the couple were 'influential Isil recruiters and extremists who actively sought to harm Western interests', adding: 'Al-Sudani was involved in planning attacks against the United States, Canada and the United Kingdom. Both al-Sudani and his wife were active in recruiting foreign fighters in efforts to inspire attacks against Western interests.' But it was not the end of Safaa's contact with Isis. Before her death, al-Amriki had put her in contact with a wider group of men and women in Syria, including a man who called himself Abu Usama al-Britani. His real name was Naweed Hussain, he was a 30-year-old from Coventry and he liked to woo the ladies. He struck up an online relationship with Safaa, who had just turned 16, communicating with her for up to 12 hours each day. After less than three months of online chats, Hussain said that he wanted to marry the teenager and could get her into Syria. In August 2016, Safaa declared that she loved him and wanted to join him in Isis' capital of Raqqa, marry and have his children, preferably twins.

Her older sister, Rizlaine Boular, had already made a similar attempt in 2014. Then aged 18, she got as far as Istanbul before being stopped by Turkish authorities and sent back to the UK, where she admitted to police that she had been trying to join Isis in Syria. Rizlaine was not prosecuted but her actions put the family on the security services' radar. She later settled down in London, married and had a child, but Safaa's burgeoning extremism rekindled her intentions. The sisters spoke about Isis and the life they wanted as women of the caliphate. Safaa was determined to go and Rizlaine decided to join her, making travel arrangements for them both with Hussain's assistance. He raised £3,000 in cash for their journey, which was sent to Rizlaine in the post by an unknown Isis supporter in the UK. In August 2016, Rizlaine purchased plane tickets to Turkey for herself, her nine-month-old baby and Safaa. Mindful of her previous botched attempt, she booked return journeys and a hotel to be used as a cover story to present the trip as a mere holiday, but the real plan was to travel to the Syrian border and pay smugglers to cross. In a Telegram message, Hussain told Rizlaine that if she was caught and prevented from reaching Isis territory, she should 'do something' in the UK, adding bomb, knife and fire emojis. 'Yes,' Rizlaine responded. He had been talking separately to Safaa about what she would be doing in Syria. 'Belts are a must,' Hussain wrote. 'Don't eva b hesitant 2 pull da pin ok. Ur honour is worth more than any *kafirs* life.' Safaa wrote that she was 'tired of it … I want *jannah* [paradise] so bad'.

But Safaa would never reach Syria and meet Hussain in real life. She was stopped under terror laws on 19 August 2016, on her way back from a holiday in Morocco with her mother. Safaa admitted that she and Rizlaine were planning to leave Britain the following week, and disclosed her plan to marry Hussain. But the sisters were not arrested, and two days later their mother reported them missing. Police tracked them to a hostel in Kilburn, where they were staying with Rizlaine's baby. This time, the sisters were arrested on suspicion of preparing acts of terrorism by travelling to join Isis in Syria. After being released on bail, Safaa resumed her contact with Hussain using a new mobile phone that she kept hidden inside a yellow cushion. With her aspirations to reach the caliphate thwarted, they fell back on Isis' playbook and started planning an attack in the UK instead. Hussain and Safaa discussed an assault on the British Museum, where she would use a gun or grenade supplied to her to murder tourists.

In December 2016, Hussain told a Telegram contact who he believed to be a would-be terrorist based in Leeds that he was planning for 'maximum carnage'. He was actually an undercover MI5 agent, who had been deployed to discover the extent of Hussain's involvement in international attack planning. It was extensive, and Safaa was far from the only person he was speaking to. Safaa took her younger sister to visit the British Museum on 4 April 2017—two weeks after the Westminster attack—and Hussain told the role-players that his unnamed London accomplice would be 'going to the place to check it out'.[13] Unknown to him, the people he believed to be accomplices who would supply Safaa with weapons and join her in the attack were also undercover agents. Hussain was killed on the same day Safaa scoped out her target, by which point MI5 had bugged the flat where the family lived in Vauxhall. The device recorded Safaa's reaction after a role-player claiming to have been Hussain's Isis commander delivered news of his death. Safaa sobbed while being comforted by her mother and sister. Safaa said she didn't want to live and Rizlaine told her that Hussain was 'waiting' for her to join him in heaven. 'I'm so proud of her,' her mother said, telling her daughter: 'May Allah raise your ranks, may Allah raise your status'.[14]

When new security service officers posing as an Isis fighter and a widowed woman contacted Safaa online, she told them of her plan to commit a terror attack and her desire to become a martyr. Days after her 17th birthday, she wrote: 'My heart has been set on this for months. Only Allah can guide me but your assistance is needed desperately.' Safaa said that Hussain had given her instructions on how to use weapons and the role-players drew details out of her by claiming they had to report the plans to Isis leaders. She told them that if a gun and grenades could not be supplied, all it would take was 'a car and a knife to get what I want to achieve'. The teenager wrote:

> I wish to be honoured by a departure purely for the sake of Allah. And I do not have time to lounge around. I simply cannot afford to waste this opportunity. So if you can assist me in any way, although it may be different to the original plans … grant me martyrdom for his sake. My heart yearns to be reunited with my dear husband for the very first time.

On 12 April 2017, Safaa was charged for her attempted travel to Syria the previous year and taken into custody. Unknown to her and her relatives, the investigation into her plot continued and they were being closely watched. On the day of her charge, a new surveillance operation began targeting Rizlaine, her mother and one of Safaa's friends, Khawla Barghouthi. It revealed that Safaa was passing the baton of violent jihad to her sister and mother. In phone calls from the Medway Secure Training Unit in Kent, which were recorded by the security services, they repeatedly discussed arranging a 'party'. Days after she was detained, Rizlaine pretended to be a friend who was planning to 'throw a party soon' and that her friend Khawla had been 'invited so that everyone can support each other, help each other out and stuff you know'.

Rizlaine, Safaa and their mother had a lengthy phone conversation on 24 April, where Rizlaine told her sister: 'It's going to be like me like and a few sisters and stuff and we're just gonna have fun erm its basically gonna be like a tea party and stuff ... it's gonna be fun it's going to be on Thursday we're gonna have this party.' Rizlaine said it would be an 'English tea party' and joked with her sister about an 'Alice in Wonderland theme'. 'You can be the Mad Hatter,' Safaa told her. The infantile code signalled that Rizlaine was going to launch her attack on 27 April. Two days before, she and her mother Mina Dich went on a reconnaissance trip to Westminster, with Dich driving them around key landmarks including the Houses of Parliament and Westminster Bridge. The following afternoon, they purchased a pack of three knives and a small rucksack from a supermarket. Dich threw away the receipts and discarded two of the knives in a public bin, keeping the largest, with a 6-inch blade. Rizlaine then went to practise for her attack at Barghouthi's flat in Willesden, north-west London.

Armed police made their move on 27 April 2017, after listening in on a conversation where Rizlaine told her friend she was going to use the knife to carry out the attack that very night. The pair laughed and joked about Rizlaine's fears that she might 'flop so badly' and cut her arm by accident. 'How are you going to do it? What if they are faster than you?' Barghouthi was recorded saying, before Rizlaine said she hoped 'Allah gives me a heart attack' if she got tasered or shot by police. 'Don't worry. Come here, want to practise on me again?' Barghouthi responded, before Rizlaine could be heard trying different stabbing techniques as her friend played a victim. Shortly afterwards, counter-terror police raided the home, shooting Boular as she shouted, 'Fuck you'. She survived her injuries and both women were arrested.[15]

A judge later found that Dich had started moving towards an 'extreme adherence to the Islamic faith' in 2012, influencing the mindset of her daughters and exposing them to a circle of like-minded friends who supported Isis. 'You must carry a heavy responsibility for the path that your two daughters have taken,' Judge Mark Dennis KC told her during a sentencing hearing. He found that the sisters' extremism was intensified by online Isis propaganda and contact from Hussain and other recruiters. He determined that while Safaa's young age had made her 'vulnerable to being influenced by others who were older and already radicalised', she became deeply committed to Isis and was dangerous. A pre-sentence report found that Safaa, then 18, presented 'a high risk of causing serious physical and associated psychological harm to indiscriminate members of the public', adding: 'Whilst the offence in the UK may not have materialised due to advanced scrutiny by the authorities, without these safeguards such an event could not be ruled out.' Judge Dennis said Safaa had only been prevented from committing an attack either in Syria or Britain because her plans were 'thwarted' in circumstances beyond her control.[16]

The judge said that by 2016, Safaa was 'old enough to make her own decisions', and had been 'well able to stand up to anyone and choose her own path'. Rather than being a duped victim, Judge Dennis said the teenager 'knew what she was doing'—but he also acknowledged that she had been influenced and drawn into her extremist mindset at an 'impressionable' age by her mother and friends, her older sister, her female mentor al-Amriki and finally Hussain.

Rizlaine and Dich admitted preparing acts of terrorism but Safaa denied the offence and was convicted following a trial. She claimed that she thought Hussain's suggestions of an attack in London were just a fantasy, and that she did not take him seriously or plan to do anything. She was jailed for life with a minimum term of 13 years, which was cut to 11 after an appeal. At the time of writing, Safaa remains Britain's youngest female terror plotter. A judge found that her sister Rizlaine, then 22, was made 'vulnerable to malign influences' by her upbringing and background, but truly intended to carry out a 'wicked' act borne of distorted views.[17] Although a defence barrister said Rizlaine had suffered an abusive marriage and had wanted to kill herself, knowing that 'as she produced a knife in the vicinity of the Palace of Westminster police officers would swoop and kill her', she was jailed for life with a minimum term of 16 years. Dich was given six years and nine months for assisting her daughter's plot and Barghouthi, then 21, was jailed for two years and four months for failing to report the plans to the authorities.

* * *

But there was someone else at the heart of this plot who was not brought to justice: Hussain. And this is far from a unique case. Safaa Boular is one of countless girls and young women who were targeted online by male Isis fighters, in a process characterised as a form of 'grooming' by some academics. The term 'jihottie' was coined to describe the young, handsome jihadists who attempted to attract female recruits to the new caliphate. It was a difficult sell. Women making the journey faced arranged or forced marriages, extreme restrictions on their movement and dress, poor living conditions and healthcare, and of course the threat of being killed in air strikes. Many had romanticised dreams of marrying a handsome Isis fighter, but would be forced to share him with multiple wives or a Yazidi sex slave. As a 2018 report by the United Nations women's authority wondered: 'How could a group that promotes women's subjugation and sexual slavery also appeal to women and seemingly offer them tools of empowerment?'[18]

The short answer is that Isis completely flipped the idea of what subjugation and empowerment were. It decreed that subjugation was the imposition of feminism on Islam, Western values, Western clothing, living in the land of disbelief. Freedom was living in a land governed only by the laws of Allah, where women could supposedly practise their religion fully, free of the false standards and restrictions imposed by Western states. There was also the thrill of defying parents, and police, by fleeing to join Isis. A propaganda article purporting to have been written by a female Muslim convert who journeyed to the caliphate from Finland said:

> Many of these obstacles are just in your head and they're the work of Satan ... unless you're living here you don't realize what kind of life you had before. The life here is so much more pure. When you're in *Dar al-Kufr* [the lands of disbelief] you're exposing yourself and your children to so much filth and corruption. You make it easy for Satan to lead you astray. Here you're living a pure life, and your children are being raised with plenty of good influence around them. They don't need to be ashamed of their religion. They are free to be proud of it.[19]

Pearson, who has infiltrated Telegram groups for female Isis supporters and interviewed the group's followers, says that both men and women worked as recruiters.[20] Several notorious blogs were run by women who lived in the caliphate, including one who went by the name Umm Layth. Her real name is Aqsa Mahmood. She had attended private school and was studying for a radiography degree at Glasgow Caledonian University when she dropped out and disappeared in November 2013. Days later, she called her family and told them she was about to cross from Turkey into Syria. Mahmood's blog and social media accounts claimed to portray her life in Raqqa, showing pictures of herself with other women, food and daily life. She issued advice on travelling to Isis territories and chastised girls for 'using their parents as an excuse' to stay at home. Mahmood suggested that they would live in comfort:

> In these lands we are rewarded for our sacrifices involved in our *hijrah* [migration], for example one is by receiving *ghanimah* [war booty]. And know that honestly there is something so pleasurable to know that what you have has been taken off from the *kuffar* [non-believers] and handed to you personally by Allah as a gift. Some of the many things include kitchen appliances from fridges, cookers, ovens, microwaves, milkshake machines etc, hoovers and cleaning products, fans and most importantly a house with free electricity and water provided to you due to the *khilafah* [caliphate] and no rent included.[21]

So effective were Mahmood's recruitment techniques that she was sanctioned by the United Nations in 2015. The listing says she became a key figure in Isis' all-female al-Khansaa Brigade, which enforced its interpretation of Sharia law. The UN said Mahmood encouraged global terror attacks and was 'responsible for recruiting others, particularly women, to join Isis and uses social media to offer advice on how to travel to Syria'.[22] Pearson says recruitment strategies would vary by the gender and nationality of the target and in Britain, discussions of Islamophobia and particularly assaults on women in traditional Muslim dress got 'a lot of traction'. Young female Isis supporters came to feel that travelling to Syria was a form of rebellion—against the West, wider society and even their families. 'You can't say objectively there's anything liberating about Islamic State but the terrifying thing is that it did feel like a form of liberation to some people,' Pearson adds:

In focus groups we saw older [Muslim] women saying, 'Why do they want to look like this, why do they want to wear these awful binbags', the kind of things you can imagine Boris Johnson saying. The young women were saying, 'We want to wear whatever we want to wear and if this is our expression of religion then who are you to tell us not to do this?'[23]

While the hyper-violence of Isis propaganda videos showing sadistic execution methods grabbed international headlines, much of its output was more mundane. In its quest to present a utopian vision of its caliphate, the group frequently released videos of daily life in its territories, showing apparently bustling markets, boys attending school, children playing and restaurants cooking pizzas. Women were rarely pictured in Isis propaganda but the male fighters featured were almost always smiling, and often handsome. One edition of its English-language propaganda magazine even showed a jihadist in battle fatigues cuddling a kitten.[24] Isis' unprecedented online presence went beyond official propaganda outlets to spawn informal pro-Isis social media groups where male and female supporters came into contact. Pearson says that 'performative purity' was common, with women discouraged from directly messaging men, but that 'what was going on behind the scenes was something a bit less ideologically pure'. One young woman from London told her that she and her friends had got into Isis because they were 'not able to date because of family and cultural reasons', and were looking for Muslim boyfriends online. Pearson recalls: 'She talked about how completely flattered they were, it just seemed incredible that there were these guys doing something really positive for Muslims.' She says that sex and dating were important parts of Isis' recruitment strategy, whether for people to join its caliphate or carry out attacks in their home countries. 'Marriage, children, those relationships were really important, the backbone of the Islamic State project was around families. That was what was going to keep the caliphate going.' Even at the height of its power, Isis knew its members had to produce children, particularly boys, to replace the men killed off in battle and bombings. By 2018, British authorities estimated that of around 900 people who travelled from the UK to Isis' Syrian territories, a fifth had been killed. While depleting Isis' strength in its territories, some of the deaths gave birth to new threats at home.

Shortly before 3pm on 28 November 2017, a young man was walking along a residential street in North Kensington, London. He was carrying a blue holdall with a padlock on it. Naa'imur Zakariyah Rahman believed it contained a pressure cooker bomb of the type used in the Manchester Arena attack, a suicide vest stuffed inside a Puffa jacket and a canister of pepper spray. He was going to use the devices to target Downing Street. First, he would deploy the pressure cooker bomb, which had a ten-second delay timer, to blow up the security gates protecting the prime minister's official residence and kill the armed police officers on guard. He would then run through the smoke of the blast to Number 10, entering in the ensuing chaos or using a hostage to bargain his way through the famous black door. Rahman was going to hunt down the then prime minister, Theresa May, and 'take her head off' using a knife before either getting shot dead by police or blowing himself up using the suicide vest. The 20-year-old had made a pledge of allegiance to Isis with an audio recording sent via Telegram. He was, as he told a contact, 'good to go'. Or so he thought. The holdall did contain a pressure cooker and Puffa jacket, but the explosives inside them were not real. The Isis 'emir' he had been talking to on Telegram was an MI5 agent, the supposed bombmaker who gave him the holdall was an undercover police officer. Rahman was under surveillance, and at the moment he left the spies' car carrying the holdall packed with fake explosives, they had all the evidence they needed to move in. Armed police swooped as he walked down the street and he was arrested. 'I'm glad it's over,' Rahman commented as he was taken into custody. When asked if he had any mental health issues, he replied: 'I was planning to die.'[25]

He had been planning the attack on Downing Street for months, but was hoping to commit some kind of action in support of Isis for much longer. In 2015, his uncle Musa had travelled to the terrorist group's caliphate in Syria with his wife. Rahman was only 17 when he left the UK and they stayed in regular contact. Defence lawyers said the teenager was effectively 'brainwashed' into jihadism by Musa and other relatives, including two uncles who were later convicted for fundraising terrorism by sending their brother £10,000.

Rahman's mother moved with him from the West Midlands to London in an attempt to lessen their influence but he continued to hero-worship Musa and started consuming more Isis propaganda himself. In June 2017, his uncle was killed in a drone strike and in the midst of grief and depression, Rahman intensified his activities. By then he was 19 and had already come to the attention of counter-terror police through his relatives. Back in October 2015, following his uncle's departure for Syria, he had been referred to the Prevent programme and put into its Channel intervention process.

Rahman initially engaged but then withdrew from the scheme and refused further contact, while attempting to make police believe he was not an extremist. But in the months following Musa's death, he came into contact with an FBI agent on Telegram. He asked for help to conduct a terror attack in London and was put in touch with an MI5 role-player posing as an Isis commander in Syria called 'Abu Anis'. Rahman made his intentions clear from the start. On the day he was put in contact with the supposed commander in September 2017, Rahman wrote: 'I want to do a suicide bomb on parliament. I want to attempt to kill Theresa May.' He suggested that an accomplice could use a gas tanker in an explosive lorry attack, adding: 'I will bomb. All I need now is a sleeper cell to lay low for now.' He said the Parsons Green underground bombing days before, where the attacker's device had only partially exploded, was just 'the start' and praised the Manchester Arena attacker. Rahman told the MI5 agent that he had been planning either to migrate to Isis territories or carry out an attack in the UK since his uncle had left for Syria and had trained him and sent bomb-making videos. 'I have no desire for this life,' Rahman wrote. 'My desire for *jannah* [paradise] makes me strong'.

The teenager quickly started discussing potential attack methods and targets, including a suicide bombing on the Houses of Parliament or drone attack on MI5's headquarters, and 'Abu Anis' introduced him to two other supposed Isis contacts that he claimed could help. The first, known as Abu Waleed, was an MI5 agent posing as an Isis security officer, while the second, Shaq, was an undercover police officer said to be able to help Rahman obtain weapons and explosives to carry out his plans. He was put into contact with the agents online and on 28 September 2017 met 'Abu Waleed' in Regent's

Park. Rahman was handed a package containing a mobile phone for securely contacting those he believed to be Isis commanders. He told the man that he was homeless and sleeping in a van parked next to a mosque because he had to move out of his shared flat in Barnet. Rahman did not trust the other worshippers in the mosque and said he hid his true beliefs from them as his attack plans progressed. A doctor he met through the mosque helped him secure work at an internet café in north London and find accommodation, but his focus remained on his attack.

In October, Rahman met 'Abu Waleed' for the second time, at a shopping centre in Shepherd's Bush. Over toast and hot chocolate in a café, Rahman emphasised his desire to carry out a bombing, but was told not to do anything until he had spoken to the supposed emir 'Abu Anis'. A week later, he was introduced to the undercover police officer going by the name Shaq, meeting in a car parked near the Westway Sports Centre in Kensington. When asked what he wanted, Rahman said he was 'desperate' to become a martyr and that the ideas for his attack had originally come from his uncle. He spewed out numerous potential methods, including drones, poison and remote-control car bombs. When asked to pick one, Rahman settled on a suicide bombing targeting Theresa May and on leaving the meeting, messaged 'Abu Anis' on Telegram, stating: 'Everything is finalised.' He had more phone calls and meetings with 'Shaq' in different parts of London, revealing his final plan to use the combination of a bomb, suicide vest, pepper spray and a knife to launch an assault on Downing Street.

At one point, doubts appeared to be creeping in. On 7 November, Rahman demanded assurances that the people he was speaking to were real Isis fighters, and asked to speak to someone who knew his uncle in Syria. 'If you can get a brother who knows my uncle ... I will carry out my *amaliya* [operation] straight away,' he wrote. Days later, he received audio messages on Telegram from a person calling themselves Abu Omar, who had enough personal and biographical information on Musa and his time in the Syrian town of al-Asharah to pass Rahman's test. He told 'Abu Anis' that his mind had been put at rest and he would be ready to carry out the attack within weeks. On a busy afternoon in November 2017, Rahman carried out reconnaissance in Westminster, walking around Trafalgar

Square, the Houses of Parliament, Whitehall and past the entrance to Downing Street. London had already been subject to four terror attacks that year and surveillance officers noticed him look closely at mounted soldiers and police officers. Rahman told 'Shaq' he had 'gone to see things' and hours later sent an audio recording of his pledge of allegiance to Isis. Three days afterwards, he met Shaq outside a PC World in Brixton and handed him a black Puffa jacket and a rucksack bought from Argos to fill with explosives.

On 28 November 2017, 'Shaq' texted Rahman telling him the items were ready and could be collected. In fact, they had been fitted with replica explosive devices and placed in the blue holdall. Rahman met his supposed Isis fixer in his car, parked in a residential London street. He was handed the holdall and given the padlock code. 'Shaq' showed him the time-delay detonation mechanism for the pressure cooker bomb and how to trigger the suicide vest hidden in the jacket. He told Rahman that he would have to source a knife himself but handed him a replica can of pepper spray. When asked if he was ready, he replied: 'Yeah. Do you know? Now I've seen everything it feels good.' He said he had to clear a few debts and 'then after that I'm good to go'. Rahman said that he would carry out the attack by the end of the week, got out of the car and was arrested minutes later.

He denied preparing an act of terrorism, claiming that he intended to throw the devices away in some woods and had no intention to carry out the attack. Defence lawyers argued that Rahman could never have harmed anyone because the devices were fake and he was under heavy surveillance. Ali Bajwa KC told his sentencing hearing that he 'was at all times planning with, preparing with, law enforcement operatives'. He said the security service role-players held 'great authority' in Rahman's eyes and claimed he had 'taken his lead' from them on methods of attack, but a judge found that the operatives did not lead Rahman into the plot and were 'careful to avoid overstepping the mark'.[26] A psychological report found that Rahman was 'highly compliant' and susceptible to exploitation, and was suffering from depression, anxiety and the ongoing grief from his uncle's death. He was said to lack confidence and self-esteem after being abused over several years by his mother's boyfriend, and was homeless and unemployed. A judge accepted that Rahman was vulnerable and 'immature'. He cited the 'baleful influence' of his uncles and said he had a 'difficult and disrupted childhood, was homeless, estranged from his family and living on a meagre income during the material time'. But Mr Justice Haddon-Cave added:

> At no relevant stage did Rahman intend to withdraw from his opera-tion, and that when he stepped out of Shaq's car on 28 November 2017 carrying the blue holdall, containing his rucksack and jacket fitted with explosive devices, he was fully committed and deter-mined to carry out his carefully planned attack on Downing Street imminently, within days ... he was absolutely intent on using these items to carry out an imminent terrorist attack on Downing Street which he hoped would lead to his infamy and martyrdom.[27]

Rahman was jailed for life with a minimum term of 30 years for preparing acts of terrorism and for helping a friend and fellow jihad-ist, Mohammad Aqib Imran, in his attempt to join Isis in Libya. Rahman had recorded a sponsorship video intended to be used after his own 'martyrdom' to gain the group's trust.

The case illustrated the fine line the security services must tread in their quest to discover a potential terrorist's intentions and capa-bility, and then prove them in court. Careful plotters like Rahman, working alone, cannot be relied upon to tell people of their plans or announce them on the internet like some of the foiled plotters earlier in this book. Agents sent in undercover must gain a target's trust and appear to share their ideology. To maintain their persona, they must not raise any alarm with potential terrorists, and it becomes difficult to obtain the necessary evidence without being seen to directly or indirectly encourage plots.

Police and MI5 know that allegations of entrapment will be used as a defence in such cases, and so they must work carefully to ensure resulting trials do not collapse.

PART THREE

DANGER AHEAD

NARROW ESCAPES AND FUTURE THREATS

Some would-be terrorists have come dangerously close to achieving their murderous aims. Several attacks have been stopped with only hours or even minutes to spare, while others were not intentionally thwarted by the security services at all, but by the attackers' own blunders. In some cases, the day was saved by the swift reaction of ordinary police officers on the ground, or the actions of members of the public who raised the alarm just in time. Mere chance can make the difference between a foiled plot of which the public is barely aware, and a deadly massacre with horrific effects on victims, survivors and their families. Such narrow escapes may reveal gaps in the knowledge of counter-terror police and MI5, who in several cases had no idea the would-be terrorists were a threat. The distinction between these incidents and attacks that have slipped through the net since 2017 is vanishingly thin, and each one holds vital lessons for the future.

There is a line, albeit a fine one, between attacks that are stopped at the last minute and attacks that are launched, but go wrong. Of the 15 incidents classified as terrorism by police since 2017, under half resulted in victims being killed. The remaining eight saw people injured, but the attackers either were shot, were arrested, ran away or took their own life before they could do further damage. The first near miss of its kind was the 2017 Parsons Green bombing. Ahmed Hassan, an Iraqi asylum seeker, told immigration officials he had been forced to train as a child soldier at an Isis camp in his home country. During an interview over a year before that attack, Hassan told officials he had been 'trained to kill' by the terrorist group and indoctrinated in 'what Allah believed was right'. This was in January 2016, but he was not investigated by MI5 and was instead referred to the Prevent programme, which he deceived. After falsely claiming to be 16 on his arrival in the UK, Hassan was enrolled at Brooklands College in Surrey, where his academic success was viewed as a 'protective factor' by counter-terror police as they decided that ideological mentoring was not necessary. But the teenager was leading a double life, and used a voucher awarded for being named 'student of the year' to buy materials for an improvised explosive device from Amazon.[1]

Hassan was able to build a huge bomb, containing 300g of powerful explosive and 2.2kg of metal shrapnel including nails, screws, bolts, knives and screwdrivers. The sophisticated device had a delay timer, which Hassan deployed when he left it in a packed London Underground carriage in the morning rush hour on 15 September 2017. Hassan calmly left the District Line train at Putney Bridge station in west London, knowing that the device would blow minutes later while he made his escape. The bomb detonated as the train pulled into Parsons Green station—but not properly. The initiation functioned as planned, causing a fireball that injured several passengers as glass flew through the air, but the main charge and surrounding shrapnel did not detonate.[2]

Experts who examined the bomb for Hassan's trial found that it was a 'matter of luck' that it did not detonate as intended, and that the initiator may have been dislodged as he carried the device to his target in a Lidl supermarket bag.[3] But dozens of people suffered burns and 28 other victims were injured during a panicked stampede to flee Parsons Green station. If Hassan's bomb had worked correctly, it could have killed everyone in the packed train carriage.[4] He fled but was caught the following day at the port of Dover, while waiting to board a ferry to France. A parliamentary report later found 'fundamental failings' in the handling of Hassan's case by the Home Office, counter-terror police and local council. It said a 'litany of errors resulted in Hassan's attack planning passing unnoticed' and demanded a review of the Prevent programme as a result of the bombing.[5] An official review has still not been published over five years after the attack.

There have been at least six more terror attacks where the perpetrators failed to achieve their murderous ambitions. On 14 August

2018, a man ploughed a car into a group of cyclists outside parliament and sped towards police officers guarding the building. But they were able to dive out of the way and Salih Khater crashed into a metal security barrier.[6] Months later, on New Year's Eve, a mentally ill man launched a knife attack at Manchester Victoria railway station, while shouting 'this is for Allah' and 'long live the caliphate'. The couple and police officer he stabbed survived and Mahdi Mohamud was quickly wrestled to the ground and detained.[7] The day after the New Zealand mosque shootings, which left 51 Muslim worshippers dead on 15 March 2019, a white supremacist went on a violent rampage in the Surrey town of Stanwell, hunting for Muslims to kill. Vincent Fuller, who had watched Brenton Tarrant's livestream of the Christchurch massacre, attacked cars with non-white drivers with a baseball bat and prowled the streets armed with a knife looking for targets. He stabbed a teenager of Bulgarian heritage in a Tesco car park, apparently in the mistaken belief that he was Muslim, but his victim survived. Fuller was arrested a short distance away, while calling police 'dirty race traitors' and saying that he hoped 'Isis comes over and rapes your children'.[8]

Then on 9 January 2020, an Isis-inspired terror attack struck in the least expected of places—inside a high-security prison. Jailed attack plotter Brusthom Ziamani and radicalised violent criminal Baz Hockton tried to murder a prison guard at HMP Whitemoor in Cambridgeshire.[9] They were wearing fake suicide vests and armed with homemade shanks, but the improvised weapons did not kill their victim and they were overpowered by his colleagues. Ziamani and Hockton struck weeks after their former prison associate, Usman Khan, murdered two people at a rehabilitation event at Fishmongers' Hall in London. A judge found the timing was 'no accident'. Less than a month later, another freed terror offender launched a stabbing spree on Streatham High Street in south London. Sudesh Amman was under surveillance and being followed by armed police officers, who shot him dead shortly after he stabbed two victims. They survived their injuries.

Yet another near miss came on 14 November 2021—Remembrance Sunday—when an asylum seeker from Jordan detonated a bomb outside the Liverpool Women's Hospital. Emad al-Swealmeen killed only himself in the blast, which went off inside a taxi as he was dropped off at the building's main entrance. The driver was injured but managed to get out of the car as it went up in flames. No further terror attacks struck Britain until almost a year later, on a quiet Sunday morning in the coastal town of Dover. On 30 October 2022, Andrew Leak, a far-right extremist with mental health issues and a history of criminal offences, threw homemade firebombs at a processing centre for asylum seekers arriving from across the English Channel—but he failed to cause any serious injuries. The 66-year-old drove away from his burning target, and killed himself at a nearby petrol station minutes later.

Although those attacks did not result in the deaths of victims, numerous people were injured, some seriously. Many survivors and witnesses suffer from trauma and long-term psychological harm. Terror, in the most literal sense, was inflicted. In the following chapter, attempted attacks were stopped short of that threshold, but only just.

6

NEAR MISSES

On 27 April 2017, a man got off the London Underground at Victoria station. He was wearing a black jacket and black trousers, and a brown rucksack displaying a British flag and the word 'London' emblazoned in white writing. To the casual observer, Khalid Ali looked like a tourist and he started walking, as many tourists do, towards Westminster. He reached the area around the Houses of Parliament shortly after 2pm but did not stop to take pictures, instead heading towards the River Thames. He went for a stroll along the scenic Victoria Embankment and sat on a bench looking at the view. After a few minutes' rest, he walked over to the river wall and seemed to lean over it. Eagle-eyed observers would have seen Ali drop a Samsung Galaxy phone into the murky water. But he didn't seem concerned about the loss, and walked back towards the Houses of Parliament. Ali threw his Oyster travel card in a bin outside Westminster underground station as he passed the entrance and made his way towards Parliament Square. MI5 and counter-terror police, who had him under surveillance, had seen enough and gave the order for armed officers to intercept. Ali was not a tourist, he was a Taliban bombmaker who had returned to the UK after five years in Afghanistan. He had three knives concealed in his clothing and he was about to use them.[10]

Officers spotted Ali in a throng of tourists about to cross a junction on the corner of Parliament Square and moved in. As he waited with the crowd for the pedestrian crossing to go green, two police cars sped in to block the road in both directions, as officers armed with semi-automatic rifles ran towards Ali. Members of the public started running away as officers shouted at the terrorist to get on the floor. He sank to his knees with his hands in the air and was quickly pinned to the ground, face down. Ali was detained five weeks after the Westminster attack, just metres away from where Khalid Masood had crashed his car and murdered PC Keith Palmer, before being shot dead by a minister's armed bodyguard. The officers hand-cuffed Ali behind his back and started searching his backpack. 'Ok mate, you're under arrest on suspicion of being a terrorist, alright?' one of the officers asked. Ali appeared unsurprised by the allegation and did not reply when he was officially cautioned. 'Do you have anything on you that may hurt us or hurt anyone else by virtue of us searching you mate?' he was asked after a search of the rucksack revealed no weapons. 'You'll see,' Ali replied.

As the body search continued, police found two black-handled kitchen knives in his left and right jacket pockets, and a larger knife tucked in the waistband of his tracksuit bottoms. It was a risky hid-ing place—police later noticed a cut in the front of his boxer shorts. Officers conducted an urgent safety interview at the scene to check for any other risks. When asked if any members of the public were in danger, Ali said he was 'not interested' in the general public. Asked if anyone else was in danger, he told police: 'You lot are carrying weapons, so you must know you are in danger.' He claimed that anyone who had stepped into a war with the *mujahideen* was in danger. Ali refused to give his name when he was taken to a police station and declined a lawyer. In a fresh interview shortly after 4pm, he claimed that it was not him but 'the West' who was a danger to the public, because it had entered Afghanistan, Iraq and Syria and 'handed Palestine to the Israelis'. The 27-year-old later told police: 'I would consider myself as a *mujahid* [holy warrior]. Jihad is what we do.' Ali declared his loyalty to the Taliban and told how he made bombs in Afghanistan, claiming that he had 'pressed the button' more than 300 times in attacks targeting American and British sol-diers spanning five years. His words may have sounded like a self-aggrandising fantasy, but they were true.

Ali's journey towards terrorism had started in 2010. He had been born in Saudi Arabia to a Somali family but moved to Britain as a young child and had never been religiously observant. He lived with his parents, four brothers and two sisters in Edmonton and trained as a plumber after leaving school. He started working with one of his brothers, but around the age of 19 his family noticed him suddenly become more religious, growing his beard and wearing traditional Islamic clothes. He started attending the mosque four or five times a week and hanging out with a new group of friends. Abruptly, he announced that he was leaving the UK to join a ship taking aid to the Gaza Strip, a Palestinian enclave that was suffering food shortages following Israeli bombardment and a naval blockade.

Just weeks later, on 12 November 2010, Ali turned up on the news—he was on a ship taken to Greece by its crew after the captain refused to sail to Gaza.[11] Then 20, he returned home to London, but left again the following year. Ali deceived his family, claiming he was travelling to Birmingham for work, before contacting them three weeks later to say he was not coming home. They reported him missing in July 2011, but after discovering Ali had flown to Abu Dhabi, police could find no further trace of him. He disappeared for five years, having no contact with his relatives until he resurfaced at the British consulate in Istanbul, Turkey.

He presented himself at the building on 31 October 2016, claiming he had lost his passport days before at a tourist landmark and needed a temporary travel document in order to return to the UK. A consulate employee thought Ali's behaviour was unusual. For one thing, he did not seem concerned that he had lost his passport. He reported him to the British government's Risk and Liaison Overseas Network and Ali was put on a register of suspicious travellers bound for Britain. Suspecting that British authorities may want to keep an eye on his movements, Ali attempted to deceive them. He presented the consulate with a booking for a flight that would arrive at Heathrow Airport at 3.30pm on 2 November, but boarded a different flight that landed three-and-a-half hours later. The ruse did not work and Ali was stopped under Schedule 7 of the Terrorism Act 2000. Officers noted that he was travelling alone and had no hand or hold luggage with him, only the clothes he was wearing.

When questioned about his travels, he told police that he had left England because he was under pressure to marry, and had travelled to Pakistan to get away. He claimed to have spent his time travelling across the region, enjoying the natural beauty of the surroundings and being put up by friendly local people. Certain Islamic sects tried radicalising him, Ali told police, but he refused to be drawn in. He had decided to return home, travelling to Turkey via Iran and losing his luggage and passport on the way. Police released Ali after four hours, but not before taking samples of his DNA and fingerprints. They would prove that the tale Ali spun of his travels was a ludicrous fabrication.

Four years earlier, on 28 January 2012, a chest-sized box had been brought into the compound used by the US Army's 720th Explosive Ordnance Disposal (EOD) Company at Spin Boldak in south Kandahar province in Afghanistan. It contained detonators, receivers and triggers for bombs that had been seized by the Afghan security forces. An examination saw fingerprints on the components taken and documented. Five months later, on 6 July 2012, another cache was handed in, this time to the 630th EOD Company, based in central Kandahar province. It contained pressure plates, landmines, firing pins, detonators and triggers. Again, the items were sent for analysis and fingerprints were taken at the time, but several sets did not match any known terrorists on international databases. Fast forward four years, and the British security services—who had their suspicions about Ali—shared the fingerprints with the FBI. They were a match to 42 prints found on the 2012 caches of bomb components. Ali had handled adhesive tape binding bundles of detonators, triggers and a circuit board chip. There was only one conclusion—he had been making remotely detonated IEDs for the Taliban in Afghanistan. His own handwriting was even visible on bomb components shown in evidence photos.

The damning analysis was not completed until several weeks after Ali had arrived in the UK, meaning police at Heathrow Airport had to let him go. He moved back in with his family, who questioned why he had disappeared for so long without a word to distraught relatives. He told them that he had been in Pakistan but claimed he could give no further details because he did not want to get them into trouble. Ali was questioned again by police on 23 November 2016, in a follow-up to the original missing person report. He repeated his claims of travel around Pakistan, but added an allegation that MI5 had attempted to recruit him as a 'James Bond'-type spy in 2010 and that he had refused. Ali claimed he was against any form of extremism, that he had no imminent plans to travel and that he was going to return to work as a plumber. One of Ali's brothers helped him to enrol on a course to renew his licence and gave him thousands of pounds and clothes. But there were arguments at home and Ali started to intermittently disappear. An old school friend offered him part-time work at a pizza shop in Ealing, and Ali took the offer while he worked on his grand plan.

His reconnaissance mission started on 18 March 2017, when Ali attempted to use an anti-racism march as cover to survey parts of Westminster, including Whitehall and Downing Street. As the protest passed the British prime minister's official residence, Ali was approached by a police officer for loitering. Asked if he was OK, Ali asked to confirm if the building behind the security gates was Downing Street and appeared to be smirking. That officer thought he might have a mental health issue. He was not moving with the protest, instead walking alone and frequently loitering, while approaching police officers and questioning them apparently at random. Four weeks later, Ali carried out another reconnaissance trip to central London. He walked past the MI6 headquarters, along the River Thames, across Westminster Bridge and past the Houses of Parliament before sitting in Parliament Square. He had traced part of the route Khalid Masood drove in his car during his deadly terror attack weeks before. Ali walked on up Whitehall, past the Cenotaph war memorial and Ministry of Defence building, which he observed for several minutes, and then on to the Metropolitan Police headquarters at New Scotland Yard. On his phone, Ali collected photos of police officers, their weapons and stab-proof vests, and vehicles.

On 25 April 2017, Ali armed himself by purchasing a set of knives and a sharpener at a discount shop called the Mighty Pound in Ealing. The following day, he went to a computer shop near his family home 15 miles away, where he asked a member of staff whether 'they' could trace the serial number on a new mobile phone if he swapped his SIM card. Ali paid for the new phone in cash. It was never recovered. By that point, MI5 and counter-terror police had stepped up their monitoring of Ali and surveillance officers were hot on his heels. After observing him putting a white plastic bag in a wheelie bin down the road from his home that night, they fished it out to find packaging for five kitchen knives and a sharpener. Ali had formulated his plan, selected his target and armed himself. But despite his battlefield experience, he had not accounted for one thing—his mother.

Fadumo Haji Adam was upset that her son had been ignoring her and had spent much of the day holed up in his bedroom using her iPad. When she asked for it back, as he headed out of the front door to dump the knife packaging, he merely raised his hand in a 'keep quiet' gesture. So Mrs Adam went up to his bedroom to look for the tablet. She saw four knives on the floor and a sharpener next to them. When Ali returned from his trip to the neighbours' wheelie bin, she confronted him but he would not answer her questions. He went up to his bedroom again and discovered the knives had disappeared, then started to shout and throw belongings around in a fit of rage. Shortly after midnight on 27 April 2017, his mother called the police. They arrived quickly and Mrs Adam, who was upset and speaking in broken English, explained that she had found knives in her son's bedroom. She feared he was going to murder the family and showed the weapons to the police. Ali came downstairs and showed he was unarmed, presenting a calm front to the local bobbies—who had no idea about the ongoing surveillance operation and the true threat that he posed—and claimed he had no idea why his mother had called the police. He stated that he had recently moved back home and merely kept all his belongings in his room. He repeated he was unsure why his mother had called the police. Mrs Adam said she heard her son putting something into a wheelie bin, but when asked what that could be, Ali replied: 'I don't know, you tell me.' Police questioned Ali on the whereabouts of his mother's iPad and he appeared 'cocky'. They asked Mrs Adam if she wanted her son to be arrested but she said she didn't, she just wanted him to leave. Before Ali left, he asked the police present about the Tasers they were armed with and how strong they were. By the time officers left, he was gone.

His mother had effectively disarmed him, forcing him to leave his knives in the family home while the police were present. He stayed up all night, journeying the 16 miles from his family home in Edmonton back to Ealing. Ali killed time in a Costa café until high street shops opened, and then set about rearming himself. Shortly after 9am, he went into a branch of the discount homeware shop Wilko and closely examined the knives on sale for seven minutes. He appeared to be attempting counter-surveillance techniques—walking into a Burger King and sitting down, but not ordering anything and then quickly moving on. Ali went to a shop called Rug Town, which had no CCTV cameras. He immediately asked for rucksacks and was directed to the brown bag with the Union Flag emblazoned on it. He paid £10 and returned to Wilko, swiftly selecting a range of knives—a Sabatier 8-inch chef's knife for £10 and two 3.5-inch paring knives at £5 each. To avoid suspicion, he threw in some cocktail sticks, a potato masher, a meat thermometer and a car cleaning cloth. Now homeless, Ali bought a £1.22 bottle of shower gel from a nearby Co-op and showered at a local gym. He stashed the Wilko bag and unnecessary kitchen tools in a locker and took the knives out of their packaging. Such was Ali's enthusiasm to free the weapons that he cut himself as he ripped the plastic open, leaving incriminating bloodstains. Now fully prepared, he headed back out of the gym wearing the rucksack and caught the train towards his target.

Despite admitting to being a Taliban bombmaker and wanting to send the British government a 'message' in his police interviews, Ali, then 28, denied all offences at his trial. He told the jury he had merely travelled to Pakistan for 'tourism and hitchhiking' but was taken captive by the Taliban and forced to make bombs at gunpoint to prove he was not a British spy. He claimed he was only carrying knives in Westminster for protection in case he was attacked while trying to deliver his 'message'. He did not react while being convicted of making explosives with intent to endanger life in Afghanistan and preparing an act of terrorism in the UK. A judge found that Ali had been viewing jihadist material before leaving home in 2011 and had deliberately journeyed to volunteer for the cause. Judge Nicholas Hilliard QC said that by the time Ali returned to the UK in 2016, he was an 'active and committed terrorist' bent on an 'act of extreme violence' to convey his supposed message. He found that there was a 'very considerable risk' of the thwarted plotter attempting further attacks in the future, and said he could not say when the risk he posed would decrease, if ever. Judge Hilliard handed Ali three life sentences—with concurrent minimum terms of 40 years for the explosives offences and 25 for the attempted terror attack. He added:

> You were obviously being followed on the 27th of April and it will be of great reassurance to the public that that was the case. The

timing of the intervention by armed officers was, in fact, before anybody was attacked by you and at a stage which had enabled the greatest amount of evidence to be gathered. That can never be an easy balance to strike, but in this case, events show that it was struck at the right stage.[12]

National Socialists Union Standing Against the New World Order

'I'm going to war tonight,' wrote 19-year-old Ethan Stables. 'There is a "pride night" with free entry. I'm going to walk in with a fucking machete and slaughter every single one of the gay bastards.'[13] It was an otherwise normal Friday afternoon in the northern port town of Barrow-in-Furness, but 23 June 2017 would see scenes unfold the likes of which it had never seen. As Stables was typing the message, in a Facebook group he created called 'National Socialists Union standing against the New World Order', he was walking towards the New Empire pub. Its landlords had planned a night to mark LGBT+ pride, which is globally celebrated in June each year. They had advertised the event on social media, hired a DJ and hung up a rainbow union flag.

Stables, a committed neo-Nazi, noticed. He lived just a 15-minute walk away and frequently passed the pub on his journey to the nearby Jobcentre—although he preferred to sit outside using its free Wi-Fi rather than seek employment. At 4.23pm, Stables wrote in his Facebook chat group: 'For fucks sake man, there's a pub across the road with an LGBT flag hanging in the window … I might make a pipe bomb when I go home.' Someone replied urging him to 'get in there and burn it down'. 'I shall,' Stables replied. 'This is a fucking disgrace, the pub has a Union Jack defaced with the gay pride colours [angry face emoji]. That's our national fucking flag.' As the minutes passed, the teenager got angrier and angrier. He walked up to the pub and took photographs of the offending flag, reading a poster about that night's planned event. At 5.01pm, he posted that he was 'going to war'.

But not everyone in the Facebook group was a like-minded neo-Nazi. Stables, who was later described in court as 'lonely and inadequate', had added several young local women to his chat. One happened to be looking at her phone when he made his bloodthirsty vow to 'slaughter every single one of the gay bastards'. 'That's not right Ethan,' she wrote. Stables was not dissuaded, replying:

> I've had enough. I don't want to live in a gay world and I sure as hell don't want my children living in one. What happened to our traditional qualities? They're fucking ruined. I don't care if I die, I'm fighting for what I believe in and that is the future of my country, my folk, and my race.

Other members of the Facebook group started piling in and trying to calm Stables down, telling him his actions would make matters worse and lend the 'Jew media' more firepower. He merely became more incensed, telling them: 'I don't care, I'll kill every feminist, every gay, every Jew, and every nigger I meet.' Stables worked himself up into a frenzy, saying it was time to take 'violent measures', that he was 'not going to sit by idly whilst my homeland is defiled by these sick fucking deviants'. By 5.20pm he appeared resolved, writing: 'I'm going to make the fucking news. I want them to know they're being targeted. Tonight is going to be a good night, and the beginning of the end. Hail victory, *Sieg heil*.'

It was far from the first time Stables had voiced his hatred for gay people. A week earlier, he had filmed himself burning a pride flag to ashes while muttering, 'That's what I think of your gay pride. Look at that rainbow, so much nicer when it's on fire. It's just like gay people, much nicer when they're on fire.' The young woman who had tried and failed to calm him down had already reported several of his vile posts to Facebook in an effort to get them taken down. After reading his messages about attacking the New Empire, she contacted the police. Having made the call at 5.25pm, she decided to put out a desperate warning on Twitter. 'If you're in Barrow-in-Furness, please do not attend the LGBT gay pride night at a pub,' she wrote. 'I've reported it to the police but still DON'T GO.' To enforce the seriousness of her message, she attached screengrabs of Stables' Facebook posts, his photograph of his target and selfies showing him posing in front of a huge Nazi flag and holding a machete. Cumbria Police took her warnings seriously and deployed armed officers to the town. Their first task was protecting the New Empire, where astounded bar staff were told they were at risk and watched the building surrounded by gun-wielding police. Stables was still at large, having returned to his nearby flat.

He had not been known as a threat to the security services, despite having made his violent neo-Nazi sentiments well known online over several months. His mother believed he had become radicalised while visiting a girlfriend in Germany, and told his trial how she struggled to cope with his behaviour and sought support for her son's autism with local mental health services. Stables, now 19, was expelled from his school after bouts of violence including one that saw him put another pupil in a headlock. When he was 17, his mother threw him out of her home after he threatened to behead her and burn the house down.[14] Alone and unemployed, he deepened his radicalisation on the internet. The teenager had attempted to join the British Army, but told police he was turned down because of his mental health issues, which included suicidal thoughts, depression and anxiety. Stables was deeply unhappy with his situation, blaming it on 'faggots, niggers, spastics' and the UK's equality laws, writing in a WhatsApp message a month before his arrest: 'My country is being raped ... I might just become a skinhead and kill people.'[15] After listening to neo-Nazi death metal songs sent by a Facebook contact, Stables said he was considering becoming a 'machete-wielding maniac' and was just 'waiting for an excuse to flip'. The tracks' lyrics described the Second World War as a 'fratricidal' conflict, suggesting it had been instigated by Jews, adding: 'The enemy is more powerful than ever, he controls world affairs ... where do you want to stand when the world goes up in flames again?'[16]

Stables' internet searches showed a deep interest in mass killing, committing terror attacks and either being shot dead by the police or jailed. In October 2016, he typed into Google: 'I want to go on a killing spree'. A month later, he wrote 'I'm close to going on a killing spree', then the day after 'I'm going on a killing spree' and 'I'm going to murder someone'. While looking up white supremacist terror attacks, the Columbine High School shooting and famous mass murderers, Stables sought information on whether armed police were stationed nearby and 'how to kill police officers'. In December 2016, he simply Googled: 'How to be a terrorist'. At points, Stables turned to Isis for inspiration, watching numerous propaganda videos showing the group's beheadings and executions alongside a series of graphic snuff and torture videos from around the world.[17]

But the teenager mainly gorged on neo-Nazi material, repeatedly searching for the National Action terrorist organisation and saving images of its flag and propaganda on his phone. Stables also looked up the KKK, violent British fascist group Combat 18 and asked Google 'how to be a white supremacist'. He even Googled a 'fascist haircut' (shaved sides, very long on top) for carefully constructed selfies that he posted on Facebook, showing him wearing a checked shirt, waistcoat and blazer. Stables researched Adolf Hitler, his religious beliefs, Aryanism and the Third Reich, as well as more modern far-right concepts. Stables looked up and shared the white supremacist slogan known as the '14 words', written three decades ago by American ideologue David Lane. It reads: 'We must secure the existence of our race and a future for white children'. The phrase has become so well known on the far right that it has been incorporated into hate symbols including the widespread 1488—14 for the slogan and then 88 for the eighth letter of the alphabet, meaning 'heil Hitler'. Stables threw himself into racist social media platforms and online forums, although his search history suggests he struggled for inspiration for posts. In 2016, he conducted a stream of searches for 'racist Muslim jokes', 'nigger jokes', 'Jew jokes' and 'Paki bashing'. Following his arrest he was claimed as 'one of us' by the British version of 4chan's notorious 'politically incorrect' board.[18] But one user was unimpressed, writing: 'When you plan a high profile killing spree you don't tell any cunt.'

A machete attack may not have been Stables' only plan. Since September 2016, he had conducted extensive online research into buying, importing, smuggling, stealing or manufacturing guns and ammunition. It was during that period where the teenager suddenly looked into joining the British Army, and how long basic training would take. Stables downloaded the 'Expedient Homemade Firearms' guides by British activist Philip A. Luty, but by the time of his arrest he had only been able to obtain an air rifle and BB gun. The teenager was also interested in explosives, and searched the internet for instructions on making a wide array of different types while Googling 'how to make an IED' and 'how to make a pipe bomb'. Hours before his arrest, Stables posted on Facebook:

I know how to create homemade explosives such as Astrolite A-1-5, Napalm, and Thermite. I can make machine pistols b getting hold of ammunition is the hard part. I'd start a resistance movement if there were anyone around here who had taken the redpill. It seems they're far more content to sit around and get butchered by Islam.[19]

When police raided his flat, they found a large number of snapped-off match heads and a carbon dioxide canister, which corresponded with bomb-making instructions Stables had acquired. But the deadliest items in his home were an array of bladed weapons, including a British Army issue machete bought from a surplus store in the Lake District days earlier. Footage taken by a police officer searching the property showed a floor-to-ceiling Nazi flag hung on a wall by Stables' bed and a dresser strewn with weapons including the axe and knives, alongside tools. His air rifle was leaning against a bookcase and the machete was discovered under a coffee table, concealed by piles of mess including clothes, CDs and a bottle of mead. Officers waited for him to leave the de-facto armoury to swoop, pouncing on Stables as he walked back towards the New Empire shortly after 10pm. He was wearing a swastika armband and carrying a rucksack, but had no weapons—prosecutors alleged he was carrying out a final reconnaissance mission.

Stables renounced his apparent beliefs at his trial, where he was convicted of preparing an act of terrorism, making threats to kill, possessing an explosive substance under suspicious circumstances and possessing information useful to a terrorist. After the jury had been shown days of evidence of his virulent hatred of gay people, he claimed he was actually a closeted bisexual and had had male sexual partners in the past. Stables pronounced that he was, in fact, politically liberal, was embarrassed by his posts and had only written them to fit in with online contacts. The account he gave on the witness stand contradicted interviews with police immediately after his arrest, where he denied that he would have harmed anyone but admitted adhering to 'Nazi principles'. Stables described them as: 'Traditional family values, sticking to my own race, preserving culture and traditional architecture kind of thing—against modernism.' He denied the Holocaust and praised Hitler as a 'charismatic' leader, who 'cared about children, about women, and he only did what was the very best'. When asked to explain his objection to gay people, Stables replied: 'It's just part of my beliefs.'

Defending Stables, a barrister said he was not a white supremacist but a 'white fantasist', describing him as 'lonely and inadequate'. He told the jury Stables would sit at night on a wall outside the Jobcentre for six hours at a time as he had no Wi-Fi at his home: 'How can that be regarded as normal?' A judge said Stables' wildly varying accounts to police, doctors and the court increased the risk he posed, but that his responsibility was partially diminished by his autistic spectrum disorder. 'The nature and degree of that make it appropriate for you to be detained in a hospital for medical treatment,' Judge Peter Collier KC told him. 'There will always be a risk when you are released'. Stables was sentenced to an indefinite hospital order, and will have to fulfil terrorist notification requirements for ten years after his release.[20]

In a Facebook post minutes after Stables was arrested, the pub's landlady called Stables an 'idiot', adding: 'I will not let the bastards beat us.'[21] The New Empire was decorated with more pride flags, and held an even bigger all-day and all-night event the following month. But if it was not for the warning issued by Stables' female Facebook contact, his plan would not have been discovered in time.

'Cardiff, are you ready for our terror'

Shortly after 4pm on 30 June 2017, armed police burst into a farmhouse in the remote Welsh valleys. It had been identified as the home of a terrorist who was planning to attack a Justin Bieber concert to be held in Cardiff that evening. His intentions had been made clear in a series of posts on an Instagram page in the name of 'Alqaeds'. 'Cardiff, are you ready for our terror', read a message from two days earlier. 'May Allah bring terrorism to Cardiff on 30th June 2017'. In another post, the words 'Cardiff are you prepared?' were overlaid on a photo of the Welsh capital's castle, along with an image of a Jeep, knife, bomb and a fluttering Isis flag. The same account had already shared a page giving instructions on launching deadly vehicle attacks from Isis' English-language propaganda magazine, along with photos of suicide vests and jihadist militants.[22] Counter-terror police and MI5 were alerted to the threats on 29 June 2017 and identified the anonymous Instagram user in just a day, but when they revealed the person behind the account it was not who they might have expected.

The poster was a teenage boy whose sole knowledge of Isis and jihad had come from internet research in his bedroom. Pale and freckly with a mop of brown hair that fell into his blue eyes, Lloyd Gunton was 17 but looked younger. He lived with his Christian parents on their country farm and had never even converted to Islam, but was about to commit a knife attack in revenge for British air strikes in Syria and Iraq.

When police searched the A-level student's bedroom, they found his school rucksack contained a knife, hammer and a martyrdom letter proclaiming his intentions. 'I am a soldier of the Islamic State and I have attacked Cardiff today because your Government keep on bombing targets in Syria and Iraq,' said the handwritten note. 'There will be more attacks in the future.' Gunton had listed bullet points including 'run down the non-believers with a car' and 'strike the infidels, who oppose Allah, in the neck' and ended with the words: 'In the name of Allah, may terrorism greet your country. May there be more bomb and vehicle attacks with Allah's permission.' The letter had been written a week earlier, around the same date that Gunton recorded himself making a pledge of loyalty to Isis in anticipation of the attack. He mimicked photos published in the Isis propaganda he had consumed, holding his knife and hammer while standing in front of a computer screen displaying the terrorist group's flag. Gunton took a photo of himself with his index finger pointed upwards, in a gesture that signifies the oneness of Allah in Islam but had been widely used by Isis militants.

When police entered his home, police found the teenager watching a documentary on British Islamist extremists, which featured clips of people praising terrorists, on YouTube. Officers asked Gunton if he had an Instagram account and he confirmed that he did and gave them the password—'truck attack'. Gunton's phone and computer showed that he had searched for information on a Justin Bieber concert taking place at Cardiff's Principality Stadium that evening, and had looked up details of its security measures. He was arrested little over a month after Salman Abedi murdered 22 victims as they left an Ariana Grande concert at Manchester Arena. A judge found that Gunton was 'within hours of committing an act of atrocity on the streets of Cardiff' when he was detained.[23]

Gunton had also researched high-profile and crowded parts of Cardiff including its Castle Quarter, New Theatre, Capitol shopping centre and Central Library. He had written his martyrdom letter in the expectation that he would die during the attack, so there could be no doubt that his actions were part of Isis' campaign of terror. He appeared to be following Isis' graphically detailed instructions to the letter. The magazines he possessed advised readers to choose a sharp and strong knife and also 'carry a baton or some other kind of concealable blunt object' to strike victims with. An article added: 'Lest the operation be mistaken for one of the many random acts of violence that plague the West, it is essential to leave some kind of evidence or insignia identifying the motive and allegiance to the Khalifah [caliphate]'.[24]

His plot demonstrated the potential speed of the new wave of terror plotters in Britain since the emergence of Isis. The evidence presented at his trial suggested that Gunton had radicalised himself in little over a year. At first, he appeared to be looking up high-profile figures and events, such as the Isis executioner Jihadi John, the murder of Lee Rigby and the 7/7 bombings, without any particular purpose. But in June 2016, when Gunton was 16 years old, his searches took a darker turn. 'Could I kill myself by suffocation,' he asked Google in a wave of queries that evolved from an interest in suicide to an interest in martyrdom in a terror attack. Later that month, Gunton started searching for Isis beheading videos and terror attacks claimed by the group, then in July 2017 he simply Googled 'join Isis' and later: 'Convert to Islam'. Gunton started looking up information on lone terror attacks carried out by non-Muslims, and then how fast armed police responded to incidents in the UK. In autumn 2016, his searches started to focus on attack methods—'Isis lorry attack', 'driving a lorry into a crowd of people', 'Isis wants lorry attacks', 'Isis how to attack non-believers', 'terrorist knife'.

The pattern continued until June 2017, when Gunton's activity accelerated following the attacks claimed by Isis in Westminster, Manchester and London Bridge. The teenager looked up information on how to pledge allegiance to Isis and tried to find out what 'getting shot feels like'. By 10 June, Gunton was seeking advice on 'how to stab someone and kill them'. He then downloaded the instructions in two editions of Isis' English-language propaganda magazines, while continuing to search for Isis propaganda videos.

On 12 June, he set up his 'Alqaeds' Instagram account and started putting violent images together for the posts that would soon alert the security services to his plans. Gunton, then aged 17, searched for '17 year old jihad' and watched footage of the Nice lorry attack, which left 86 victims dead in July 2016. As he started narrowing in on potential targets in Cardiff, he used Google Maps to scope out its Castle area and other landmarks, as well as where 'metal poles' had been erected to protect the city's pedestrian zones.

By 18 June, Gunton was trying to teach himself how to drive with online manuals and looking up how to steal a car and 'what happens if a car hits a traffic bollard'. The following day, the teenager was searching for information on children killed in British air strikes in Syria—echoing claims made by Isis in its repeated calls for revenge attacks on Westerners in their home countries. By 23 June, Gunton had gathered his weapons and was posing with them in a series of selfies and the video recording his pledge of allegiance. He tried to translate the phrase 'I will kill the non-believers' into Arabic and searched for photos of victims killed in knife attacks. Gunton did not have a copy of the Quran, so tried to use Google to find passages of the holy book on martyrdom instead. On 28 June, he appeared to settle on a concert by Canadian pop star Justin Bieber to be held at Cardiff's 74,000-capacity Principality Stadium as a target. Gunton downloaded a promotional poster for the event and hunted for information on security measures.

The knife stashed in his rucksack was 'particularly sharp' and designed for cutting meat, while the heavy, clawed hammer was a potentially deadly weapon in itself. Gunton had been carrying the items around all day at school, and on his walk home that afternoon he had searched unsuccessfully for a car to steal. Gunton admitted to police that he had made the searches and Instagram posts, and put the knife and hammer in his bag, but denied intending to hurt anyone. The teenager claimed he had been conversing on Instagram with someone going by the name 'al-Baghdadi', like the leader of Isis, in the week leading up to his arrest. He claimed the man had told him he would go to hell because he did not believe in Islam and instructed him to Google Isis and its Rumiyah propaganda magazine. Gunton said the man claimed that he needed to commit an act of terrorism if he wanted to go to paradise. At a different point, the

teenager claimed he had only made Instagram posts glorifying Isis
and terror attacks to somehow provoke a negative reaction to the
terrorist group. Jurors and a judge rejected his explanations.[25]
Gunton was convicted of the plot, possessing two editions of Isis'
English-language propaganda magazine—which contained instructions on knife and vehicle attacks—and two counts of encouraging
terrorism with his Instagram posts. 'There was nothing about what
appeared on that page or the way in which that account was run by
you to suggest that you had anything but admiration for the actions
of Isis,' Judge Mark Wall KC told him:

> You told the jury in evidence that you had been conversing through
> Instagram with someone calling himself al-Baghdadi, the same name
> as that used by the leader of Isis. You sought to blame him for
> encouraging your actions. I do not doubt that you were able to find
> support and encouragement from what you were doing from those
> who read and liked your posts on Instagram. However, I am equally
> certain that by the time you set up that account your views had
> already become radical in nature and that therefore those who made
> contact with you were reinforcing the views which you had already
> taken up off your own bat.[26]

The judge said Gunton appeared to have started with general
searches for beheadings and gruesome material, before his internet
activity became 'more and more focused' on Isis. The teenager
claimed that he merely had a 'macabre interest in the gruesome' but
Judge Wall said he was committed to carrying out an attack, adding:
'You were dedicated to the cause for approximately one year. This
was no passing phase.' The judge found that Gunton's planned
attack had two phases, where he would first steal a vehicle and drive
into a crowd of people, and then produce his knife and hammer to
inflict as much harm as possible before being stopped—in line with
Isis' advice.

The judge said he doubted the 'viability' of Gunton's plan for an
initial vehicle attack on crowds, given that he only had a provisional
driving licence and had driven only a few minutes in a small car
along his parents' driveway. But there were no such doubts about
the viability of the second part of Gunton's plot. Judge Wall said the
teenager would have been 'quite capable of inflicting death and seri-

ous injury' with the knife and hammer, and planned to kill multiple victims. 'Whether you would have targeted people attending that concert or others going about their lawful businesses in Cardiff is not certain,' he added. 'It is not possible to estimate how many people would have been murdered or seriously injured by your actions as the attack was foiled before you could undertake it.' He described the teenager as 'something of a loner' and said that his autism, which was formally diagnosed after his arrest, made him easily impressed by what he read online. But a psychological report found that Gunton posed a high risk of further terrorist offending and that he was vulnerable to outside influences. Because Gunton was still only 17, he was sentenced to 'detention at Her Majesty's Pleasure'—a type of prison term reserved for minors who commit serious crimes—with a minimum term of 11 years before he could be released.

In the year his attack was stopped, Gunton was one of 27 under-18s arrested, 13 charged and ten convicted of terror offences in Britain.[27] At the time, the figures were a record high since such statistics started to be recorded on 11 September 2001. Before 2016, arrests of children under terror laws rarely rose out of single figures, but since then the number has not fallen below 12 and teenagers have made up an increasing proportion of suspected terrorists. In the year to September 2022, 31 under-18s were arrested on suspicion of terror offences, meaning that one in six suspects detained in Great Britain was a child. In another sign of shifting trends, white people have made up the largest single ethnic group arrested for terror offences for five consecutive years. Three quarters of suspects arrested in 2022 considered themselves to be British or dual nationals, compared to just a third in the year following the 9/11 attacks.[28] Dean Haydon, the UK's former Senior National Coordinator for counter-terrorism policing, is aware of children as young as 12 being arrested for terror offences.

'We're seeing the age profile of terrorists going down and becoming younger because of the accessibility of the internet, but also people experimenting with all sorts of different ideologies,' he adds. 'The internet has changed people's lives and the access to material. You don't have to travel anymore [for terrorist training], there's no real command and control, you don't need the approval to say "go and do an attack", you self-radicalise looking at material online.' Haydon says the challenge for counter-terror police is distinguishing between children who may be consuming terrorist propaganda and violent material online as they 'find their way in life', and those who are becoming a real-world threat.[29] Counter-terror police were sure that despite his age, autism and completely online interaction with jihadist ideology, Gunton had become a real threat.

The Windsor Castle

At 6.30pm on 25 August 2017, an Uber driver left his home in Luton and started driving towards Windsor. He put a location in the SatNav, placed a sharpened sword on the seat next to him and started playing inspirational lectures by jihadist preacher Anwar al-Awlaki on his car stereo. Mohiussunnath Chowdhury was about to carry out a terror attack, where he would murder soldiers outside the Queen's famed residence. He was not shy of expressing his intentions to those who knew where to look. Hours earlier, Chowdhury changed his WhatsApp profile image to a green bird—a symbol of martyrdom—replacing the black Isis flag used before. A note left behind for his sister made his plan explicitly clear. It read:

To my dearest sister,

By the time you read this *inshallah* [God willing] I will be with Allah. Do not cry and be strong. The *shaheed* [martyr] will take 70 members of his family with him to paradise. I will take you there *inshallah*. Tell everyone that I love them and that they should struggle against the enemies of Allah with their lives and their property. The Queen and her soldiers will all be in the hellfire, they go to war with Muslims around the world and kill them without any mercy. They are the enemies that Allah tells us to fight. Please make *dua* [prayers] for me that Allah accepts my efforts. I have left you all the money I had left in the bank which was £200, I know I didn't pay you back the full amount I borrowed but I had the intention to do so please forgive me of this debt.

I love you the most in the world shrimp.

Peace be upon you.[30]

Chowdhury selected Windsor Castle as the target where he would murder soldiers guarding the royal family. In carrying out his plan, he would elevate himself to the ranks of *mujahid*—a holy warrior—and be rewarded with palaces and wives in paradise. Chowdhury had been doing his research on such matters by listening to Awlaki's lectures, imbibing material by hate preachers and gorging on Isis propaganda. Hailing from a British-Bangladeshi family in Luton, he had not always been a practising Muslim but knew how to make amends, after watching other Isis-inspired atrocities hit the UK and commending them as a 'good way to go'. Now, he was ready.

Everything was going to plan as Chowdhury drove towards the scenic Berkshire town and approached his historic target. But instead of launching the attack at Windsor Castle, he drove straight past the historic royal residence and arrived at the destination put into his SatNav—a nearby pub of the same name. It was filling up with Friday night drinkers and diners, but Chowdhury was not there for them. He had resolved to martyr himself taking soldiers guarding the Queen to 'the hellfire', and was not to be deterred by a simple SatNav error. Instead of redirecting himself to the castle, or simply asking a local for directions, he drove all the way to Buckingham Palace. He arrived shortly before 8.30pm on the warm summer's night and started driving in a loop as unsuspecting tourists, dog-walkers and Londoners were milling around the park outside the royal landmark. But the string of terror attacks that had struck during the previous months had sparked an increase in security, and roads outside the palace had been partly closed to traffic amid enhanced police patrols. As Chowdhury drove his blue Toyota Prius along its perimeter scanning for potential targets, a marked police van came in the other direction and he saw his chance.

He swerved through traffic cones into the path of the van, which braked to avoid a crash. PC Gavin Hutt hadn't initially taken any notice of the car, which is a routine model for Uber drivers in London and a common sight on Friday nights. After watching it crash through the traffic cones and jolt to a stop, he decided to check it out in the belief that a drink-driver could be behind the wheel. He got out of the police van's passenger seat and walked towards the stationary vehicle, unarmed and wearing only a stab vest over a thin white shirt because of the heat. As PC Hutt walked towards the driver's side, the officer noticed that the window was open and the driver was staring intently at him, which he thought was a bit strange. He asked Chowdhury what was going on, and he replied: 'It's all a bit fucked up.' Again, the officer thought his behaviour strange, but not threatening. Alarm bells only started to ring as Chowdhury turned his back and reached towards the passenger side of the car. PC Hutt tried to halt him with a hand on his shoulder, telling him, 'Mate, whatever you're trying to do, just leave it and speak to me'. Chowdhury started loudly chanting 'Allahu akbar' and grabbed his sword, at which point the penny dropped for PC Hutt and a frantic struggle began.[31]

The officer started to repeatedly punch the attacker in the face to subdue him, as his colleagues ran into the fray. PC Ian Midgley sped around to the passenger side of Chowdhury's car and wrenched open the door. In the darkness, he could see the driver was holding some sort of large, T-shaped object. Not realising what it was, PC Midgley grabbed it with both hands and felt the sharpened blade cut into the flesh of his palm. As he heard Chowdhury shouting 'Allahu akbar' and struggling against his colleague, PC Midgley realised they weren't dealing with a drink-driver—they were face-to-face with a terrorist and fighting for their lives. PC Midgley started trying to hit Chowdhury's arms and legs but he fought back, punching the officer in the head and keeping a grip on his sword. PC Hutt managed to pin Chowdhury's right arm to the car's roof as a third police officer ran in to help. 'Just fucking spray him,' PC Hutt screamed, and Chowdhury was doused with CS gas. As he shut his eyes in pain and was distracted from his struggle for the sword, the officers were finally able to handcuff and subdue him.

The would-be terrorist was taken out of the car and arrested, as PC Midgley carried the sword away from the scene. The weapon, with a 42-inch blade, was an ornamental sword he had bought in 2013. Originally blunt, Chowdhury had sharpened it to a deadly point with a £5 tool bought from Sainsbury's the day before his failed attack. During his trial, he claimed to have purchased it because he was interested in Japanese anime and thought it would be 'pretty cool' to have a sword like those seen in the Lord of the Rings films.

The Uber driver, then 26, was not known to the security services and his murderous plans had gone undetected. If it had not been for the bravery and quick-thinking of the police officers Chowdhury targeted, and his bungling SatNav error preventing him from reaching Windsor Castle, he might have achieved his aims. The wannabe terrorist had not raised official concerns despite sending Isis propaganda to friends and defending the terrorist group's atrocities in Iraq and Syria. Chowdhury had conducted numerous internet searches for Isis beheading videos and the British executioner known as Jihadi John. Prosecutors said he had shown a 'great interest in Islamist terrorism', while declaring the British government a 'Zionist force' and soldiers and police officers the 'enemies of Allah'. Even after being thwarted, arrested and put on trial, he almost got away with it.

A jury was discharged after failing to reach a verdict on a single charge of preparing an act of terrorism in June 2018. Chowdhury told the court that he had not attempted a terror attack and was trying to get himself killed by being shot by police. He said he had been feeling lonely and depressed, and had 'so many chances' to get out of the car and kill the officers but chose not to. Confronted with his numerous messages declaring support for Isis, he told the jury they were merely 'in jest'. His defence, albeit completely false, was fatal to the requirement under British law to prove that Chowdhury was attempting an act of violence 'for the purpose of advancing a political, religious or ideological cause'. Prosecutors applied for a retrial, but that saw Chowdhury acquitted of preparing an act of terrorism in December 2018 and freed from custody.[32]

Chowdhury seemed surprised by the not guilty verdict himself, raising his eyebrows and saluting jurors before walking out of the court. But his intentions remained unchanged. In the months he was held on remand at HMP Belmarsh during his first two trials, he had made some new friends. Chowdhury networked with terrorists including the Parsons Green bomber, Ahmed Hassan, Erol Incedal, who he believed to know the Isis executioner Jihadi John. He received advice from his 'like-minded brothers' on how to fool the jury. During Chowdhury's first trial, he had a long beard and appeared unkempt.[33] After those jurors failed to reach a verdict, extremist inmates urged him to shave his beard off to appear more secular and neat at the retrial—more befitting of the character painted by his defence. In prison, Chowdhury was not so careful. While sat inside his cell, he made graphic drawings including one depicting a terrorist shouting 'Allahu akbar' and firing at a police officer outside 10 Downing Street, and another showing the 9/11 attacks. Prosecutors said a stash of 12 documents in total celebrated and provided a justification for violence against the UK, its government, army and police. But the evidence didn't win the day, and the experience of his arrest and detention didn't seem to have deterred Chowdhury. Speaking to his ten-year-old cousin following his release, he said prison was 'scary' on his first night but added: 'The next day was alright. It was normal, I met loads of Muslims there it was all good ... at the end of the day I did it for Allah right, so Allah protected me.'

Within days of being freed on 20 December 2018, Chowdhury was planning new attacks, but this time the security services were ready. On the surface, things looked normal. Chowdhury moved back in with his family in Luton and got a job at a peri peri chicken shop near his home. A colleague described him as a 'quiet, non-offensive person' who was 'very childish but professional with customers'. Among those customers were three men who introduced themselves as Hamza, Mikael and Zulf, who were in fact undercover police officers. They befriended Chowdhury and talked about his Bangladeshi heritage, and over time he opened up to them. He told them of his love of Isis, of the attack he tried to commit at Buckingham Palace, of how he had been inspired by Anwar al-Awlaki. But he did not restrict himself to the usual diet of al-Qaeda and Isis-linked propaganda. Chowdhury was also inspired by the counter-jihadist far right, whose depiction of an inherently violent Islam fitted his aspirations perfectly.[34]

On 31 March 2019, he met his supposed friends Hamza, Mikael and Zulf at a local mosque. After greeting the trio and sitting down, Chowdhury presented a book—*Mohammed's Koran: Why Muslims Kill for Islam*. It was co-written by Tommy Robinson, real name Stephen Yaxley-Lennon, the Luton-born founder of the English Defence League. Published in 2017, it was not well reviewed, and was later removed by Amazon and other mainstream retailers for violating their hate speech policies.[35] But Chowdhury was a fan. Despite his low-paid job, he shelled out £39.95 for a signed collector's edition of the work, and told his new friends it had 'decoded' the Quran. 'If you read it in chronological order you will find that the majority of the peaceful verses have been cancelled out by the later verses commanding violence,' he enthused. When questioned later about his unusual choice of reading material, Chowdhury praised Robinson, telling the court the anti-Muslim figurehead 'understands jihadi doctrine'. He told how he had deliberately sought out 'anti-Isis ideology' on the Jihad Watch website founded by American activist Robert Spencer, who Chowdhury hailed as a 'scholar'. In a Telegram chat group with the undercover police officers, he also shared videos made by a Christian preacher who claimed to 'explain jihad' and vehicle attacks by presenting Islam as inherently violent. Chowdhury described American David Wood as a 'hardcore enemy of Allah', adding: 'Some videos I don't watch where he mocks Islam but his other videos are more truthful than the majority of Islamic speakers.'[36]

Chowdhury told the undercover police officers that he had not completed the mission he started at Buckingham Palace, and that he had new aspirations to attack potential targets including a gay pride parade, Madame Tussauds and a London tourist bus. Police and MI5 were taking no chances. They bugged his home and car, and then watched and waited as he engaged in physical training by acquiring wooden swords, practised stabbing techniques, enrolled on a shooting course and obtained a replica pistol while seeking a live firearm and ammunition. On 20 June 2019—six months after his acquittal—a covert recording showed Chowdhury telling his sister that he was quitting his job. When she asked why, he told her: 'I'm doing another attack … I'm serious bro. It's about time now.' He affectionately nicknamed his sister, Sneha Chowdhury, 'shrimp', and confided in her as they both remained living in their family home with their ill mother.

Single and overweight, Chowdhury had written down plans for his anticipated arrival in heaven as a martyr and stuck them to his bedroom door. One handwritten list was entitled 'plans for *jannah*', meaning paradise. His number-one priority was to 'tour entire property' and 'choose main palace'. Chowdhury, who had spoken to undercover police of his struggle to meet a girlfriend, named his second priority as 'meet all wives and name and choose main two'. He was then to 'decorate main palace', meet family and friends, feast repeatedly, go to the market, 'spend time with wives' and embark on quests. Meeting Allah did not make the list until point number seven. But Chowdhury did not get a chance to make his second attack attempt before being arrested by armed police and put on trial once more.

The jihadi's third time in court was not so lucky, and jurors saw through his barrage of lies to convict him of preparing an act of terrorism in July 2020. Sneha was convicted for failing to warn authorities of her brother's plans, but denied discussing Isis or jihadist ideology. She told the court: 'Me and my brother are just weird, we miaow at each other and stuff ... it's not normal.' She was spared jail, because of the 'controlling behaviour by male members of her family', but Chowdhury was jailed for life with a minimum term of 25 years. He was returned to HMP Belmarsh and, as future trials would show, he was welcomed straight back into the fold of his 'like-minded brothers'.

7

PLOTTERS OF THE FUTURE

The profile of attack plotters has transformed in the UK since 2017, becoming less organised, less ideologically homogenous and less predictable than their predecessors. They are also increasingly likely to be young, vulnerable and British. The evolution of the threat has not stopped and the ground is ever-shifting between the security services' feet. For now they are sure that self-initiated terrorists, or 'lone wolves' as they are sometimes known, will be behind the majority of attacks for the foreseeable future. They are defined officially as people 'without material support or personal direction from a terrorist organisation; but who may still be influenced or encouraged by the rhetoric or ideology of a group'.[1]

At the time of writing, less than half of Prevent referrals see a fixed ideology identified, with a quarter linked to far-right extremism and 22 per cent of them suspected Islamists. Although Prevent is a voluntary scheme, completely dependent on police, schools, health workers, councils, prisons and members of the public deciding to make reports, its referral statistics have proved to be an early indicator of shifting terror threats in England and Wales. In 2017—before many of the extreme right-wing plots in this book were detected or even formed—the number of people flagged over far-right extremism rocketed by 36 per cent as jihadists started to drop. If the latest figures are an accurate forecast, many plotters of the future will be teenagers and vulnerable people with autism or mental health difficulties, whose motivations and methods look set to become increasingly varied.

If the deadly attacks of 2017 became a blueprint for the dozens of plots that followed, more recent terrorist incidents in the UK could set a concerning precedent. On Remembrance Sunday 2021, a taxi was booked to take a passenger to Liverpool Women's Hospital. As the vehicle pulled up to the entrance to the maternity facility, it exploded. Inside was Emad al-Swealmeen, a 32-year-old asylum seeker. While living in government-provided accommodation, he had managed to build a homemade bomb and tried to deploy it on 14 November 2021. Months of planning and preparations had gone undetected and at the time of writing, his aims and motivations are still not known. It is assumed that al-Swealmeen's device was detonated accidentally as he arrived at his assumed target, and he killed only himself as the taxi driver managed to escape the car before it completely went up in flames. The failed bombing was declared a terror attack because of the methods used, but police have not announced any ideological allegiance. Dean Haydon, who was the senior counter-terror officer charged with formally deciding whether the incident was terrorist in nature, admits that 'even to this day, we don't know the motivation behind his intention or his target'. Haydon calls the Liverpool attack 'a bit of a strange one', but says it is symbolic of the changing picture. 'You take individuals such as that, they're really difficult to detect and disrupt,' he adds. 'Quite clearly he's got some instructional material in relation to how to make an IED [improvised explosive device] and then he's selected his target and off he's gone.' Haydon says the methodology suggests al-Swealmeen must have had access to terrorist propaganda and instruction material, but the bit police are missing is 'around motivation, ideology and targeting—we may potentially never know'.[2]

An inquest into the bomber's death heard that a copy of the Quran and a prayer mat were found at his home, despite the fact al-Swealmeen had openly converted to Christianity in 2015 and declared his commitment to the faith in a ceremony at Liverpool Cathedral. The coroner said he had 'carried out the religious duties of someone who is a follower of Islam, notwithstanding the reported conversion'. A police officer giving evidence to the inquest said it was possible that al-Swealmeen was trying to strengthen his asylum claim, which was turned down after his arrival in Britain in 2014, by claiming that as a Christian he would be liable to persecution on return to Syria or Iraq. An immigration tribunal previously ruled

that al-Swealmeen had lied about being from Syria in his initial asylum claim and was in fact a Jordanian national who previously lived
in the United Arab Emirates.

The bomber was not known to Britain's security services but had
a criminal record after being prosecuted for brandishing a knife in
public in 2015. Al-Swealmeen had admitted that offence and was
detained under the Mental Health Act, being diagnosed as suffering
from depression, anxiety and post-traumatic stress disorder. The
coroner who oversaw the brief inquest into his death did not make
any findings on what role, if any, his mental health played in the
attack. But al-Swealmeen is one of numerous terrorists and plotters
who have a history of psychological issues. MI5 has acknowledged
that mental health can be a factor in the motivation behind attacks,
but cautions that it is 'often not possible to determine the extent to
which an attack was motivated exclusively by an extremist ideology,
or was exacerbated by complex mental health issues'.[3]

Several violent incidents have taken place in the UK which have
appeared, on the face of them, to be terror attacks, but have not
been officially declared as such because the security services have
assessed that mental health issues or personal grievances were a
greater motivator than ideology. They include a mass stabbing in a
Glasgow hotel that was being used to accommodate asylum seekers
in June 2020. As Ken McCallum, the director general of MI5, told
a parliamentary committee: 'For the first few hours it was not clear
to Police Scotland colleagues, or to ourselves, what really we were
dealing with here: was this, as it turned out, a desperate man in
some form of deranged state, or was this an ideological attack?'[4] The
former won out after it emerged that the rampage had been
prompted by a row between the knifeman and a fellow asylum
seeker over noise.

Perhaps the most controversial decision not to declare an attack
terrorism was a mass shooting in the Devon city of Plymouth on
12 August 2021. Jake Davison, 22, murdered his mother before
roaming the streets with a shotgun and killing a three-year-old girl,
her father and two other passers-by. It was the worst mass shooting
in Britain in more than a decade, and social media posts quickly
emerged suggesting that Davison identified as an 'incel'. Short for
'involuntary celibate', the term describes a loose online movement

that originated in North America and sees men forge a 'sense of identity around a perceived inability to form sexual or romantic relationships'.[5] Incels blame society at large and specifically women for their situation, which they see as inescapable, and are characterised by virulent expressions of misogyny. Although not explicitly violent, the movement has already been linked to several mass shootings that have left more than 50 people dead in the US and Canada since 2015.

An inquest in 2023 will probe Davison's ideology and the extent to which it affected his actions, and proceedings have already revealed that he had been reported to the Prevent programme by his mother—but counter-terror police involved in categorising his killing spree have defended their decision. Haydon believes that the attack was primarily driven by a 'mental health crisis'. 'Incel ideology was not the driver for him to kill his mother and the people in the street—if it was it would fall under the definition of terrorism,' he says:

> I took the decision that it wasn't, and I'll stand by this decision to this day. The circumstances were that an individual who has mental health issues has gone through a mental health crisis to the point he's picked up a shotgun and killed his mother, and then gone out onto the street and started shooting random people. If you look at his motivation for doing that it was a mental health crisis driven by a falling out with his mother. There was no other ideology or direction, inspiration or control. That's not terrorism.[6]

The decision not to declare Davison's shooting as a terrorist attack sparked a widespread public backlash, but the security services have insisted that they were not ruling out incels as a terrorist threat as a whole. MI5's position is that incel ideology should not be 'treated automatically as single-issue terrorism, but recognised as a potential terrorist motivation and assessed case by case against terrorism thresholds'.[7] Haydon says that if a shooting spree was 'driven' by incel ideology it would have met the legal definition of terrorism, adding: 'Incel can be terrorism but under the circumstances of Plymouth it wasn't, because it was a mental health crisis that drove him to kill.' The former senior officer, who retired from policing in July 2022, admits that the Terrorism Act provides quite

a 'loose definition' that requires 'professional judgement' to inter-
pret. 'It's quite a fine line sometimes around "is it terrorism or is
it not?",' he says.[8] The line is set to become even more blurred in
future, as MI5 casework, referrals to the Prevent programme,
arrests and court cases all point to a rising cohort of mentally ill
terror suspects.

The security services assess that mental health issues particularly
overlap with extreme right-wing terrorists. Europol's 2022 report
on international terrorism trends warned: 'Mental health issues are
of growing concern to law enforcement agencies, as they may make
individuals more susceptible to right-wing extremist ideas. This has
been enforced by the Covid-19 pandemic measures, such as school
closures and prolonged social isolation.'[9] Learning difficulties and
autism have become an increasingly frequent occurrence in cases
involving young terror plotters, like Isis fanatic Lloyd Gunton and
teenage neo-Nazi Paul Dunleavy, as well as teenagers arrested for
less serious offences such as collecting terrorist propaganda. The
prevalence, and relevance, of autism in the cohort is a matter of
professional debate, but a 2021 assessment by the British government's Homeland Security Group found that jailed extreme right-
wing terror offenders were five times more likely to be diagnosed
with autism spectrum disorder than other inmates.[10]

Jonathan Hall KC, the Independent Reviewer of Terrorism
Legislation, has said that despite a 'very real and respectable fear
that making any sort of link will lead to stigma', the prosecution of
autistic children and young people for terror offences must be spoken about. He says that neuro-diversity can be 'strong mitigation'
for people who have developed a special interest in cataloguing
material, such as on weapons or the Second World War, that may
ultimately lead to criminal charges, adding:

> In terms of risk and carrying out attacks I don't think the presence
> of autism means that police can discount the risk or that they ought
> to feel it is enhanced … people who have in the real world lacked
> friends and not been part of a group can feel immensely seduced by
> the friendliness and group mentality they encounter online.[11]

Hall wants to see British authorities consider more inventive solu-
tions, beyond current criminal prosecution and punishment, to

combat the 'phenomenon of autistic children being in their bedrooms for hours at a time, accessing material and persuading themselves that they are soldiers of Allah or soldiers of Hitler'. But the way forward is not easy, and new prosecutions are already underway for alleged terror plots mounted by autistic teenagers.

Counter-terror police working in the Prevent programme, which aims to intervene before people become a security threat or commit offences, talk of autism as one of many 'vulnerabilities' that they work to address. They have set up a series of regional 'CT Vulnerability Support Hubs' that see police sit alongside health nurses, psychologists and forensic psychiatrists to identify factors that may be feeding into or exacerbating people's path towards terrorism.[12] They can refer extremists into mental health treatment, as well as support for substance misuse or issues with housing, education and employment. In the year ending March 2021, more than half of the suspected extremists referred to the Prevent programme in England and Wales ended up being signposted to other services—mainly mental health providers—and only 27 per cent were taken forward for ideological mentoring.[13] Children under the age of 15 made up a fifth of all Prevent referrals, and 15- to 20-year-olds accounted for another third. More than half of people assessed were deemed to have a 'mixed, unstable or unclear ideology', which can include people whose allegiances are conflicted, undetermined or not explicitly terrorist—such as obsessions with mass violence or school shootings. The category also includes mentally ill people who may be vulnerable 'out of a desire for belonging'.

Cases are beginning to emerge of terror offenders switching from one driving ideology to another, and even flipping between completely opposed ends of the extremist spectrum. At least one case has been officially recorded of a jailed neo-Nazi transforming into a jihadist while in prison, and more could follow the same route. In 2020, the teenager officially named only as 'X', who had been sentenced to 18 months in youth detention for encouraging far-right terrorism, had his release delayed over security concerns. The Ministry of Justice made a rare application to a youth court for a two-month extension to his time in custody because of the 'increased risk to the public posed by X and the urgent need for further offending behaviour work to be carried out before his release'. He had converted to Islam while being held at HMP Belmarsh ahead of his trial, a month after telling the author of a pre-sentence report that no one would ever change his neo-Nazi worldview. Prison intelligence suggested that X was practising an 'extreme form of Islam' and associating with Isis supporters including Sudesh Amman, a terrorist inmate who would go on to launch the Streatham stabbing. A psychological assessment concluded that he was 'emotionally and psychologically damaged and vulnerable to being groomed into doing something significantly more serious than the offences of which he had been convicted'. Authorities issued the teenager a letter saying he was being kept in custody for longer because of his 'exceptional circumstances', including his vulnerability to ideological grooming, his conversion to Islam, his association with Amman and the spate of recent terror attacks by convicted terrorists. X was put into two government deradicalisation schemes and is not known to have reoffended since his eventual release.[14]

No cases of jihadists switching to the far right inside prison have been officially recorded and a 2022 review of terror offending inside British jails found that there was yet 'no comparable threat' to Islamists. But it added: 'The right-wing terrorist offender population is increasing and there is no reason why gang-type behaviour should not in due course pivot towards different ideologies that are conducive to terrorism ... failure to address the power of Islamist groups may encourage different prisoners with different ideologies to adopt similar mechanisms.' As of 30 September 2022, 239 people were being held in British prisons for terrorism-connected offences, with 65 per cent categorised as holding Islamist extremist views, 28 per cent far right and 7 per cent labelled 'other'.[15]

* * *

The ambiguities and fluidities around the motivations behind attempted attacks have started to impact on prosecutions. Since 2017, Britain has seen charges against at least four failed plotters in the category of a 'mixed, unstable or unclear ideology'—and none of them, ultimately, could be charged with preparing acts of terrorism. The first case saw two boys, who were arrested when they were aged just 14 in October 2017, jailed for planning a mass shooting at their Yorkshire secondary school. Thomas Wyllie and Alex Bolland idolised the Columbine High School shooters and a judge found that they wanted to create 'terror on the scale of the school shootings that have been seen in America'.[16] The pair drew up a hit-list of targets including fellow pupils and teachers to murder, collected materials and manuals to make explosives and planned to steal shotguns from Wyllie's girlfriend's home. The plot was only detected because Bolland spilled their plans to a schoolfriend on Snapchat, and the girl raised the alarm with her mother and teachers. Police uncovered a diary where Wyllie espoused far-right ideology and discussed his motivations for wanting to carry out an attack. The first page read: 'If this is found I have committed one of the worst atrocities in British history or I killed myself.' Wyllie wrote that humans were a 'vile species' and that he would get to 'play the role of God' and decide who lived and died. 'Fuck, I hate my school. I will obliterate it. I will kill everyone,' he vowed.[17] Bolland had been bullied by fellow pupils for years and wanted revenge, so the pair joined forces to get it. Counter-terror police led the investigation, but the boys were charged with conspiracy to murder rather than preparing acts of terrorism because the Crown Prosecution Service did not believe the case passed the necessary threshold of the use or threat of violence 'for the purpose of advancing a political, religious, racial or ideological cause'.[18] Their primary motivation was seen as revenge for the wrongs they felt had been done to them by teachers and pupils, as well as an obsession with school shootings—which is not classed as a terrorist ideology or form of extremism in the UK.

The second plot to fall into the 'mixed, unstable or unclear ideology' bracket was mounted by an unemployed, self-described 'loner' who planned to ram a van loaded with explosive gas canisters into crowds attending a sporting event in his Cumbrian hometown. Shane Fletcher, then 20, held a violent hatred for the people of Workington, who he blamed for school bullying and his inability to get a job. He made the mistake of voicing his aspirations to a probation worker who was working with him after a previous arson offence, and in police interviews following his arrest in March 2018 he described himself as a 'big fan of Hitler'. Fletcher's phone and iPad contained selfies showing him perform Nazi salutes and photos of the Ku Klux Klan, and he had written in a journal of his hatred of 'degenerates' from different religious and ethnic groups, women and gay people. But he also idolised the Columbine killers and other mass shooters, and told police he had been watching snuff videos and documentaries about serial killers since the age of 13 because he 'had not gone out much', and was excited by violence. Again, Fletcher was not charged with preparing an act of terrorism, although he was convicted of two counts of possessing terrorist information over bomb manuals. He was jailed instead for soliciting to murder, after trying to convince his only friend to commit the massacre with him. Fletcher wrote to the man that he wanted to go on a 'massive killing spree' that would 'destroy all [his] problems at once', adding: 'Im sick of seeing ppl who have mistreated us in so many ways living happy and healthy lives ... Workington and humaninty living in it needs to be wiped off the face of the earth n I will be the one to do it'. A prosecutor told Fletcher's trial that he was not motivated by terrorism, but hatred and a desire for revenge. Jonathan Sandiford KC added:

> In part, the defendant's hatred was borne of his racist belief that people who were Jewish and not white were responsible for his inability to find work and to make any kind of a meaningful life for himself. However, the main source of his hatred was that he had or felt that he had been bullied throughout his teen years and was looked down on and victimised by the people of Workington where he had grown up. His hatred was flamed by his own feelings of worthlessness, inadequacy and inability arising from his inability to find work or make any kind of meaningful life or relationships for himself.[19]

A judge found Fletcher had an 'unhealthy interest' in murder, torture and rape, and he admitted feeling 'aroused by acts of cruelty to animals', but adjusted his nine-year jail sentence on account of his youth, mental health issues and potential undiagnosed developmental disorder that 'may have affected the way in which [Fletcher] perceived the world'.[20]

In June 2018, another shooting plot was foiled when US Homeland Security officers intercepted a package containing a Glock handgun and five rounds of ammunition at Newark Airport,

New Jersey.[21] It was bound for Kyle Davies, an 18-year-old student studying for his A-levels who had ordered the items to be delivered to his home in Gloucestershire. Davies had carried out extensive online research into mass shootings including Columbine and the Norway attacks of 2011 by white supremacist Anders Breivik. He had a handwritten shopping list entitled '*Gotterdammerung*', meaning 'the end of time', including firearms, a gas mask, body armour, a trench coat—as worn by the Columbine shooters—and the ingredients needed to make explosives. He had already obtained guides on how to build bombs and carry out attacks. Davies was depressed and had been bullied at school, and had also been collecting indecent images of children on his computer. Again, he was not charged with terror offences, but jailed for the alternative offence of attempting to possess a firearm with intent to endanger life—namely a mass shooting.

The fourth person charged with a 'mixed, unclear or unstable ideology' plot was Gabrielle Friel, a 22-year-old man from Edinburgh who had collected an arsenal of weapons including a machete, a high-powered crossbow and a ballistic vest. He was convicted of possessing the items for the purposes of terrorism, but acquitted of preparing a terrorist act following his arrest in August 2019. Friel, who had previously served time in a psychiatric hospital after stabbing a police officer at his sixth-form college in 2017, was again fixated on the Columbine shooting and other massacres. He felt a particular affiliation for the Californian mass shooter Elliot Rodger, who was an incel, and told his trial that he fantasised about spree killings. Jailing Friel for ten years, a judge found he suffered from depression and told him: 'Whether it is a cause or symptom of illness, spending 12 hours and more each day surfing the internet has been extremely damaging for you.'[22]

* * *

We have already seen plots on the borderline of terrorism involving incels and those motivated by a generalised hatred or sense of victimhood, and terrorism prosecutions in the UK look set to expand beyond the jihadist and far-right tribes responsible for most plots in this book. The first case of its kind for an alleged terror offender holding a 'left-wing anarchist ideology' ended in 2020 when the defendant killed himself in prison, three months before his trial was due to begin. Dominic Noble, 32, was being held at HMP Leeds charged with 14 counts of possessing or accessing documents useful to a terrorist. He had researched bomb-making and attacks, and wrote online posts about a 'list of potential targets' who he perceived to have wronged Wikileaks founder Julian Assange. Had the trial gone ahead, conviction was uncertain. Jurors may have been reluctant to class Noble's beliefs as terrorist in nature, or convict him in light of a history of mental illness. An inquest found that he was an 'isolated individual with anger issues from a young age', who had mental health problems and used cannabis to self-medicate.[23] At the time of his death, he had been waiting more than a month for a psychiatric appointment and his mother had warned the prison of 'paranoid and bizarre' phone conversations.

While Noble was the first modern British terror case with a left-wing motivation, it was not thought by the security services to indicate any broader trends, or a rising threat from the far left as a whole. A 2022 report by parliament's Intelligence and Security Committee said that left-wing groups such as animal rights campaigners, 'rarely cause [anything] more than occasional public order concerns' in the UK.[24] Separate research carried out for the Commission for Countering Extremism said revolutionary socialists, communists, anarchists and other strands of the far left had no 'realistic prospect of direct organisational involvement in any sort of imminent terrorist activity in the UK' and 'no history of using terrorist tactics in the hope of precipitating revolution'. But the report cautioned: 'The objective of revolution and the construction of narratives in which certain social groups are positioned as the enemy of the majority, as well as the categorisation of the UK and its allies as a threat to world peace, can potentially act to legitimate certain forms of violence.'[25]

Some academics and law enforcement officials have posited that climate change and its associated harms could also be used to justify violence in Britain, following significant waves of protest and civil disobedience by groups including Extinction Rebellion and Just Stop Oil. The first 'eco terrorist' incident in the UK took place in Scotland in 2018, when 35-year-old Nikolaos Karvounakis left a homemade bomb next to a bench in a busy Edinburgh park. Karvounakis, who previously carried out national service in the Greek Army, claimed to be acting on behalf of Individualists Tending to the Wild (ITS), a self-described 'eco extremist' group that originated in Mexico.[26] He had assembled a viable pipe bomb and put it in a cardboard box, but without any method of detonation. Inside the lid was a message scrawled in black marker pen: 'FUCK YOU ALL!' After the device was discovered, ITS issued a claim of responsibility by Karvounakis. Writing under the name Misanthropos Cacogen, he said he had left a 'package bomb totally indiscriminately at a central location' and described himself as a 'lover of nihilist anti-political violence'.[27]

Karvounakis' motivations were difficult to understand, even by his own account. His three-page screed did not contain any explicit mention of the environment or climate crisis, but accused humanity of 'indiscriminate destruction and murder'. His splurge of angry pseudo-philosophy concluded: 'I am not an eco-extremist, I am a nihilist misanthrope as I like to call myself.' Karvounakis was jailed for eight years and four months for possessing items for a terrorist purpose.

While ecological activism has historically emanated from left-wing groups, recent years have seen a melding with far-right ideas to create a surge in 'eco-fascism'. Among those adopting the label was Brenton Tarrant, the white nationalist who murdered more than 50 victims in the March 2019 shootings at two mosques in Christchurch, New Zealand. In his lengthy manifesto, he described himself as an 'eco-fascist' three times, writing:

> For too long we have allowed the left to co-opt the environmentalist movement to serve their own needs ... the environment is being destroyed by over population, we Europeans are one of the groups that are not over populating the world. The invaders are the ones over populating the world. Kill the invaders, kill the overpopulation and by doing so save the environment.[28]

A gunman who murdered 22 victims in a Texas supermarket five months after Tarrant's shooting said he supported the Christchurch attacker and his manifesto, although his massacre was specifically 'a response to the Hispanic invasion of Texas'. Patrick Crusius titled his manifesto 'An Inconvenient Truth', in an allusion to Al Gore's famous 2006 documentary on climate change. He argued that American lifestyles were 'destroying the environment of our country' and because individuals, the government and corporations were not voluntarily making the changes necessary, the 'next logical step is to decrease the number of people in America using resources'. Crusius concluded: 'If we can get rid of enough people, then our way of life can become more sustainable.'[29] English-language far-right movements are heavily internationalised through their shared online spaces, and the influence of eco-fascism is likely to grow in the UK as climate change remains an issue of significant public concern. As Europol's 2022 terror threat assessment stated:

> Environmental developments might have an influence on the, albeit small, faction of eco-fascists within the right-wing extremist spectrum. Climate change may deepen dystopic views that some right-wing extremists are emphasising, such as the collapse of current societal systems, social-Darwinist ideas of the survival of the fittest, and the preservation of humankind.[30]

Another potential terror threat comes from anti-vaxxers. Previously a fringe movement concentrated online in the UK, it has pulled crowds of thousands at regular protests in London since the start of the Covid pandemic. Present at those demonstrations were a substantial number of activists who have campaigned against 5G communications technology and used Covid to expand their audience. They claimed that 5G was spreading the virus, that the waves were otherwise harmful or even deadly, and that people were unknowingly being implanted with 'nano material antenna'. To the uninitiated, the claims appear bizarre and perhaps humorous. But they have been inspiring direct action by believers, with dozens of phone masts vandalised and set on fire in the UK. Shortly before this book was published, a man went on trial for the UK's first terror plot said to be directly inspired by conspiracy theories. Oliver Lewin, a former audio-visual engineer who lived with his mother and stepfather despite being in his late 30s, had joined conspiracist communities on Telegram. He came to believe that it was his duty to fight the 'emergence of a Chinese communist system', which had supposedly been triggered by the coronavirus pandemic. Lewin was accused of attempting to topple the British government by recruiting a militia to commit coordinated attacks on phone masts, radio transmitters and other critical national infrastructure across Britain.[31] His trial was a test case with huge significance for the scope of terrorism laws in the UK—would jurors be persuaded that his belief system fell within the definition of a 'political, religious, racial or ideological cause'? They were. Lewin was convicted of preparing acts of terrorism, and the verdict could open the door for terror charges against more conspiracy theorists in the future.

Haydon says counter-terror police are starting to see 'some casework in the conspiracy theorist space' and fears that theories that may appear ideologically neutral can bring people into contact with far-right and jihadist propaganda online.[32] A report by parliament's Intelligence and Security Committee cited 5G conspiracy theories as a potential threat, and said that wider national infrastructure such as transport, electricity and utilities could be targeted by the far right. It said: 'It is possible that national infrastructure is seen as a legitimate target in order to accelerate the fall of a modern Western state and thereby instigate a "race war" in order to create a fascist, white ethno-state.'[33]

* * *

Some experts are growing concerned that the current interpretation of the UK's legal definition of terrorism means that the potential for attacks driven by inceldom, obsessions with school shootings and other forms of mass violence is not being addressed. Researchers who have been chronicling the impact of online subcultures at the Institute for Strategic Dialogue think-tank found that the gap means that violent material relating to incels and school shootings remains more easily accessible than equivalent videos and posts classified as terrorist propaganda, even though both have the potential to motivate people to kill.

Milo Comerford argues that the solution is not to 'massively expand the counter-terrorism apparatus to include all other violent threats', but that Britain needs a 'much better and broader violence prevention architecture that is able to anticipate, respond to and intervene in threats in a much more upstream way that isn't just counter-terrorism policing and a very narrow Prevent-type focus.

That is only ever going to address a small part of these issues.' His colleague Tim Squirrell adds: 'We need to understand mass violence and targeted violence as issues in themselves, rather than as issues only insofar as they fit into an ideological framework.' He believes the current machinery to prevent mass killings is stymied by its roots in the post-9/11 understanding of the terror threat posed by al-Qaeda, and will struggle to adapt to the new 'post-organisational' landscape.[34]

A 2021 report by the UK's Independent Reviewer of Terrorism Legislation issued a warning over the emerging trend, saying that while jihadists remained the principal threat, the 'internet is a cornucopia of violent ideologies'. Hall wrote that 'novel cause terrorism such as attacks by incels and school shooters' was on the rise. He identified that by 2019, a problem was emerging of proving offences where people seemed to be motivated by clashing ideologies, personal grievances or mass violence as ends in themselves. Hall said:

> The Columbine High School shooting and its perpetrators exercise a powerful pull towards emulation. The ideological component is less clear, appearing (superficially at least) to be a form of violent nihilism, although in practice individuals often have a strong identitarian attachment. It has something akin to the incel's revolution of the unhappy or 'beta' uprising.[35]

The watchdog said that authorities were becoming concerned about a significant number of people who did not fall within the 'traditional categories' of extremism, and that distinguishing those planning attacks out of pure hate from those advancing a cause was increasingly difficult. Hall said that counter-terror police were still able to investigate incels or wannabe school shooters, but that prosecutors later faced the 'challenge' of proving a terrorist motivation beyond reasonable doubt. He pointed out that the legal definition of terrorism does not require a set 'ideology'—just a desire to advance a 'cause'. The report concluded that the existing definition was 'sufficiently broad to capture modern phenomena such as incel violence', and that an extension of terror laws beyond what wider society commonly understands as terrorism might cause juries to refuse to convict.

The Crown Prosecution Service overstretched the definition in a series of terror prosecutions between 2017 and 2020 for people who had joined or supported Kurdish groups fighting against Isis in Syria. The Kurdish People's Protection Units (YPG) were armed and backed by the US-led coalition and successfully drove the jihadist group out of much of its territories, with support from British air strikes. So when volunteers, including two former British Army soldiers, were charged for a variety of offences, including preparing acts of terrorism, it came as something of a surprise. The cases were a disaster. In 2019, a judge ruled that one volunteer prosecuted for joining the YPG in Syria had 'no case to answer', when the group was 'supporting the policy of the United Kingdom and other allies by fighting Isis'.[36] Prosecutors dropped charges against another man for attending a YPG training camp in 2018, and the previous year saw a jury acquit a third volunteer fighter of a terror charge over possessing *The Anarchist Cookbook*.

The ill-fated attempts ended in July 2020, when prosecutors discontinued similar pending cases. Defence lawyers demanded an explanation for the U-turn, which came after they made a formal application for prosecutors to disclose 'information relating to diplomatic pressure placed on the UK government by Turkey to treat the Kurdish YPG as terrorists'. But the Crown Prosecution Service merely said there was 'insufficient evidence to sustain a reasonable prospect of conviction'.[37] An unimpressed judge adjourned the case to check whether he had powers to compel 'more meaningful or detailed explanations', noting that one of the innocent defendants had been held in prison for seven months on remand.[38] He found he did not and the men and their families were left angry and confused. One of the defendants wrote on Facebook: 'They fucked all my shit up and got away with it scot-free. No reason, no compensation, no law to stop them from doing it again.'

An explanation was also denied to Hall, who found that fighting for the YPG actually does fit the legal definition of terrorism in the UK and there appeared to be no applicable defences. He surmised that 'prosecutorial discretion' must have been at work and called the lack of transparency 'regrettable'. Hall said that the YPG prosecutions 'pushed to limit what might be considered in ordinary language terrorism' and warned that an 'incremental approach is desirable' in any extension of terror laws, adding:

External demands for deviant behaviours to be recognised as terrorism should be resisted. A decision to treat something as terrorism should never be paraded as a sign of strength or virtue. The use of terrorism powers is better considered as a necessary but regrettable response to behaviour when ordinary criminal law and processes are insufficient.[39]

In her official response to the report, then home secretary Priti Patel called Hall's assessment of the increasing threat from mixed, unstable or unclear ideologies and incels 'interesting' but insisted that the UK's existing framework was effective in 'countering all forms of terrorism, irrespective of the ideology that inspires them'.[40]

* * *

As security services try to monitor potential threats from the increasingly disparate pool of unknown and volatile people, they are also watching known terror offenders who are coming up for release from jail. Several terror attacks have been launched by freed terrorists, such as Usman Khan—who had his first terror plot foiled in 2010 but went on to murder two people at a prison education event in London in 2019. The government responded to the attack, and the subsequent stabbing by another previously jailed plotter in Streatham, by tightening the law to mean that terror offenders could no longer be released automatically half-way through their sentences and must have the risk they pose assessed by the Parole Board. Published assessments by the body provide stark evidence of the dangers at play.

In July 2022, the Parole Board refused to release a man who had been the highest-ranking al-Qaeda operative in Britain when he was jailed in 2008. Rangzieb Ahmed was sentenced to life with a minimum term of ten years for directing an al-Qaeda cell, being a member of al-Qaeda and possessing terrorist articles.[41] The Parole Board found that despite undertaking an 'accredited programme to address extremist offending' and working with imams in prison, there were still concerns about Ahmed's 'attitudes, beliefs and behaviour in custody'. Officials said that even with strict limitations on his contacts, movements and activities, it was too dangerous to release him.[42] In another case, the Parole Board refused to

177

free a man jailed in 2007 for his part in an al-Qaeda-linked plot to bomb potential targets including London's Ministry of Sound nightclub and the Bluewater shopping centre in Kent. While Jawad Akbar had presented 'no behavioural concerns' in custody, the British government had issued an order attempting to deport him to Italy on release. The Parole Board found that Akbar could not be 'safely managed' in Italy, because the controls limiting the risk he posed were not sufficiently 'robust' in the country and it has no information-sharing agreement with the UK for released prisoners. 'The Parole Board's assessment of risk must consider the risk to the public, whether they are in the United Kingdom or elsewhere,' the body said.[43]

Released terrorists make up the bulk of MI5's priority four SOIs, and have their 'risk of re-engagement assessed'. That workload is set to get bigger, as a large cohort of Isis supporters come up for release from 2023 onwards. Since the terrorist group emerged in 2014, record numbers of people have been jailed for terror-related offences in England and Wales—but the vast majority were handed sentences of under ten years. From 2014 to 2017, the most common terms were between one and four years, meaning the security services had to decide in many cases whether—on balance—it would be more dangerous to put terrorists in prisons where they were more likely to associate with like-minded extremists than be meaningfully deradicalised, or to delay arrests in the hope of securing a more serious conviction. 'Before 2017, we saw a lot of individuals that were consuming extremist material online, both collecting and disseminating it,' Haydon recalls. 'Some were being arrested and facing the courts but the sentences were pretty weak.'[44]

The number of terror offenders being jailed surged to new highs in 2017 and 2018 as the security services thwarted numerous plots, caught people trying to travel to join Isis, cracked down on those spreading terrorist material online and responded to the ban of neo-Nazi terrorist group National Action. Then in 2019, the British government increased the punishment for offences including collecting and sharing terrorist material, and encouraging terrorism, to 15 years. Haydon says the legislation enabled police to 'intervene at an early stage rather than let a job run', but even those longer terms have been coming to an end. Between 40 and 60 terrorist prisoners are released from custody every year in Britain and Haydon says police are 'doing more and more work around the prison estate and probation and individuals being released back into the community'. He adds:

If you wind the clock back five or 10 years we saw a period where we were convicting lots of individuals that were all in prison, and now they're coming up for release. There's a new bucket of individuals there who are coming back into the community who potentially, a bit like Fishmongers' Hall and Streatham, could also pose a threat.[45]

* * *

Rather than a single ideology or political cause, a mix of social and psychological factors seem to be increasingly relevant as indicators of propensity toward terrorist violence, and police and the security services have been trying to adapt accordingly. Julia Ebner, a United Nations counter-terrorism adviser who has embedded herself in online communities ranging from Isis brides to neo-Nazis, says that across the spectrum of extremism, online radicalisation tends to share a common path where people either chance across or seek out material because of a personal grievance—such as civilian deaths in the Syrian civil war, or the sexual grooming of white girls by Asian men—and then start interacting with others in a linked network or social group. Ebner believes people are 'socialised into' extremism and that a sense of belonging and friendship is a powerful motivator. Once people feel part of a group, perceived attacks on it become personal and people become 'more willing' to take violent action against any supposed threats, Ebner says: 'The whole social aspect of it plays a major role in going the step further to violence.'[46]

Issues around identity, belonging and status are among the red flags British authorities perceive as exacerbating a person's risk of terror offending. They are some of the 22 factors listed in an official assessment used since 2011, which sees them graded 'strongly present', 'partly present' or 'not present' in order to rate an individual's engagement with extremism, intent and capability.[47] Issues listed in the ERG22+ as contributing to engagement include a 'need to defend against threats', as well as 'excitement, comradeship and adventure', and 'political, moral motivation'. The assessment lists mental health issues as a factor, as well was 'susceptibility to indoctrination' and 'group influence as control'. Key signposts for intent include over-identifying with a particular group or ideology, 'us and them thinking' and dehumanising perceived enemies, while capability is judged by a person's knowledge and skills, their access to real-world networks, funding and equipment, and any prior criminal history.

The success of the ERG22+ is a matter of debate, after a government review found that some assessments had 'seriously minimised the seriousness of terrorist offences, and accepted the offender's characterisation (and in some cases denials) of offences of which they had been convicted'. But if adopted as a framework to understand the varying factors that may drive people towards terrorism, the ERG22+ is instructive. All plotters in this book, whatever their ideology, share many of the same characteristics—a desire for belonging, a belief in a threat that must be violently defended against, the division of the world into 'us' and 'them'. Whatever changes rock the global political landscape in the coming years, the warning signs for future plotters will be visible to those who know where to look.

CONCLUSION

PLOTS OF THE FUTURE

In the five years covered by this book, terror attacks have transformed in the UK—the targets, methods and motivations have all evolved. They will do again, and bloodshed in Britain will continue to be inspired by events far outside its borders. Sir Mark Rowley, the former head of UK counter-terrorism policing and commissioner of the Metropolitan Police as of late 2022, describes terrorism as being driven by 'political grievance'. 'Ideological seeds are being thrown into the wind that turn regional disputes into terrorism,' he warns.[1] A prime example is the Syrian civil war, which started in 2011. Bashar al-Assad's crackdown on a democratic uprising fractured into a multi-faceted conflict that spawned Isis, triggered the largest terrorist migration from Europe ever recorded and inspired jihadists around the world.

The 2019 defeat of the territorial Islamic State of Iraq and Syria—which had proved so potent a motivation for foreign fighters and terrorists around the world—was hoped by many to end its deadly thrall. But while its influence has been undermined, it is still alive and kicking. Isis had capitalised on its real-world caliphate but it did not depend on it for its online propaganda strategies, and started making ideological preparations for the loss of physical ground years before its main territories were eradicated. The last edition of its English-language magazine contained a lengthy article entitled: 'Why we hate you and why we fight you'. Over four pages directly addressed to 'the disbelieving enemies of Allah', Isis vowed that its followers would never stop attacking Western countries in alleged revenge for 'the crimes of the West against Islam and the Muslims', such as air strikes in Syria and Iraq or Quran burnings. 'Jihad will continue to be a personal obligation on every single Muslim,' Isis declared:

As much as some liberal journalist would like you to believe that we do what we do because we're simply monsters with no logic behind our course of action, the fact is that we continue to wage—and escalate—a calculated war that the West thought it had ended several years ago. We continue dragging you further and further into a swamp you thought you'd already escaped only to realize that you're stuck even deeper within its murky waters.[2]

While governments and technology giants have worked for years to limit the availability of Isis propaganda, it remains accessible online to those who know where to look, and appears set to continue as a dominant inspirational force for jihadists in the UK and around the world. Issues of al-Qaeda's English-language *Inspire* magazine, particularly those featuring articles by ideologue Anwar al-Awlaki and a notorious manual on how to 'make a bomb in the kitchen of your mom' also remain in rampant circulation. Successive international operations against the leaders of both terrorist groups—which saw al-Qaeda leader Ayman al-Zawahiri killed in a drone strike in Afghanistan[3] in July 2022 and Isis' third caliph eliminated in Syria three months later—have disrupted organisational structures, but appear to have done little damage to the movements' enduring ideological appeal. Nor has the real-world threat from Isis dissipated.[4]

Thousands of men, women and children captured in its last territories are still being held captive by Kurdish authorities in Syria. Pleas by the Syrian Democratic Forces to repatriate foreign nationals from prisons and camps for trials in their home countries have been ignored by the UK. But the group is clear that it will not be able to hold the jihadists forever, amid waves of riots, escapes and violent break-out attempts that have been directly encouraged by Isis. The British government has been seeking to block the return of anyone considered a security threat by removing British citizenship from dual nationals and obtaining court orders to legally prevent suspected Isis brides and foreign fighters from entering the country. Some ministers have floated the possibility of trials in Iraq or Syria, but there are significant logistical and legal barriers and neither country's government has declared any willingness to facilitate such a scheme. Dean Haydon, who was the UK's Senior National Coordinator for counter-terrorism policing until July 2022, says his officers were 'very alive to the fact there are foreign terrorist fighters still overseas that want to come back', warning: 'Whatever happens to those camps in the future will have a major impact around the world.'[5]

Any violent action by Isis and its supporters will continue to be seized upon by far-right movements to fuel attacks from the opposite side of the spectrum. The feedback loop of extremism created since 2014 continues to generate violence by people claiming to defend or avenge their country, race or religion—often spurred into action by the news events of the day. At the time of writing, an alleged neo-Nazi is to go on trial accused of attempting a terror attack at a London legal firm that had garnered media coverage for representing asylum seekers. He arrived at its offices on 7 September 2020 armed with a knife and handcuffs, while carrying the flags of Nazi Germany and US Confederates. The man is accused of plotting to kill a senior lawyer because of his involvement in legal challenges that prevented the British government from deporting migrants. His alleged attack attempt came amid a surge of small boat crossings over the English Channel, which have been characterised as an 'invasion' by far-right extremists in the same way the exodus from Syria was years before.

The Syrian war has not stopped, but a different conflict is now dominating the concerns of Western intelligence agencies—Ukraine. The full consequences of the Russian invasion on 24 February 2022 are yet to be seen. Millions of Ukrainians have fled the country, which looks set to be mired in conflict for years to come. War crimes are already under investigation,[6] and Russian forces are unleashing the kind of indiscriminate bombardment they became bitterly known for in Syria. An unknown number of British volunteers have already travelled to Ukraine to fight for the country's forces, against government advice. Jonathan Hall KC, the Independent Reviewer of Terrorism Legislation, says joining the conflict appears to be captured by the definition of terrorism in British law—violence 'for the purpose of advancing a political, religious, racial or ideological cause'. Charges of preparing acts of terrorism have been used against numerous men and women who have attempted to travel to Syria, even when they were fighting against Isis,[7] but the watchdog believes they are unlikely to be applied to Ukraine. 'Russia's aggression is against the international legal order,' Hall says. 'Given the government's support [for Ukraine], prosecution of foreign fighters against Russia under terrorism legislation appears to be a non-starter, even if the broad statutory definition of terrorism is satisfied in these cases. But there is always the possibility of less desirable cases at the edges—individuals who travel to Ukraine under false pretence either to support Russia or fight with an ideological group such as the neo-Nazi Azov battalion.'[8]

The difference in the British authorities' approach to the Syrian and Ukrainian wars became immediately apparent. Daniel Burke, a former British Army paratrooper, was charged with preparing acts of terrorism after fighting against Isis with the Kurdish People's Protection Units (YPG). The Crown Prosecution Service dropped the case, along with several other terror charges related to anti-Isis volunteers, without explanation in July 2020.[9] Two years later, Burke was leading a group of foreign military volunteers called 'The Dark Angels' fighting against Russian Forces in Ukraine.[10] Sam Newey, whose brother Daniel fought with Burke in Syria, was among his troops. Sam was known to counter-terror police after a failed prosecution for assisting his brother to join the YPG, but neither man has so far faced police action for their activity in Ukraine.

In July 2022, the executive director of Europol predicted that the fallout from the war would 'have a lasting impact on the EU's security for years to come'. Catherine De Bolle, executive director of Europol, warned:

> This war has already attracted several radicalised individuals from member states who have joined the fight on both sides. Moreover, the ongoing war is likely to spark violent extremist reactions and mobilisation, particularly in the online domain. We must continue to closely monitor these developments while taking heed of the lessons learnt in the past in dealing with foreign fighters returning from battlefields in the Middle East.[11]

Haydon says that an immediate concern is the transportation of weaponry from Ukrainian battlefields. 'There is some really heavy weaponry in circulation in that country at the moment and if you look forward into the future, what happens to that weaponry and whose hands it gets into is also a concern for us at the moment,' he warns. 'We are worried about events in Ukraine, quite clearly ... at some stage we will have individuals coming back with combat training as well.'[12]

It is possible that Russian targets, such as embassies or government officials, will be targeted abroad by people unsatisfied by the international economic, legal and cultural sanctions taken in the early part of the invasion. The security services are keeping a close eye on the potential for international spill-over, while trying to fend off any moves by Russia to target Britain and other nations working to thwart its ambitions in Ukraine. MI5's annual threat update for 2022 was heavily focused on state threats—not just from Russia but also from China and Iran. Director general Ken McCallum said the security service's 'prioritisation choice' was becoming harder, as it was still receiving hundreds of fragmentary leads on potential terrorist activity:

> How do we balance effort between, say, detecting teenage would-be terrorists radicalised in extreme right-wing spaces online, and protecting the UK's military secrets from Russian cyber hackers? How to prioritise combatting repression of the Chinese diaspora or of Iranian dissidents here against the need to keep degrading al-Qaeda overseas? The complexity we face is huge.[13]

The invasion of Ukraine happened less than four years after Russian GRU agents used a nerve agent to try to assassinate former double agent Sergei Skripal in Salisbury. It had been assumed, following longstanding international convention, that the former double agent would be safe in Britain after a spy swap agreed with the Kremlin. But the rules, unwritten as they are, were ripped up on 4 March 2018. The brazen chemical attack left its target alive but cruelly caused the death of a local woman who believed the discarded novichok—concealed in a counterfeit Nina Ricci bottle—was perfume. The Salisbury poisonings were not declared a terror attack, but several MPs labelled them 'state-sponsored terrorism' in Parliament.[14]

Hall says a 'very strong policy decision' was taken at the time not to treat the attack on the Skripals as terrorism, but that a different decision could be taken in the future. 'We have thought very much in terms of individuals and groups committing acts of terrorism,' he says. 'But are we going to start thinking more in terms of state terrorism, bearing in mind some of the atrocities Russia has been committing as a state?' The death of Dawn Sturgess was thought to be an accidental result of Russia's recklessness in 2018, and a public inquiry will examine that further, but Hall says that a similar attack affecting the general population could be viewed as explicitly terrorist in nature. He adds: 'There is a particular potency about the word terrorism because it reflects the harm that terrorism causes, which is a state of terror resulting in the population being more cautious and inhibited. When you think about Salisbury, it was so absolutely shocking we almost lack the terminology to define it.'[15]

The Russian state has long been fuelling various forms of extremism in the UK as part of its information and influence operations. A report on extreme right-wing terrorism by parliament's Intelligence and Security Committee found that it has a 'longstanding history of using proxy actors to exert political influence and cause social unrest, and it is highly likely that it perceives exerting influence via far-right groups as an effective way to exacerbate tensions in the West'.[16] Russian disinformation campaigns using social networks and state-controlled media exploded in the wake of the 2017 terror attacks in London and Manchester. Researchers at Cardiff University found that 'sock puppet' Twitter accounts, controlled by the St Petersburg-based Internet Research Agency, tried to fuel social division and religious tensions—including by spreading a viral photograph falsely claiming to show a Muslim woman 'paying no mind to the terror attack, casually walking by a dying man' on Westminster Bridge.[17]

More and more seeds of grievance are being thrown into the wind, which now blows internationally. The effects can be seen in many attacks. The 2018 Christchurch shootings, for example, saw an Australian man massacre Muslims in New Zealand mosques, inspired by a conspiracy theory that originated in France, and using a gun with the name of a British town scarred by grooming gangs scratched into it. Numerous attacks have been launched in the UK as revenge for civilian deaths in Syria, Iraq and Afghanistan, by people who have no connection to the countries but feel they must act as part of a global Muslim community. The British security services talk of 'micro' and 'macro' motivations—the individual and the transnational over-arching narratives that dominate terrorist propaganda on all sides. In 2021, an assessment by the Homeland Security Group—which brings together intelligence agencies, counter-terrorism police and government departments—warned: 'Given that the current threat is predominantly from self-initiated terrorists, not groups, individual micro motivations (e.g. an individual's employment status) are as likely to influence the threat as macro ones (e.g. increasing levels of immigration into Europe).'[18]

There is no shortage of either type of motivation, and the intensifying cost-of-living crisis is expected to fan the flames. The same Homeland Security Group report warned that 'economic decline caused by Covid-19 is a likely driver of increased threat', and the UK's financial situation has worsened significantly since it was written. As Europol forecast in its 2022 annual terrorist threat assessment:

> Although social, political and economic inequalities are neither necessary nor sufficient to fuel radicalisation process [sic] among individuals, violent extremist groups may use perceived inequalities to promote divisive messages, and exacerbate polarisation and further violent extremism in societies … The increasing cost of living, combined with the new challenges to the economy posed by the Russian war of aggression against Ukraine, may be used as leverage in terrorist and violent extremist groups' propaganda to promote their narratives and undermine societal shared values.[19]

As well as individual grievances, the security services perceive a deepening anti-establishment sentiment from all political tribes in Britain, fuelled by mounting anger and distrust at the government. Other threat drivers included 'identity politics', a reduction in trust in the state and mainstream institutions, including reputable news outlets, and the increasing prevalence and reach of conspiracy theories.

Since the start of the coronavirus pandemic in early 2020, the online visibility of such theories has exploded. Jacob Davey, who has been tracking the phenomenon for the Institute for Strategic Dialogue, says Covid had sparked the 'coming together of quite loose communities, which manage to bridge the gap between extremist movements on the right, established conspiracy theorist movements and the anti-vaxx community, and the left'. Some factions used the pandemic to leverage hatred against Jews, Muslims and other minorities, while a common denominator has been the 'widespread and rampant amplification of disinformation'. Davey says the burgeoning conspiracy theorist scene is a 'movement of the likes we have never seen before, a physical manifestation of the online world'.[20]

While no incidents related to the Covid anti-vaxx movement in Britain have yet been declared as terrorist in nature by police, it has generated threats of violence towards healthcare workers, arson attacks, vandalism and intimidation targeting vaccination facilities, as well as threats towards healthcare workers. In Germany, a man embedded in far-right and conspiracy theorist Telegram communities shot a petrol station attendant dead after being asked to wear a face mask in September 2021. Davey's colleague, Milo Comerford, warns that the dropping of Covid-related restrictions has not dissolved online conspiracist movements, but merely seen them pivot towards broader talking points such as the 'new world order', 5G and climate change. 'This will be impacting our lives in different ways for years and years,' Comerford says. 'The pandemic provided the platform and opportunity to mainstream ideas to a wider audience. Pandora's box has been opened.'[21]

Dame Sara Khan, who formerly headed Britain's Commission for Countering Extremism, says conspiracy theories can be one manifestation of broader narratives that drive terrorism in the UK. 'There is an entire space of underlying extremism that doesn't cross over into terrorism but is creating an environment that's conducive to it,' she explains.

> You've got extremist organisations who don't advocate violence but are promoting the same ideology, the same narratives, as terrorists. They are radicalising people into hateful extremism, recruiting people to those causes, spreading that ideology and inevitably some people will then get pushed into terrorism.[22]

Khan, currently the British government's independent adviser on social cohesion and resilience, warns that there is 'no legal or operational framework' to deal with the issue, and that efforts to fix it by introducing more and more counter-terror laws have been failing. Her work has found that as well as the terror threat, hateful extremists are also driving wider harmful activity such as abuse, harassment and intimidation, while exacerbating racial and religious tensions and driving local communities apart.

Tackling extremism and the harm it causes outside of terrorism was one of the core aims of the Commission for Countering Extremism.[23] It was set up by the British government with great fanfare in the months following the wave of terror attacks that struck Britain in 2017, but then ignored by ministers. In February 2021, Khan co-authored a review with Sir Mark Rowley that warned that extremists were still 'operating with impunity' and exploiting gaps between hate crime and terror laws. Their report suggested that some terrorists, such as the ringleader of the London Bridge attack, could have been arrested earlier if tighter laws had been in place, and made a series of urgent recommendations for change.[24] Two years later, there has been no response from the government. It has also failed to act on the commission's flagship report from October 2019, which called for significant action including the adoption of a suggested definition of hateful extremism that could be used by police, authorities and social media companies to clamp down on it.[25] The commission has appealed for the government to implement its recommendations and 'take this threat to our citizens, our communities and our democracy seriously',[26] but the warnings have not triggered any response. Khan says the government must finally act, not only to tackle existing extremism but to futureproof the UK against emerging threats, adding:

> If the government has a very clear position on hateful extremism and a legal and operational infrastructure to tackle it, it doesn't matter if that activity is what we understand extremism to be in the traditional sense, or it is coming from hateful conspiracy movements, or some other weird, wacky, new thing that might emerge in two years' time.[27]

The possibilities for new types of terror attacks, against new targets, by new groups of plotters, are endless but the security services' resources are finite and prioritisation has to occur. For MI5, that means balancing its responsibility for counter-terrorism against its responsibility for hostile state threats and espionage. Extra demand was also added when primacy for handling the far right and other domestic terror threats was fully handed over by police in 2020.

MI5's G Branch, which deals with terrorism, remains extremely busy but since the Ukraine invasion and an uptick in hostile activity by China, the work for its K Branch, which deals with state threats, has increased dramatically. Giving a speech alongside the director of America's FBI in July 2022, MI5 director general Ken McCallum admitted that his agency was 'having to stretch itself as never before—in multiple different directions'. He said:

> While our countries strain every sinew to support Ukraine in resisting appalling overt aggression, we're also working to safeguard our homelands from covert threats from the Kremlin. Meanwhile, MI5's counter-terrorist work remains intense. Syria, Somalia and Afghanistan continue to generate threats. Our most immediate UK challenge is lone terrorists—Islamist extremist and right-wing extremist—radicalised online, acting at pace, in unpredictable ways.[28]

Whatever subset or mix of extremism they are driven by, the plots of the future will be dominantly driven by online radicalisation. As the cases in this book show, real-world planning and networking increases the risk of detection, and terrorists are becoming wise to that risk. The online world, with its police role-players, undercover agents and security monitoring, is not risk-free but remains the easiest and most effective way of acquiring the motivation and means to carry out a terror attack. The past decade has seen intensifying efforts to take terrorist propaganda and extremist material off mainstream internet platforms and social networks, starting with Isis and spreading to the far-right. But the efforts merely promoted the creation of 'replacement platforms' that deliberately shun moderation and refuse to co-operate with requests by international governments and law enforcement.

Julia Ebner, who plunged into internet subcultures for her book *Going Dark: The Secret Social Lives of Extremists*, describes a 'whole alternate universe' that has been built online. She says different tribes of extremists have created or hijacked their own social media networks, crowdsourcing platforms and even dating websites, meaning they can operate almost entirely in a 'disinformation ecosystem' where their views are not challenged. Although she does believe in the value of removing radicalising and hateful content, she also warns of the adverse effects. Ebner explains:

One of the biggest negative consequences is it's got a lot harder for the security services to really keep an overview of what's happening. It suddenly became a lot more chaotic because you have all these encrypted small groups where people might be plotting attacks and if you don't happen to have someone undercover in there, you're just not going to know about it. That has been a major risk factor that has come out of the removal policies.[29]

A 2022 report by parliament's Intelligence and Security Committee warned that propaganda and rhetoric posted on both mainstream and ideologically specific social media networks 'could inspire a self-initiated terrorist to commit an attack'. It said that following a succession of takedowns, extremists no longer felt the need to 'self-censor' on mainstream social media platforms in a bid to retain a presence. Instead, they can use 'safe havens' such as Telegram for networking and more direct expressions of their views. Far-right extremists in particular have embraced fringe social networks and forums, such as the Twitter-esque Gab website and 8kun, formerly known as 8chan.

However, in late 2022, there was much excitement in extremist circles about the prospect of a 'Twitter amnesty' following the platform's takeover by billionaire Elon Musk. Several groups and prominent figures who were previously banned under hate speech policies attempted to have their accounts reopened, or to start new ones, but saw little immediate success. In an email to followers in December 2022, far-right group Britain First said 'social media alternatives' like Gab, Gettr or Telegram were not enough. It explicitly admitted that mainstream takedowns had stifled its reach and created 'very small right-wing echo chambers', adding:

> The ordinary man and woman on the streets across Britain are not on those platforms. The only noteworthy users of the alternative platforms are existing nationalists and patriots, those who are already signed up to our accounts and who already follow our party ... we need to get back to where we used to be, reaching millions of ordinary Britons every week. The only way we can do that is to get back on the mainstream social networks.[30]

Such overt outreach tends to be the preserve of extremist groups that stop short of direct support for terrorism, while those following explicitly violent ideologies are more likely to hide from the authorities online. Evidence suggests that many young neo-Nazis have at least a rudimentary knowledge of the 'dark web' and use of Virtual Private Networks, which encrypt online activities to make users anonymous and make their activity harder to track.[31]

The security services expect gaming platforms to play a greater role in future extreme right-wing terrorism. A 2021 assessment by the UK's Homeland Security group said that young people interested in far-right ideas were 'over-represented' in the gaming space, and that some platforms facilitate online radicalisation. In-built text and voice chat facilities can be used as an alternative means of communication and to recruit new followers and disseminate propaganda. Discord, designed initially for the gaming community, has had its ability to build private, invite-only groups hijacked by neo-Nazis and white nationalists. The Steam, Twitch and DLive gaming platforms have also been used. The UK's Joint Terrorism Analysis Centre assesses that:

> It is plausible that some right-wing terrorists began using Discord due to a background in online gaming. This is reflected in the common parlance of right-wing terrorists, where phrases such as 'NPC' (Non-Player Character) are used to refer to an individual who does not partake in enough right-wing terrorist activity. John Earnest, the San Diego shooter, made reference to getting a 'high score' (by context, causing many deaths) in the letter he released prior to carrying out his attack.[32]

Researchers at the Institute for Strategic Dialogue found little evidence that the games being played were themselves part of serious strategies to radicalise and recruit new people, but said that gaming and the culture around it are used 'primarily as a way of finding common ground'.[33]

As they move into more secretive online spaces, terrorists are set to move even further away from involvement with or direct affiliation to groups. Isis has already pioneered a hands-off approach to directing and inspiring attacks by its followers, with none of the plotters who wanted to act in its name in this book being a 'member' in any meaningful sense. Far-right groups are now moving in the same direction, following intensifying moves by British authorities to ban neo-Nazi terrorist organisations and arrest and prosecute members. The UK's Joint Terrorism Analysis Centre, led by MI5, assesses that the 'external pressures' from waves of legal proscription and arrests has 'resulted in individuals active in the online space becoming increasingly cautious about joining established terrorist groups'.[34] While having a positive outcome in hampering the organised activity of organisations like National Action and allowing the prosecution of members and influential figures, the bans further reduce the security services' ability to infiltrate terrorist networks and detect plots. In two cases in this book alone, plotters were chanced upon by undercover police who had been deployed to broadly monitor the neo-Nazi groups they had joined on Telegram, while a third attack was thwarted after police worked their way into a jihadist chat. If terrorists move completely away from those formal or informal online groupings, the loss of intelligence could be catastrophic.

Terrorists are also learning from each other's mistakes. Ali Harbi Ali, an Isis supporter who murdered a Conservative MP in October 2021, told police how he researched previous attacks in London, Manchester and across Europe 'as sort of examples'. Ali selected a soft target, an unguarded constituency surgery inside a methodist church in the quiet Essex town of Leigh-on-Sea, for his attack. He decided to 'keep shtum' about his aspirations and views, telling police he was careful not to discuss his attack plans with anyone because he had seen news of 'so many raids' on other terror plotters. 'As soon as you open up that sort of other person you're twice as, sort of, susceptible to being found out,' he added. 'People can turn, y'know?'[35] In some cases, the learning happens in person, such as Buckingham Palace attacker Mohiussunnath Chowdhury's court coaching from his 'like-minded brothers' inside HMP Belmarsh.

Haydon says that new plots are still being foiled 'all the time' and attacks were even thwarted during the Covid pandemic. The security services are alive to a 'copycat attack issue', after runs of successful and attempted attacks using similar methods and targets such as knife rampages at crowded London landmarks, vehicle-rammings on bridges and terrorists using fake suicide vests to delay intervention in their atrocities. 'We're always alive to the fact that when an attack happens, is there another attack coming, does it galvanise other individuals?' Haydon asks.[36] Recalling his time as head of UK counter-terrorism policing, Sir Mark Rowley feels there is 'an expectation that none of this will ever happen, that you'll stop everything. The politicians want perfection, the public wants perfection. You are aiming for perfection but everyone knows that it isn't quite possible'.[37] In private, counter-terror police and MI5 agents admit that perfect coverage does not exist, that they can never understand the totality of an individual's intentions and capabilities, that their resources only stretch so far. In public, they tend to be much more defensive.

A public inquiry into the Manchester Arena bombing that began in 2020 is considering whether failings by MI5 contributed to the deaths of 22 victims, including children. The service received two pieces of intelligence on Salman Abedi, who had already appeared on the radar for links to Isis supporters, in the months prior to the attack, but did not share them with police or open an investigation. He was able to travel to and from Libya while preparing for the attack, and stored the components of a huge bomb in a car parked in plain sight on a housing estate. While being questioned by a lawyer representing bereaved families, an MI5 officer repeatedly refused to agree that the agency had 'failed'.[38]

The atrocities of 2017 prompted an internal review of how MI5 and counter-terror police detect and prevent terror attacks in the UK. It sparked significant changes to the way the security services worked together, monitored closed 'subjects of interest' and divided up responsibility for jihadists and far-right terrorists. An unclassified review of progress in 2019 said a 'stepped-up radar' was being put in place, which attempts to use data to identify emerging threats and set 'tripwires' that will flag preparations for attacks. David Anderson KC, the former Independent Reviewer of Terrorism Legislation who carried out the review, wrote: 'Though it will never be possible to prevent every attack, the measures being taken will, in my opinion, strengthen the existing ability of MI5 and CTP to stop most of them.' Agencies have been experimenting with using artificial intelligence and behavioural analytics to assess existing SOIs and discover new leads—searching for 'pre-attack behaviour, such as attempts to obtain firearms or researching attack methodologies'.[39]

Rowley believes that the world of counter-terrorism is switching from a case-by-case approach to a 'volume business'. 'The volumes of potential threats are so big just nosing case by case with humans isn't enough,' he says:

> Where we know someone is up to something and we're after them, the system works. But you've got thousands of lower-priority investigations and then tens of thousands who are not in investigations but have some form of ideological support for terrorism, they're just not acting on it. It's in those thousands and tens of thousands that somebody's life changes. Spotting the one who's making that transition is a completely different task than just dealing with old-fashioned al-Qaeda or IRA networks.[40]

The security services were caught off-guard by the 2017 attacks, and then were too slow to adapt to the changing landscape of terrorism in the UK. The question is how quickly they will adapt to what comes next.

TIMELINE OF TERROR ATTACKS IN BRITAIN
SINCE 2017

Terrorist incidents declared by police in Britain between March 2017 and December 2022.

22 March 2017: Westminster attack

Khalid Masood used a car to plough into pedestrians on Westminster Bridge, before attacking a police officer guarding the Houses of Parliament with a knife. He was shot dead by police at the scene.

Deaths: Five victims, one perpetrator

Ideology: Jihadist

Weapons: Car and knife

Perpetrator: Khalid Masood, 52, British citizen

Status at time of attack: Closed MI5 subject of interest, previous criminal convictions

22 May 2017: Manchester Arena bombing

Salman Abedi detonated a large homemade pressure cooker bomb among crowds of people leaving an Ariana Grande concert at Manchester Arena. He was carrying the bomb in a rucksack and died at the scene.

Deaths: 22 victims, one perpetrator

Ideology: Jihadist

Weapons: Bomb

Perpetrator: Salman Abedi, 22, British citizen

Status at time of attack: Closed MI5 subject of interest, previous criminal cautions

3 June 2017: London Bridge and Borough Market attack

Khuram Butt, Rachid Redouane and Youssef Zaghba used a van to plough into pedestrians on London Bridge, before going on a knife rampage targeting people around bars and restaurants in nearby Borough Market. They were shot dead by police at the scene.

Deaths: Eight victims, three perpetrators

Ideology: Jihadist

Weapons: Van and knives

Perpetrator: Khuram Butt, 27-year-old British citizen born in Pakistan, Rachid Redouane, 30-year-old Moroccan citizen, Youssef Zaghba, 22-year-old Italian-Moroccan citizen

Status at time of attack: Butt—open subject of interest (SOI) with previous criminal cautions. Redouane—never an SOI, known to police in Morocco. Zaghba—never an SOI and no criminal record

19 June 2017: Finsbury Park mosque attack

Darren Osborne ploughed a van into a crowd of Muslims who were leaving prayers near two mosques in Finsbury Park. He was detained by survivors and arrested at the scene.

Deaths: One victim

Ideology: Extreme right-wing

Weapon: Van

Perpetrator: Darren Osborne, 47, British citizen

Status at time of attack: Never a subject of interest, previous criminal convictions

15 September 2017: Parsons Green attack

Ahmed Hassan left a homemade bomb on a rush-hour London Underground train, set to detonate on a timer. The bomb malfunctioned and he was arrested while trying to flee the UK.

Deaths: None

Ideology: Jihadist

Weapons: Bomb

Perpetrator: Ahmed Hassan, 18 (disputed), Iraqi citizen

Status at time of attack: Not an open subject of interest, no previous convictions

14 August 2018: Westminster car attack

Salih Khater ploughed a car through cyclists waiting at traffic lights outside the Houses of Parliament, driving towards police officers before hitting a metal security barrier. He was arrested at the scene.

Deaths: None

Ideology: Unconfirmed

Weapons: Car

Perpetrator: Salih Khater, 29, British citizen born in Somalia

Status at time of attack: Not an open subject of interest, no previous convictions

31 December 2018: Manchester Victoria railway station attack

Mahdi Mohamud stabbed a man and woman at Manchester Victoria railway station on New Year's Eve, before turning the knife on a police officer who tried to subdue him. He was arrested at the scene.

Deaths: None

Ideology: Jihadist

Weapons: Knife

Perpetrator: Mahdi Mohamud, 25, Dutch citizen

Status at time of attack: Not an open subject of interest, known to police in Somalia

16 March 2019: Stanwell attack

A day after the Christchurch mosque shootings, Vincent Fuller attacked cars with non-white drivers with a baseball bat in Stanwell, Surrey, then prowled the streets armed with a knife and stabbed a man he believed to be Muslim. He was arrested at the scene.

Deaths: None

Ideology: Extreme right-wing

Weapons: Knife, baseball bat

Perpetrator: Vincent Fuller, 50, British citizen

Status at time of attack: Never a subject of interest, previous criminal convictions

9 November 2019: Fishmongers' Hall attack

Usman Khan launched a knife attack at a prison education event, targeting people associated with the Cambridge University Learning Together programme he had attended in jail. He was chased outside by attendees and shot dead by police on London Bridge.

Deaths: Two victims, one perpetrator

Ideology: Jihadist

Weapons: Knife, fake suicide vest

Perpetrator: Usman Khan, 28, British citizen

Status at time of attack: Open subject of interest, previous terror convictions

9 January 2020: HMP Whitemoor attack

Brusthom Ziamani and Baz Hockton attempted to murder a prison officer at the high-security HMP Whitemoor prison in Cambridgeshire. They were overpowered by his colleagues and prosecuted.

Deaths: None

Ideology: Jihadist

Weapons: Homemade bladed weapons, fake suicide vests

Perpetrators: Brusthom Ziamani, a 24-year-old British citizen, and Baz Hockton, a 26-year-old British citizen.

Status at time of attack: Ziamani—a closed or low-priority subject of interest, previous terror convictions and admitted involvement in robbery and fraud. Hockton—unknown to security services, previous criminal convictions

2 February 2020: Streatham attack

While being trailed by armed police, Sudesh Amman stole a knife from a hardware shop and launched a stabbing attack on members of the public on a high street in south London. He was shot dead at the scene.

Deaths: No victims, one perpetrator

Ideology: Jihadist

Weapons: Knife

Perpetrator: Sudesh Amman, 20, British citizen

Status at time of attack: Open priority one subject of interest, previous terror convictions

20 June 2020: Reading attack

Khairi Saadallah launched a stabbing attack in a park in Reading, targeting groups of friends who were socialising after coronavirus lockdown laws were eased. He was arrested near the scene.

Deaths: Three victims

Ideology: Jihadist

Weapons: Knife

Perpetrator: Khairi Saadallah, 25, Libyan citizen

Status at time of attack: Open subject of interest, previous criminal convictions

15 October 2021: Sir David Amess murder

Ali Harbi Ali stabbed Conservative MP Sir David Amess to death after booking an appointment at a regular session for his constituents in Leigh-on-Sea, Essex. He was arrested at the scene.

Deaths: One victim

Ideology: Jihadist

Weapons: Knife

Perpetrator: Ali Harbi Ali, 25, British citizen

Status at time of attack: Not a subject of interest but referred to Prevent, no convictions

14 November 2021: Liverpool Women's Hospital bombing

On Remembrance Sunday, Emad al-Swealmeen got into a taxi carrying a homemade bomb and asked to be taken to Liverpool Women's Hospital. His device partially detonated as the car pulled up at the entrance, while he was still inside the vehicle.

Deaths: One perpetrator

Ideology: Unconfirmed

Weapons: Bomb

Perpetrator: Emad al-Swealmeen, 32, Jordanian citizen

Status at time of attack: Not a subject of interest, previous criminal convictions

30 October 2022: Dover firebombing

A man drove 120 miles from his home in High Wycombe to the coastal town of Dover, where he threw homemade firebombs at a reception facility for asylum seekers crossing the English Channel in small boats. The devices set alight the barriers around the centre, but only caused minor injuries. The attacker drove to a nearby petrol station and killed himself.

Deaths: One perpetrator

Ideology: Extreme right-wing

Weapons: Homemade incendiary devices

Perpetrator: Andrew Leak, 66, British citizen

Status at time of attack: Not a subject of interest, previous criminal convictions

NOTES

INTRODUCTION

1. Chief Coroner of England and Wales: 'Inquests Arising from the Deaths in the Westminster Terror Attack of 22 March 2017: Regulation 28 Report on Action to Prevent Future Deaths', December 2018, page 2.
2. Speech by Neil Basu at the National Security Summit, London, 9 October 2018.
3. Speech by Ken McCallum, London, 16 November 2022.
4. Speech by Ken McCallum, London, 14 July 2021.
5. Westminster Bridge inquests, transcript of evidence heard on 12 October 2018.
6. Anderson, D., 'Attacks in London and Manchester, March–June 2017', December 2017, page 13.
7. Westminster Bridge inquests, transcript of evidence heard on 26 September 2018.
8. Author interview with Dean Haydon, New Scotland Yard, London, 26 May 2022.
9. English translation of Zawahiri's letter to Zarqawi published by the US military academy's Combating Terrorism Center. Available at: https://ctc.usma.edu/harmony-program/zawahiris-letter-to-zarqawi-original-language-2/
10. Statement by Isis spokesman Abu Muhammad al-Adnani, 22 September 2014. Translated into English by Pieter Van Ostaeyen.
11. 'HM Government Transparency Report: Disruptive Powers 2018/19', March 2020, page 31.
12. Anderson, D., 'Attacks in London and Manchester', page 70.
13. Intelligence and Security Committee of Parliament, 'Extreme Right-Wing Terrorism', July 2022, page 83.
14. Author interview with Dean Haydon, London, 20 December 2021.
15. Author interview with Sir Mark Rowley, London, 14 March 2022.

PART ONE: NIPPED IN THE BUD: FALSE FRIENDS AND FAILURES

1. 'I-S-I-S, YOU LIKE THAT?': THE 2017 DOMINO EFFECT

1. Author interview with Sir Mark Rowley, London, 14 March 2022.

2. Statement by Isis spokesman Abu Muhammad al-Adnani, 22 September 2014. Translated into English by Pieter Van Ostaeyen.

3. Author interview with Dean Haydon, London, 20 December 2021.

4. White House transcript of remarks by President Barack Obama on 30 September 2011.

5. Author interview with Alexander Meleagrou-Hitchens, conducted via video call on 5 March 2022.

6. Meleagrou-Hitchens, 2020, *Incitement: Anwar al-Awlaki's Western Jihad*, Harvard University Press.

7. Issue 1 of AQAP propaganda magazine *Inspire*, July 2010.

8. 9/11 Commission Report, chapter 7. Available at: https://govinfo.library.unt.edu/911/report/911Report_Ch7.htm

9. Anwar al-Awlaki, *44 Ways to Support Jihad*.

10. Issue 2 of Isis propaganda magazine *Rumiyah*, October 2016.

11. Issues 2 and 3 of Isis propaganda magazine *Rumiyah*, October and November 2016.

12. Author interview with Sir Mark Rowley.

13. Author interview with Dean Haydon.

14. Hill, M., 'The Terrorism Acts in 2016: Report of the Independent Reviewer of Terrorism Legislation', January 2018, page 60.

15. R v Haroon Ali Syed, transcript of sentencing remarks by Judge Michael Topolski KC at the Central Criminal Court on 3 July 2017.

16. Ibid.

17. Court of Appeal judgment in R v Haroon Ali Syed. [2018] EWCA Crim 2809 (18 December 2018).

18. 'CONTEST: The United Kingdom's Strategy for Countering Terrorism', June 2018, page 18.

19. Author interview with Sir Mark Rowley.

20. Speech by Neil Basu at the National Security Summit, London, 9 October 2018.

21. Author interview with Dean Haydon.

22. R v Abuthather Mamun et al., transcript of sentencing remarks by Mr Justice Haddon-Cave at the Central Criminal Court on 27 March 2018.

23. Statement by Isis spokesman Abu Muhammad al-Adnani, 21 May 2016. Translated into English by Isis.

24. It was not argued in court or elsewhere what 'it' referred to.

25. Prosecution opening note in Abuthather Mamun et al. Delivered at the Central Criminal Court on 9 January 2018.

26. R v Abuthather Mamun et al. sentencing remarks.

27. Prosecution opening note in R v Munir Mohammed and Rowaida el-Hassan. Delivered at the Central Criminal Court on 19 October 2017.

28. R v Munir Mohammed and Rowaida el-Hassan, transcript of sentencing remarks by Judge Michael Topolski KC at the Central Criminal Court on 28 February 2018.

29. BBC News: 'West Yorkshire family fear Iraq suicide bomber was son', 22 March 2016. https://www.bbc.co.uk/news/uk-england-leeds-35876460

30. R v Mohammed Abbas Idris Awan, transcript of sentencing remarks by Judge Watson KC at Sheffield Crown Court on 20 December 2017.

31. Bryson, R. (2017) 'For Caliph and Country: Exploring how British jihadis join a global movement'. Available at: https://institute.global/policy/caliph-and-country-exploring-how-british-jihadis-join-global-movement

32. *How to Survive in the West: A Mujahid Guide (2015).*

33. Prosecution opening note in R v Farhad Salah and Andy Star. Delivered at Sheffield Crown Court on 3 June 2019.

34. Author interview with Detective Chief Superintendent Martin Snowden, conducted by telephone, 8 July 2019.

35. R v Farhad Salah and Andy Star, transcript of sentencing remarks by Judge Paul Watson KC at Sheffield Crown Court on 24 July 2019.

36. Kenney, M., 'What is to be done about al-Muhajiroun? Containing the emigrants in a democratic society', October 2019, page 1.

37. HMG list of proscribed terrorist groups or organisations. Available at: https://www.gov.uk/government/publications/proscribed-terror-groups-or-organisations—2/proscribed-terrorist-groups-or-organisations-accessible-version

38. Kenney, M., 'What is to be done about al-Muhajiroun?', page 12.

39. R v Lewis Ludlow, transcript of sentencing remarks by Judge Nicholas Hilliard KC at the Central Criminal Court on 6 March 2019.

40. Author's email correspondence with Dr Michael Kenney, 11 August 2018.

41. Prosecution opening note in R v Lewis Ludlow. Delivered at the Central Criminal Court on 1 October 2018.

42. R v Lewis Ludlow sentencing remarks.

43. Speech by Ken McCallum, London, 16 November 2022.

44. Sudesh Amman inquest, transcript of evidence heard at the Royal Courts of Justice on 3 August 2021.

45. Azazel Anti Jihad Blogger, 8 April 2018. Available at: http://azazelantijihadblogger.blogspot.com/2018/04/speakers-corner-in-hyde-park-londen.html

46. Counter Terrorism Policing statement on Streatham incident, 3 February 2020. Available at https://www.counterterrorism.police.uk/streatham/

47. Author's notes of evidence heard at the Sudesh Amman inquest on 3 August 2021.

48. Author's notes of evidence heard at the Sudesh Amman inquest on 5 August 2021.

49. Author's notes of verdict in the Sudesh Amman inquest on 20 August 2021.

50. Author interview with Jonathan Hall KC, 6KBW College Hill, London, 10 May 2022.

2. REVENGE, RAMIFICATIONS AND THE RISE OF THE NEO-NAZIS

1. Author's notes of evidence heard in R v Darren Osborne at Woolwich Crown Court on 23 January 2018.

2. Prosecution opening note in R v Steven Bishop. Delivered at Kingston Crown Court on 8 April 2019.

3. R v Steven Bishop, transcript of sentencing remarks by Judge Peter Lodder KC at Kingston Crown Court on 11 April 2019.

4. https://twitter.com/i/events/867116415752568832

5. Author interview with Julia Ebner, London, 2 March 2022.

6. Brenton Tarrant's manifesto.

7. Author interview with Matthew Feldman, York, 7 January 2022.

8. Southern Poverty Law Centre: James Mason. Available at: https://www.splcenter.org/fighting-hate/extremist-files/individual/james-mason

9. *Siege* by James Mason.

10. Author interview with Detective Chief Superintendent Kenny Bell, head of Counter Terrorism Policing West Midlands, conducted by telephone on 12 March 2020.

11. Prosecution opening note in R v Jack Reed. Delivered at Manchester Crown Court on 10 October 2019.

12. R v Jack Reed, transcript of sentencing remarks by Judge David Stockdale KC at Manchester Crown Court on 7 January 2020.

13. Hall, J., 'The Terrorism Acts in 2020: Report of the Independent Reviewer of Terrorism Legislation', April 2022, page 95.

14. Speech by Jonathan Hall KC at Bright Blue event, London, 7 July 2021.

15. Author interview with Jonathan Hall KC, 6KBW College Hill, London, 10 May 2022.

16. R v Paul Dunleavy, transcript of sentencing remarks by Judge Paul Farrer KC at Birmingham Crown Court on 6 November 2020.

17. Prosecution opening note in R v Paul Dunleavy. Delivered at Birmingham Crown Court on 17 August 2020.

18. R v Paul Dunleavy sentencing remarks.

19. R v Paul Dunleavy, perfected advice and perfected grounds of appeal against conviction, presented at the Court of Appeal on 19 May 2020.

20. Court of Appeal judgment in R v Paul Dunleavy. [2021] EWCA Crim 39 (21 January 2021).
21. Copy of Stephan Balliet's 9 October 2019 post on Meguca, supplied to author by Dr Rajan Basra, senior research fellow at the International Centre for the Study of Radicalisation.
22. Koehler, D., 'The Halle, Germany, Synagogue Attack and the Evolution of the Far-Right Terror Threat'. *CTC Sentinel*, Volume 12, Issue 11, December 2019.
23. Counter Terrorism Police South East press release: 'Extreme right-wing terrorist sentenced to 23 years following trial—Somerset', 14 June 2021.
24. Prosecution opening note in R v Samuel Whibley et al. Delivered at Sheffield Crown Court on 20 January 2022.
25. Prosecution opening note in R v Matthew Cronjager. Delivered at the Central Criminal Court on 24 August 2021.
26. R v Matthew Cronjager, transcript of sentencing remarks by Judge Mark Lucraft KC at the Central Criminal Court on 19 October 2021.

PART TWO: ARMS RACE: INTERCEPTING ADVANCED PLOTS

3. BLINDSPOTS AND BUGS

1. Intelligence and Security Committee of Parliament, 'Extreme Right-Wing Terrorism', July 2022, page 83.
2. Intelligence and Security Committee of Parliament, 'Extreme Right-Wing Terrorism', page 84.
3. Anderson, D., 'Attacks in London and Manchester, March–June 2017', December 2017, page 8.
4. 'HM Government Transparency Report: Disruptive Powers 2018/19', March 2020, page 31.
5. Intelligence and Security Committee of Parliament, 'The 2017 Attacks: What needs to change?', November 2018, page 64.
6. Anderson, D., 'Attacks in London and Manchester', page 8.
7. Author interview with Dean Haydon, New Scotland Yard, London, 26 May 2022.
8. Transcripts of police interviews with Ali Harbi Ali, as shown in evidence to the trial of R v Ali Harbi Ali at the Central Criminal Court on 25 March 2022.
9. Author interview with Sir Mark Rowley, London, 14 March 2022.
10. West Midlands Counter Terrorism Unit press release: 'Four men have been jailed for plotting to carry out a terrorist attack in the UK', 3 August 2017.

11. R v Naweed Ali, Khobaib Hussain, Mohibur Rahman and Tahir Aziz, transcript of sentencing remarks by Mr Justice Globe at the Central Criminal Court on 3 August 2017.
12. Author interview with Alexander Meleagrou-Hitchens, conducted via video call, 5 March 2022.
13. R v Naweed Ali, Khobaib Hussain, Mohibur Rahman and Tahir Aziz sentencing remarks.
14. Court of Appeal judgment in R v Aziz et al. [2018] EWCA Crim 2412 (2 November 2018).
15. Casciani, D., BBC News: 'Birmingham terror plot: Inside the sting that caught four jihadis', 2 August 2017.
16. R v Naweed Ali, Khobaib Hussain, Mohibur Rahman and Tahir Aziz sentencing remarks.
17. Ministry of Justice: 'Summary of the main findings of the review of Islamist extremism in prisons, probation and youth justice led by Ian Acheson', August 2016.
18. Author interview with Ian Acheson, London, 2 March 2022.
19. Author interview with Sir Mark Rowley.
20. Author interview with Peter Clarke, conducted via telephone, 21 February 2022.
21. Home Office: Operation of police powers under the Terrorism Act 2000 and subsequent legislation: Arrests, outcomes, and stop and search, Great Britain, quarterly update to September 2022. Available at: https://www.gov.uk/government/statistics/operation-of-police-powers-under-the-terrorism-act-2000-quarterly-update-to-september-2022/operation-of-police-powers-under-the-terrorism-act-2000-and-subsequent-legislation-arrests-outcomes-and-stop-and-search-great-britain-quarterly-u
22. Author interview with Jonathan Hall KC, conducted by telephone, 25 January 2021.
23. Hall, J., 'Terrorism in Prisons', April 2022, page 3.
24. Hall, J., 'Terrorism in Prisons', page 15.
25. 'Hansard: Terrorism in Prisons Update', statement made by Dominic Raab on 27 April 2022.
26. Ministry of Justice: 'Tackling Terrorism in Prisons: A Response to the Independent Reviewer of Terrorism Legislation's Review of Terrorism in Prisons', April 2022, page 21.
27. Author interview with Jonathan Hall KC, 6KBW College Hill, London, 10 May 2022.
28. British National Party 2010 general election manifesto. Available at: https://general-election-2010.co.uk/bnp-manifesto-2010-general-election/bnp-manifesto-2010-british-national-party-key-pledges/

29. BNP Youth—Fight Back, May 2014. Removed from YouTube because of hate speech but available at: https://web.archive.org/web/20140611143903/https://www.youtube.com/watch?v=oczj6thd4CY

30. https://twitter.com/labourpurges/status/486912195201339393

31. Local Elections Archive Project: Local by-elections, 9 October 2014, Blackpool—Waterloo. Available at: https://www.andrewteale.me.uk/leap/by/201-10-09/

32. Author's email correspondence with BNP press officer David Furness, 3 April 2019.

33. Prosecution opening note in R v Alex Davies. Delivered at Winchester Crown Court on 20 April 2022.

34. Prosecution opening note in R v Ben Raymond. Delivered at Bristol Crown Court on 2 November 2021.

35. Ibid.

36. Home Office press release: 'National Action becomes first extreme right-wing group to be banned in UK', 16 December 2016.

37. Initial details of prosecution case in R v Jack Renshaw and others. Delivered at Westminster Magistrates' Court on 27 October 2017.

38. Author interview with Robbie Mullen, Warrington, 4 January 2022.

39. Author notes of R v Ben Raymond trial, 4 November 2021.

40. Prosecution opening note in R v Jack Renshaw and others. Delivered at the Central Criminal Court on 18 February 2019.

41. Author interview with Robbie Mullen.

42. Initial details of prosecution case in R v Jack Renshaw and others.

43. R v Jack Renshaw, sentencing remarks by Mrs Justice McGowan, at the Central Criminal Court on 17 May 2019.

44. Author interview with Sir Mark Rowley.

45. Author interview with Dean Haydon, and speech by Ken McCallum, London, 16 November 2022.

46. Speech by Ken McCallum, London, 14 July 2021.

47. Author interview with Matthew Feldman, York, 7 January 2022.

48. Author research using Wayback Machine.

49. Prosecution opening note in R v Alex Davies.

50. Prosecution opening note in R v Andrew Dymock. Delivered at the Central Criminal Court on 6 May 2021.

51. HMG list of proscribed terrorist groups or organisations. Available at: https://www.gov.uk/government/publications/proscribed-terror-groups-or-organisations—2/proscribed-terrorist-groups-or-organisations-accessible-version

52. Intelligence and Security Committee of Parliament, 'Extreme Right-Wing Terrorism', July 2022, page 53.

53. Author interview with Matthew Feldman.

54. Author interview with Superintendent Anthony Tagg, conducted via telephone on 12 May 2022.

4. CRIMINAL PASTS, TERRORIST FUTURES

1. Prosecution opening note in R v Sahayb Abu and Muhamed Abu. Delivered at the Central Criminal Court on 9 February 2021.
2. Prosecution opening in R v Abu and Abu.
3. The Counter Terrorism Division of the Crown Prosecution Service—successful prosecutions since 2016: R v Aweys, Munye and Aweys. Available at: https://www.cps.gov.uk/crime-info/terrorism/counter-terrorism-division-crown-prosecution-service-cps-successful-prosecutions-2016
4. *Ilford Recorder*: 'Jailed: Three family members including Chadwell Heath man sent to prison for owning Islamic State propaganda', 25 January 2019. Available at: https://www.ilfordrecorder.co.uk/news/2118 9559.jailed-three-family-members-including-chadwell-heath-man-sent-prison-owning-islamic-state-propaganda/
5. Prosecution opening in R v Abu and Abu.
6. Author's notes of evidence heard in R v Sahayb Abu at the Central Criminal Court on 17 February 2021.
7. Author's notes of evidence heard in R v Sahayb Abu at the Central Criminal Court on 23 February 2021.
8. R v Sahayb Abu, transcript of sentencing remarks by Judge Mark Dennis KC at the Central Criminal Court on 13 April 2021.
9. Author's notes of remarks by Commander Richard Smith, head of the Metropolitan Police Counter Terrorism Command, at a press conference on 5 March 2021.
10. Naweed Ali, Khobaib Hussain, Mohibur Rahman and Tahir Aziz, Khalid Masood, Salman Abedi, Khuram Butt and Rachid Redouane, Darren Osborne, Steven Bishop, Mahdi Mohamud, Vincent Fuller, Safiyya Shaikh, Usman Khan, Brusthom Ziamani and Baz Hockton, Sudesh Amman, Khairi Saadallah, Sahayb Abu, Emad al-Swealmeen.
11. Transcript of meeting between Sahayb Abu and Rachid on 30 June 2020.
12. Author interview with Rajan Basra, London, 3 March 2022.
13. Issue 4 of AQAP propaganda magazine *Inspire*, January 2011.
14. Author interview with Rajan Basra.
15. Issue 8 of Isis propaganda magazine *Rumiyah*, April 2017.
16. Author interview with Rajan Basra.
17. ICSR: 'Criminal Pasts, Terrorist Futures: European Jihadists and the New Crime-Terror Nexus', October 2016, page 44.

18. Intelligence and Security Committee of Parliament, 'The 2017 Attacks: What needs to change?', November 2018, page 85.
19. ICSR: 'Criminal Pasts, Terrorist Futures', page 24.
20. R v Safiyya Shaikh, sentencing remarks by Mr Justice Sweeney at the Central Criminal Court on 3 July 2020.
21. Basra, R: 'The YouTube Browsing Habits of a Lone-Actor Terrorist', 22 June 2020. https://gnet-research.org/2020/06/22/the-youtube-browsing-habits-of-a-lone-actor-terrorist/
22. Author's email correspondence with Metropolitan Police, 22 June 2020.
23. Author's notes of remarks by Commander Richard Smith, head of the Metropolitan Police Counter Terrorism Command, at a press conference on 18 June 2020.
24. Author's notes of sentencing hearing in R v Safiyya Shaikh at the Central Criminal Court on 2 July 2020.
25. R v Safiyya Shaikh, sentencing remarks by Mr Justice Sweeney.
26. Basra, R., 'Drugs and Terrorism: The Overlaps in Europe', November 2019, page 22.
27. Court of Appeal judgment in R v Mohammed Abdul Kahar and others. [2016] EWCA Crim 568, 17 May 2016.
28. Author, 'German police may have 'covered up' repeated failure to arrest Berlin attacker before Isis massacre', 18 May 2017. Available at https://www.independent.co.uk/news/world/europe/berlin-lorry-christmas-market-attack-anis-amri-germany-police-cover-up-failures-investigation-latest-a7743536.html
29. Basra, R., 'Drugs and Terrorism: The Overlaps in Europe', page 19.
30. Author interview with Rajan Basra, London, 3 March 2022.
31. Combating Terrorism Center: 'The Caliphate's Global Workforce: An Inside Look at the Islamic State's Foreign Fighter Paper Trail', April 2016, page 18.

5. LOVE AND LIES

1. Prosecution opening note in R v Madihah Taheer. Delivered at Woolwich Crown Court on 5 October 2017.
2. Casciani, C.: 'The Birmingham couple who put IS at the heart of marriage', BBC News, 26 October 2017.
3. Prosecution opening note in R v Madihah Taheer.
4. R v Ummariyat Mirza and others, sentencing remarks by Judge Christopher Kinch KC at Woolwich Crown Court on 13 December 2017.
5. Ibid.
6. Issue 7 of Isis propaganda magazine *Dabiq*. February 2015.

7. Europol: 'Women in Islamic State propaganda: Roles and incentives', June 2019, page 20.

8. Europol: 'Women in Islamic State propaganda', page 23.

9. Author notes on *al-Naba*, issue 100.

10. Author notes on 'Inside the Khilafah 7'.

11. Author interview with Dr Elizabeth Pearson, conducted via video call, 12 April 2022.

12. Prosecution opening note in R v Safaa Boular. Delivered at the Central Criminal Court on 10 May 2018.

13. R v Safaa Boular, sentencing remarks by Judge Mark Dennis KC at the Central Criminal Court on 3 August 2018.

14. R v Mina Dich and Rizlaine Boular sentencing remarks.

15. R v Mina Dich and Rizlaine Boular, transcript of sentencing remarks by Judge Mark Dennis KC, delivered at the Central Criminal Court on 15 June 2018.

16. R v Safaa Boular sentencing remarks.

17. R v Mina Dich and Rizlaine Boular sentencing remarks.

18. Lahoud, N., 'Empowerment or Subjugation: A Gendered Analysis of ISIL Messaging', June 2018, page 1.

19. Issue 15 of Isis propaganda magazine *Dabiq*, July 2016.

20. Author interview with Dr Elizabeth Pearson.

21. Hoyle, C., Bradford, A. and Frenett, R., 'Becoming Mulan? Female Western Migrants to Isis', January 2015, page 21.

22. UN Security Council sanctions list entry for Aqsa Mahmood. Available at https://www.un.org/securitycouncil/sanctions/1267/aq_sanctions_list/summaries/individual/aqsa-mahmood

23. Author interview with Dr Elizabeth Pearson.

24. *Dabiq* 15.

25. Prosecution opening note in R v Naa'imur Zakariyah Rahman and Mohammad Aqib Imran. Delivered at the Central Criminal Court on 18 June 2018.

26. Author's notes of sentencing hearing in R v Naa'imur Zakariyah Rahman at the Central Criminal Court on 31 August 2018.

27. R v Naa'imur Zakariyah Rahman, transcript of sentencing remarks by Mr Justice Haddon-Cave at the Central Criminal Court on 31 August 2018.

PART THREE: DANGER AHEAD: NARROW ESCAPES
AND FUTURE THREATS

6. NEAR MISSES

1. Author's notes of evidence heard in R v Ahmed Hassan at the Central Criminal Court on 7 March 2018.

2. R v Ahmed Hassan, transcript of sentencing remarks by Mr Justice Haddon-Cave at the Central Criminal Court on 23 March 2018.

3. R v Ahmed Hassan.

4. Author interviews with explosives experts, conducted by telephone, 16 September 2018.

5. Intelligence and Security Committee of Parliament, 'The 2017 Attacks: What needs to change?', November 2018, page 96.

6. Author's notes of evidence heard in R v Salih Khater at the Central Criminal Court on 8 July 2019.

7. R v Mahdi Mohamud, sentencing remarks by Mr Justice Stuart-Smith at Manchester Crown Court on 27 November 2019.

8. Author's notes of evidence heard in R v Vincent Fuller at Kingston Crown Court on 16 August 2019.

9. R v Brusthom Ziamani and Baz Hockton, sentencing remarks by Mrs Justice May at the Central Criminal Court on 8 October 2020.

10. Prosecution opening note in R v Khalid Ali. Delivered at the Central Criminal Court on 5 June 2018.

11. BBC News: '"Captive" aid workers arrive in Greece after ship trip', 12 November 2010. Available at: https://www.bbc.co.uk/news/uk-11742063.

12. R v Khalid Ali, transcript of sentencing remarks by Judge Nicholas Hilliard KC at the Central Criminal Court on 20 July 2018.

13. Prosecution opening note in R v Ethan Stables. Delivered at Leeds Crown Court on 23 January 2018.

14. Sandiford, J: 'Terrorist Prosecution for Planned Attack on Pride Event', 25 March 2019. Available at: https://www.stpaulschambers.com/terrorist-prosecution-for-planned-attack-on-pride-event/

15. Transcript of evidence heard in R v Ethan Stables, at Leeds Crown Court on 25 January 2018.

16. Ubermensch, 'Bruderkrieg'.

17. Prosecution opening note in R v Ethan Stables.

18. https://archive.4plebs.org/pol/thread/162492335/

19. Prosecution opening note in R v Ethan Stables

20. R v Ethan Stables, transcript of sentencing remarks by Judge Peter Collier KC at Leeds Crown Court on 30 May 2018.

21. https://www.facebook.com/newempirebarrow/posts/pfbid023j-fogJLRwy5XWZ7DNNA7giyYzua1L2dfhinb8nvJxapcVveV9LnQt-8VpR9FfprnVl

22. Prosecution opening note in R v Lloyd Gunton. Delivered at Birmingham Crown Court on 14 November 2017.

23. R v Lloyd Gunton, transcript of sentencing remarks by Judge Mark Wall KC at Birmingham Crown Court on 2 March 2018.

24. Issue 2 of Isis propaganda magazine *Rumiyah*, October 2016.

25. Prosecution opening note in R v Lloyd Gunton.

26. R v Lloyd Gunton sentencing remarks.

27. Home Office: Statistics on the operation of police powers under the Terrorism Act 2000 and subsequent legislation, year to March 2022: annual data tables.

28. Home Office: Operation of police powers under the Terrorism Act 2000 and subsequent legislation: Arrests, outcomes, and stop and search, Great Britain, quarterly update to September 2022. Available at: https://www.gov.uk/government/statistics/operation-of-police-pow-ers-under-the-terrorism-act-2000-quarterly-update-to-septem-ber-2022/operation-of-police-powers-under-the-terrorism-act-2000-and-subsequent-legislation-arrests-outcomes-and-stop-and-search-great-britain-quarterly-u

29. Author interview with Dean Haydon, New Scotland Yard, London, 26 May 2022.

30. Prosecution case summary in R v Mohiussunnath Chowdhury. Delivered at Westminster Magistrates' Court on 31 August 2017.

31. Transcript of evidence heard in R v Mohiussunnath Chowdhury, at the Central Criminal Court on 11 December 2018.

32. Author's notes of evidence heard in R v Mohiussunnath Chowdhury at the Central Criminal Court on 19 December 2018.

32. Prosecution opening note in R v Mohiussunnath Chowdhury. Delivered at Woolwich Crown Court on 8 January 2020.

34. Prosecution opening in R v Chowdhury (2020).

35. Tell Mama: 'Amazon removes Tommy Robinson's book on Islam from sale', 27 February 2019. https://tellmamauk.org/amazon-removes-tommy-robinsons-book-on-islam-from-sale/

36. Author's notes of evidence heard in R v Mohiussunnath Chowdhury at Woolwich Crown Court on 27 January 2020.

7. PLOTTERS OF THE FUTURE

1. Intelligence and Security Committee of Parliament, 'Extreme Right-Wing Terrorism', July 2022, page 15.

2. Author interview with Dean Haydon, New Scotland Yard, London, 26 May 2022.

3. Intelligence and Security Committee of Parliament, 'Extreme Right-Wing Terrorism', July 2022, page 30.

4. Ibid.

5. Institute for Strategic Dialogue, 'Incels: An overview of online "involuntary celibate" subcultures', April 2022, page 3.

6. Author interview with Dean Haydon.
7. Intelligence and Security Committee of Parliament, 'Extreme Right-Wing Terrorism', July 2022, page 27.
8. Author interview with Dean Haydon.
9. Europol, 'EU Terrorism Situation and Trend Report 2022', July 2022, page 44.
10. Intelligence and Security Committee of Parliament, 'Extreme Right-Wing Terrorism', July 2022, page 31.
11. Author interview with Jonathan Hall KC, 6KBW College Hill, London, 10 May 2022.
12. National Police Chiefs' Council, 'Report published into the functioning of vulnerability support hubs', 18 November 2020.
13. Home Office, 'Individuals referred to and supported through the Prevent Programme, England and Wales, April 2020 to March 2021', 18 November 2021.
14. High Court judgment in the Queen on the application of X Claimant and Ealing Youth Court. [2020] EWHC 800 Admin. (3 April 2020).
15. Hall, J., 'Terrorism in Prisons', April 2022, page 7.
16. R v Thomas Wyllie and Alex Bolland, sentencing remarks by Mrs Justice Cheema-Grubb at Leeds Crown Court on 20 July 2018.
17. Material provided by Counter Terrorism Policing North East. Some photographs of evidence can be seen here: https://www.independent.co.uk/news/uk/crime/yorkshire-columbine-massacre-teenager-jailed-northallerton-boys-latest-updates-a8456571.html
18. Section 1 of the Terrorism Act 2000.
19. Prosecution opening note in R v Shane Fletcher. Delivered at Manchester Crown Court on 16 January 2019.
20. R v Shane Fletcher, transcript of sentencing remarks by Judge Patrick Field KC at Manchester Crown Court on 30 April 2019.
21. Crown Prosecution Service, 'Teenager jailed for 19 years after researching mass shooting', 13 September 2019.
22. HMA v Gabrielle Friel, sentencing statement by Lord Beckett. Delivered at the High Court in Edinburgh on 12 January 2021.
23. Senior coroner for West Yorkshire: 'Inquest touching the death of Dominic Robert NOBLE—Regulation 28 report to Prevent Future Deaths', July 2022.
24. Intelligence and Security Committee of Parliament, 'Extreme Right-Wing Terrorism', July 2022, page 4.
25. Allington, A., McAndrew, S. and Hirsh, D.: 'Violent extremist tactics and the ideology of the sectarian far left', July 2019, page 6.
26. HMA v Nikolaos Karvounakis, sentencing statement by Lord Braid, delivered at the High Court in Edinburgh on 16 February 2022.

27. ITS: 'Communiques of the Individualist Tending Towards the Wild From 46 to 60'
28. Brenton Tarrant's manifesto.
29. Patrick Crusius' manifesto.
30. Europol, 'EU Terrorism Situation and Trend Report 2022', July 2022, page 78.
31. Prosecution opening in R v Oliver Lewin. Delivered at Birmingham Crown Court on 18 November 2022.
32. Author interview with Dean Haydon.
33. Intelligence and Security Committee of Parliament, 'Extreme Right-Wing Terrorism', July 2022, page 67.
34. Author interview with Tim Squirrell and Milo Comerford, conducted by video call 10 August 2022.
35. Hall, J., 'The Terrorism Acts in 2019: Report of the Independent Reviewer of Terrorism Legislation', March 2021, page 6.
36. R v Aidan James, sentencing remarks by Mr Justice Edis at the Central Criminal Court on 7 November 2019.
37. Author's notes of submissions heard in R v Sam Newey, Daniel Burke and Paul Newey at the Central Criminal Court on 3 July 2020.
38. Author's notes of submissions heard in R v Sam Newey, Daniel Burke and Paul Newey at the Central Criminal Court on 10 July 2020.
39. Hall, J., 'The Terrorism Acts in 2019: Report of the Independent Reviewer of Terrorism Legislation', March 2021, page 121.
40. Home Office, 'Response to the annual report on the operation of the terrorism acts in 2019', February 2022.
41. High Court judgment in Rangzieb Ahmed v Director General of the Security Service et al. [2020] EWHC 3458 (QB). (16 December 2020).
42. Parole Board decision summary for Rangzieb Ahmed.
43. Parole Board decision summary for Jawad Akbar.
44. Author interview with Dean Haydon, London, 20 December 2021.
45. Ibid.
46. Author interview with Julia Ebner, London, 2 March 2022.
47. Ministry of Justice, 'The Structural Properties of the Extremism Risk Guidelines (ERG22+): a structured formulation tool for extremist offenders', July 2019, page 1.

CONCLUSION: PLOTS OF THE FUTURE

1. Author interview with Sir Mark Rowley, London, 14 March 2022.
2. Issue 15 of Isis propaganda magazine *Dabiq*, July 2016.
3. White House: Remarks by President Biden on a Successful Counterterrorism Operation in Afghanistan, 1 August 2022. Available

at: https://www.whitehouse.gov/briefing-room/speeches-remarks/
2022/08/01/remarks-by-president-biden-on-a-successful-counterter-
rorism-operation-in-afghanistan/

4. US Central Command: 'Death of Isis Leader', 30 November 2022.
Available at: https://www.centcom.mil/MEDIA/PRESS-RELEASES/
Press-Release-View/Article/3232259/death-of-isis-leader/
5. Author interview with Dean Haydon, London, 20 December 2021.
6. International Criminal Court: Situation in Ukraine. Available at: https://
www.icc-cpi.int/ukraine
7. For example, Daniel Burke. *The Independent*: 'Terror charges dropped
against British ex-soldier who fought against Isis in Syria', 3 July 2020.
https://www.independent.co.uk/news/uk/crime/daniel-burke-ter-
ror-charges-dropped-soldier-isis-syria-news-a9599561.html
8. Author's email correspondence with Jonathan Hall KC, 27 February
2022.
9. *The Independent*: 'Prosecutors refuse to explain why they dropped terror
charges against Kurdish YPG supporters', 10 July 2020. https://www.
independent.co.uk/news/uk/crime/ypg-syria-kurdish-terror-charge-
cps-daniel-burke-sam-newey-paul-a9612226.html
10. Daniel Burke Facebook posts.
11. Europol, 'EU Terrorism Situation and Trend Report 2022', July 2022,
page 3.
12. Author interview with Dean Haydon, New Scotland Yard, London,
26 May 2022.
13. Speech by Ken McCallum, London, 16 November 2022.
14. 'Hansard: Salisbury Incident 2018', debated on 21 September 2021.
15. Author interview with Jonathan Hall KC, 6KBW College Hill, London,
10 May 2022.
16. Intelligence and Security Committee of Parliament, 'Extreme Right-
Wing Terrorism', July 2022, page 50.
17. Cardiff University Crime and Security Research Institute, 'Russian influence and interference measures following the 2017 UK terrorist attacks',
April 2018, page 3.
18. Intelligence and Security Committee of Parliament, 'Extreme Right-
Wing Terrorism', page 18.
19. Europol, 'EU Terrorism Situation and Trend Report 2022', July 2022,
page 76.
20. Author interview with Jacob Davey and Milo Comerford, conducted by
video call, 10 February 2022.
21. *Der Spiegel*: 'Das »Sündenbock-Narrativ« des Todesschützen an der
Tankstelle', 1 July 2022. https://www.spiegel.de/panorama/justiz/

idar-oberstein-toedliche-tankstellenattacke-was-eine-kriminalpsy-chologin-ueber-mario-n-sagt-a-6a3eaa0b-2c7-46a-89ac-5ab083267c5e

22. Author interview with Dame Sara Khan, conducted by video call, 12 April 2022.

23. Home Office, 'Factsheet on the Commission for Countering Extremism', 25 January 2018. Available at: https://homeofficemedia.blog.gov.uk/2018/01/25/factsheet-on-the-commission-for-countering-extremism/

24. Commission for Countering Extremism, 'Operating with Impunity: Hateful extremism—the need for a legal framework', February 2021, page 13.

25. Commission for Countering Extremism, 'Challenging Hateful Extremism', October 2019, page 10.

26. Commission for Countering Extremism, 'Commission for Countering Extremism: Three years on', March 2021, page 23.

27. Author interview with Dame Sara Khan.

28. Speech by Ken McCallum, 6 July 2022. Available at: https://www.mi5.gov.uk/news/speech-by-mi5-and-fbi

29. Author interview with Julia Ebner, London, 2 March 2022.

30. Email from Britain First to mailing list, titled 'Twitter amnesty is happening', 22 December 2022.

31. Intelligence and Security Committee of Parliament, 'Extreme Right-Wing Terrorism', page 56.

32. Intelligence and Security Committee of Parliament, 'Extreme Right-Wing Terrorism', page 59.

33. Institute for Strategic Dialogue, 'Gaming and Extremism: The Extreme Right on Discord', August 2021, page 7.

34. Intelligence and Security Committee of Parliament, 'Extreme Right-Wing Terrorism', July 2022, page 62.

35. Transcripts of police interviews with Ali Harbi Ali, as shown in evidence to the trial of R v Ali Harbi Ali at the Central Criminal Court on 25 March 2022.

36. Author interview with Dean Haydon.

37. Author interview with Sir Mark Rowley.

38. Manchester Arena inquiry, transcript of evidence heard on 25 October 2021.

39. Anderson, D., '2017 Terrorist Attacks MI5 and CTP Reviews: Implementation Stock-Take', June 2019, page 16.

40. Author interview with Sir Mark Rowley.

INDEX

INDEX

INDEX

INDEX